The Billion-Dollar Battle

The Billion-Dollar Battle

Merck v Glaxo

MATTHEW LYNN

HEINEMANN : LONDON

William Heinemann Ltd
Michelin House, 81 Fulham Road, London SW3 6RB
LONDON   MELBOURNE   AUCKLAND

First published 1991
Copyright © Matthew Lynn 1991

A CIP catalogue record for this book
is held by the British Library
ISBN 0 434 43924 X

Phototypeset by Wilmaset, Birkenhead, Wirral
Printed in Great Britain
by Clays Ltd, St Ives plc

Contents

Acknowledgements

Thanks are due to many people for their help with this book, some in small ways, some in major. At Merck, the company's international press officer Russ Durbin was tireless in his efforts to line up information and interviews. Without him, and without approval from Dr Roy Vagelos, the Merck chapters would have been both shorter and less interesting. At Hoffmann - La Roche, Dr Dieter Bothe was a source both of contacts and background material. Requests for detailed co-operation with Glaxo, negotiated through its press officer Geoffrey Potter, were turned down by the company, much to my regret. One useful interview was finally arranged, for which thanks are due. Greater debts of gratitude, however, are owed to the many former Glaxo employees, some junior, some very senior, who gave their time freely. Many are not mentioned by name, at their request; they will recognise themselves, however. Others helped in different ways. My employers at *Business* allowed me time off to complete the book, and at Heinemann, my editor, Tom Weldon, handed over the cheque and left me alone.

Author's note

This is a story about the drugs industry: about its heroes and demons; about its dramas and dénouements. But it is something else as well: it is a story about the soul of capitalism.

Matthew Lynn
London, December 1990

Oh bitter; very bitter!
                    And more bitter,
To fear a deeper curse, an inner ruin,
Plague beneath plague, the last turning the first
To light beside its darkness. Let me weep
My youth and its brave hopes, all dead and gone
In tears which burn! Would I were sure to win
Some startling secret in their stead, a tincture
Of force to flush old age with youth, or breed
Gold, or imprison moonbeams till they change
To opal shafts! – only that, hurling it
Indignant back, I might convince myself
My aims remained supreme and pure as ever!
Even now, why not desire, for mankind's sake
That if I fail some fault may be the cause
That, though I sink, another may succeed?
O God, the despicable heart of us!
Shut out this hideous mockery from my heart!

From 'Paracelsus' by Robert Browning

Introduction: The molecular casino

Paris, June 1990

The men filed into the hall slowly, silently, hesitantly that morning; their feet shuffled and their heads were bowed. They were grey-looking characters, with grey suits, grey hair, grey skin and grey expressions, and they fumbled towards their seats, sitting down in long, neat rows, facing forwards, like a congregation awaiting the Word. Strips of bright, neon tubing shone down on them, filling the room with a dazzling artificial glare. The light was everywhere, a fierce, intense, revealing light. Yet there was also darkness that morning. Not in any of the open, public spaces, but creeping into the most distant and secluded corners of the hall. There was a darkness in their minds.

I sensed it as soon as I walked into the conference room: a sort of tension, an edginess, mixed with an air of foreboding. The hall was in truth more of a basement, a room sunk into the depths of a smart Parisian hotel, the Meridien Montparnasse. Outside were dull streets lined with concrete blocks, and the hotel itself was an ugly slab of seventies concrete: the type of place always chosen by business groupings for their conferences.

The grey men were lined back in twenty rows. There were papers on their desks: transcripts and agendas. There were headphones and dials: dial one for English interpretation; dial two for French; dial three for German; and so on. At ten minutes past nine in the morning, they were already deep into Euroland.

They were there, holed up close to the sewers of Paris for three days, to attend the Eighteenth Annual International Pharmaceutical Conference. It is a yearly gathering, a chance to meditate, ruminate and reflect on the state of their industry. An opportunity to assess the health of the drugs business, to check its pulse, and to run over its cholesterol level. The organisers were resolutely upbeat: their optimism almost military in its precision. And yet, as the event dragged on, it was to become clear that this is not a happy business.

Up on the platform, the proceedings are about to crank into action. A man called Pierre Joly starts to speak. He is the President of the International Federation of Pharmaceutical Manufacturers and, judging by the sheer weight and length of his title, a man who should carry some authority. Joly is old; his craggy, caved-in face has a punched and beaten surface; and, like many Frenchmen of his generation, he both looks and sounds like a rough, heavily tarred Gauloise cigarette. His words, croaked and harsh, are dense and bristling with nerve-endings.

'Our industry is going through great changes, and is on the eve of even deeper changes,' he tells his audience. I look around. There are nods of agreement at this thought, nods that are wise and peaceful – polite even. 'The great competitors of our industry are now facing each other for domination of the world market,' he continues. More nods, but this time less polite, this time edged with uncertainty. Joly casts his heavy eyes around the hall and decides it is time to speed up. He skips past markets and capacities, the stuff with numbers and charts, and moves on to his real point. He starts to explain how eighty per cent of the world's drugs are consumed by only twenty per cent of its people. They are, not surprisingly, the rich ones. The others – the poor ones – lie around dying from stupid, needless diseases. It gets worse. In another ten years, by the end of the millennium, there will be another billion of these people, dying all over the world, messily and inconveniently and in poverty. And could this be the fault of the men sitting so peacefully in this room? Joly seems to think so.

'One of these days this situation will lead to an explosion,' he warns. 'Perhaps the health industry should start on a solution.'

It is a strangely political point on which to open an industrial conference: a point, on the face of it, far removed from the ordinary concerns of manufacturing and marketing, of production and profits. Inside this room, however, one of the witty paradoxes of modern capitalism is well demonstrated. Meeting here are men of considerable power: representatives of all the major companies – European, American, Japanese – in one of the world's largest industries. Yet despite this, they are constantly gripped by a sense of their own powerlessness.

The power they possess is both subtle and extensive. It is the power of transformation: a mysterious ability to alter completely the world we live in. In the past, it was the sort of power held by armies, churches, states, or political parties: each of those were institutions which could mobilise ideas, manpower, technique and strategy to reshape the world in their own preferred shape. In our times, however, that power has shifted to the corporation. The motor industry, through the cheap automobile, redefined the shapes of cities and communities, altering the very nature of people's lives and work; the airline industry tore down the barriers of distance between countries and continents; the communications industry delivered new relationships between the individual and society; the computer industry challenged perceptions of knowledge and intelligence. And the drugs industry? It, too, had a revolution to wreak: in a style that was very carefully and neatly plotted, it abolished death.

Or, if not death itself, at least its intimate companion, disease. In the period since 1920, known in the drugs industry as the era of the 'wonder drugs', a morbid cluster of lethal conditions were conquered: cholera, plague, diphtheria, syphilis, smallpox, meningitis, scarlet fever, typhoid, tuberculosis, and so on. The consequences of those victories showed up immediately in the figures for average life expectancy. In the United States, which scores no more than average in the health charts, a white male can now expect to live to close on seventy, compared with around fifty-five in 1920; a female can expect to live to about eighty compared with fifty-five only seventy years ago. Some of that increase is due to better diet, better sanitation, and so on. Yet it is mostly due to new and better medicines, which means it is the result of the work done by the people in this room.

It has been some achievement; indeed, it is the most eloquent testimony to the powerful triumph of modern technology and modern capitalism. But there is more to this story than simple statistics reveal. There is a psychology as well, a perception. In the past, disease was one of mankind's great obsessions: an alien, hostile force which was feared but also respected. Disease had an image – not a very positive image, it's true – but it had a place and a role in society. Yet, as the years of the twentieth century clocked by, a series of medical breakthroughs gradually peeled away the mystique surrounding disease. It became less of a just retribution for past sins and more of a technical nuisance; it was more likely to provoke irritation than fear.

Look at the anger any intrusion by disease now creates. Cancer, when it was the last of the great, incomprehensible killers, became a modern taboo, something too awful even to discuss. The arrival of AIDS, a flashback to the wild and lethal plagues that haunted our ancestors, prompted mass fear. But it also prompted mass indignation. It was as if people had been cheated and duped.

It illustrated perfectly the way our mental universe had shifted. Disease had exited, vanished, disappeared. It had been defeated. We believed we were immune. It was, of course, never a strictly accurate perception. There were always lots of diseases still around, hanging out, waiting to get you. But they at least had the decency to wait until you were old: until it seemed reasonable to suppose your number had been called. This perception – a powerful one – had been created by the drugs industry.

All industries have an idea that propels them forward; all products, inevitably, contain within them an image of how the world should be. The motor industry revolves around the idea that mobility is good, that it liberates us, and allows us to express ourselves. It is a clever idea, and it strikes a chord within us. The communications industry spins on the idea that knowledge is good, that it advances us, and makes us complete. The point about these ideas is not that they are false, not that they are a trick foisted on a beguiled public. They are true, or at least they are a kind of truth. The clever part is convincing people that the industry can deliver, in creating the impression that the promise can be fulfilled.

The drugs industry had an idea, and it was one of the simplest, smartest, and most attractive ever invented. Its idea was this: it would make us safe from disease. Trust it, and we would feel secure and safe, comfortable and at ease. The message of the product boiled down to one easily understood thought: you have a problem, we have a pill.

It succeeded brilliantly, and the rewards for that idea were very rich. Starting with the era of the wonder drugs, the medicine business not only grew into one of the world's largest industries but also became its most profitable legitimate trade. In other industries, profit margins of around ten per cent of sales were considered normal and acceptable. But not in the drugs industry – there, the average profit margins were around thirty per cent: three times the money everyone else was making.

All of which was quite a power, and quite an achievement: to discover both great good and great riches. So why the nervousness this morning? Why the edginess? And why the darkness?

The mood around the hall is subdued and quiet now. Perhaps it is the time: it is Wednesday morning and there are still three days of this stuff to get through. Or perhaps it is Joly's talk: it was, after all, a bit of a downer. However, up on the stage the organisers are rumbling into action again. Wheeled into view is a man called Gerald J. Mossinghoff, the president of the Pharmaceutical Manufacturers Association, the US trade grouping, representing the most powerful collection of drug manufacturers anywhere. Mossinghoff has both the look and the manner of a Yankee. He is tall, his shoulders are wide and his back is broad. His hair is closely cropped, curling around a thick, blunt instrument of a head, the sort of head used for butting other heads. The sort of head that enjoys butting other heads. He is a tough guy, tough but still gentle, a familiar figure from American folklore. Today, however, his appearance has a strange dissonance to it. He creates an impression of American optimism, boundless, expansive, and all-conquering: an optimism which sees ceaseless improvement in the human condition as no more than a matter of time and technology and the American Way. It's what you expect, but he doesn't deliver. Like a badly dubbed movie, there is a mismatch between the way he acts and what he says. His thoughts and actions have become strangers to one another. There is a reason: Mossinghoff has succumbed to European neurosis and uncertainty.

It could be the place. Paris is a city where gloomy, self-important waffle is treated as wisdom. Or it could be a mark of America's transition from optimistic new civilisation to a pessimistic old one. Both factors probably play a part. But, more likely, his gloom today results from the plague of troubles his association members keep bringing to him. For the drugs industry, these are troubling times.

During a talk lasting about an hour, Mossinghoff casts his eye around a panorama of terrors. Here is a small selection. There is the European Community, and the coming integration of the twelve member economies. Generally, business types see this as a good thing, but for the druggies it is a nasty intrusion into their comfortable universe. Free trade in drugs – one of the proposals coming out of Brussels – threatens the delicate pricing structure which has made this the most profitable of all the world's industries. They appear to have two options. They can play wimp and let the upcoming EC rules eat savagely into their profits. Or they can play tough and let sick people in certain countries die. And keep dying until the EC lets them go back to their profitable pricing structure. That would be good, hard negotiating, but awful public relations – the sort of PR which brings people out into the streets baying for your blood. It's a tough choice.

Secondly, prices everywhere are under attack. Mossinghoff mentions a few countries. In the United Kingdom the government has stated its intention to focus on what it perceives as doctors' over-prescribing of drugs. In a flash of wayward optimism, the American suggests the industry should focus on its own problem of under-prescribing. Not much of a meeting of minds there. In Japan, the world's second largest drugs market, the government keeps on slashing drug prices. And in the United States, the biggest cherry in the pie, there are rising protests against the cost of drugs: protests fuelled by the evidence of escalating medical expenditure, and by the dismal fact that in ghetto areas health standards and life expectancy are down to Third World levels. Again, there is a difficult choice to be made. Do we humour these people and let them eat into our profits? Or do we ignore them, play tough, and wait until they get really mad? Nobody really knows.

There is a resentment here: I can read it in the scowls and frowns on the faces of the audience. It is as if there were a suspicious whispering floating through the hall. What the heck is going on here? Don't those people like us any more? Can that be? After all we did for them? After all the diseases we killed?

Mossinghoff ends with a quotation from Martial, the first-century Roman poet. He wrote: 'Life is not to live, but to be well.' It isn't a particularly striking quote, or even particularly clever. But he is making a point, which is that people are not as happy with the industry as they once were: this security you have given us – we're not so sure we like it any more. Industries, along with everyone else who pitches their stall in the market, have to stay tuned to the tastes and prejudices of the ordinary public. And the industrialists sense, those tastes and prejudices may be running away from them; may, even, be heading off in another direction.

That direction – not just in medicine but throughout the whole range of manufactured products – is away from mindless material-ism and towards something called the quality of life. In the drugs business, this phrase has a specific meaning; it means less emphasis on the endless keeping alive of empty, broken shells of human beings, and more emphasis on making life worth living. 'Adding life to years, rather than years to life,' as one expert has put it. Whatever the definition, however, it doesn't sound too good for the industrialists of the chemical manipulation of the human body. But so it goes. An industry rises, and becomes, briefly, glorious. And then, like a used up strip of neon tubing, it starts to flicker and fade away.

Welcome to the molecular casino: a place ruled by chance and by arcane rules, where corporations take the place of punters, science the wheel, patients the chips and death the croupier.

The delegates have broken for lunch now and the straight rows of grey figures have been swapped for circular tables ringed by the same characters. Over the food they sit around gossiping, exchanging jokes and stories and nuggets of information. It hasn't really been a good morning: too much doom and gloom, too many nerves touched. But these are resilient people: like boxers, they know that taking a few blows is just part of the routine of doing business. A glass of wine numbs the pain, and soon they are back on form, talking deals, talking strategies and talking money.

The man on my left is an American, about thirty-five, and fairly typical of the day's congregation. He works for one of the major drugs combines, the third company he has worked for. Like most of the executives within the industry, he has job-hopped within it, yet stays firmly inside its closed circle. People don't move in or out of the drugs business very much. It is a narrow and insular community, and one with few contacts beyond the triangle of drug companies, physicians and regulators: a fact which explains the obsessive secrecy and protectiveness of the industry.

He is talking about risk. The conversation started when I asked him what he was up to, and he started describing the deal his company had struck with 'a little biotechnology outfit – some bunch of crazy scientists'.

'The deal goes like this,' he explains. 'We give them the money and then they spend it.'

'And what do you get?' I asked.

'We get to give them more money,' he answers.

'But what's your pay-off?'

He shakes his head softly before replying. 'In an ideal world these guys discover an amazing drug, and we get to sell and make lots of money.'

'And is this an ideal world?'

'Are you kidding?'

'So it might happen and it might not. You take that chance?'

'Right.'

'Is that a fun way to make a living?'

'No.' He pauses before continuing. 'It's terrifying.'

Pharmaceutical chemists used to have a term for their work. They called it 'molecular roulette', and it neatly captured the process of drug discovery. Essentially, hundreds upon hundreds of chemical formulations would be carefully prepared and then tested. The tests consisted of pumping the chemicals into a laboratory rat and seeing what happened to the little guy. If he keeled over, you knew it was a dud. If, alternatively, he jumped up, shook your hand and wrote out a cheque, you knew the molecule had some interesting possibilities. That was the molecular roulette and the way to play was to keep spinning until you ran out of money or you found a winner. At a rough average, the chemists figured they would find something interesting once in every ten thousand tries.

From the mid seventies onwards things started changing; advances in biological technology made the process of discovering a drug a little less random. But the metaphor of molecular roulette still grips the industry. Except now it is a better description of the commercial game than of the chemical game.

Drug executives – no less than penguin-suited men sitting around a casino table – are gamblers. More than most major businesses the drugs industry is a crap shoot; the profits are determined by the tumbling of the dice. Vast sums – well over $500 million each year at the big companies – are poured into research, with very little in the way of certain return. Developing a new marketable product will cost somewhere in the region of

£230 million, a price to be paid for entry into a market worth $120 billion each year worldwide. If it works then the profits can be huge: say, one billion dollars a year in pure profit, year in, year out. But if if doesn't work there is no fall back position, and no way of recouping any of the outlay. The money just sinks down the test tubes.

Even after a drug is discovered, the risks just go on and on. Drugs companies make extraordinary profits because they have patents on their products; discover it and it's yours, and you can charge what you like for it. Like most great gifts, however, this one comes with a heavy price attached; the patent lasts for only twenty years. After that, it's gone. And the drugs company has to haul itself back into the process of finding another successful drug: it has to step back into the casino and start spinning again. And so it goes on, around and around.

This characteristic, this dual blessing and curse, sets the drugs industry aside from its rivals. The seeming immortality of most major companies – the big motor companies, the big oil combines, the tobacco and food conglomerates – is unknown to these men. Instead, they know that each of the corporations, no matter how big and no matter how powerful, has to re-invent itself within the relentless twenty-year life cycle. And that knowledge, that premonition of their own impending demise, fills the industry with its own brand of commercial neuroticism; that of the organisation which knows that it might die at any moment.

Day two of the conference starts in lighter mood. The delegates shuffle into their seats between nine thirty and nine forty-five, some – the fitness freaks – bouncing in bright and early, the rest – the eaters, smokers and drinkers who make up the majority – straggling in later, looking the worse for a night's wear. Up on the stage a large, round man with wisps of grey hair hanging over his forehead has arrived on the stage. He looks friendly and sweet. Appearances are deceptive, however. His name is Armin Kessler and he is a board member of F. Hoffmann-La Roche. Just the name, printed blandly on the agenda papers in front of us, is enough to send a shiver of anticipation down the spines of the audience. Anticipation touched with a little fear: fear from the past, and fear of what may yet happen.

Hoffmann - La Roche is a monumental, almost mythical, force within the drugs industry. The company was creator of Valium – still, a decade after its fall from grace, the best known and most celebrated brand-name drug in the world. With it, Hoffmann - La Roche became the biggest and most profitable drugs company ever. Since then, in the eyes of the rest of the industry, they have had a charisma about them that belongs only to the creators of an industry. There were plenty of drugs companies before Roche, and there will be plenty more after them. But for a couple of decades the company drew all the strands together and wove them into a sturdy rope. And then, strangely, it turned the rope into a noose.

Like the people in the audience, Kessler has peered into the future and found it irksome. He is bugged by the Japanese, in the way that most business types in most industries are. He thinks they are out to get him, and he is probably right. After all, how could they resist? This is the most profitable industry in the world: whoever thought they would leave it to the West?

'Methodically, for the past few years, their government has been working with them,' he starts to beef. 'They give better patent protection, they give higher prices to new products, they discourage generics. And that is why they will be all over us soon. Here in Europe we are doing the exact opposite. We are giving it to them.'

There is a hint of foul play here. The Japanese are cheating, Kessler suggests. Or at least playing too hard and too rough. Coming from Roche, this is rich stuff. Back there in the sixties and seventies, before it blew the whole caboodle away in a whirlwind of misshapen desire, Roche was a walking caricature of capitalist evil. It carved the tablets on Unfair Competition; it wrote texts on Monopoly Pricing; and so on. Yet now it is reduced to whingeing senselessly about unfair competition from others: it is a bully stripped of its powers and stranded, complaining about the other thugs, which is about as sad a picture as the commercial world ever conjours up.

Over lunch, however, the pathos of the talk has little effect on the delegates around the tables. Instead the chatter is concentrated on its content. The Japanese have them bothered too. Phrases like 'protected home market' and 'just like the car industry' filter through the conversation. And a man on the other side of the table says simply: 'As if things weren't tough enough already.'

He looks as if he is in his mid forties, and is wearing the standard middle-ranking executive kit: greying hair, double-breasted suit, moustache, striped tie, and slightly saggy eyes. A decent enough man in a difficult world. I ask him what he means.

'Look at how it stacks up against us,' he starts to explain. 'Begin with the costs side of the equation. More and more has to be put into research before we can come up with anything. Okay, we can live with that. But then look at the revenue side. Increase our prices and everyone jumps up and down about how we are exploiting the sick. But then they want us to increase the amount of testing we do to make drugs safer, and they want us to discover new drugs for everything under the sun. They want to reduce the patents on the drugs as well. They want to sue us for compensation every time something goes wrong. From where I'm sitting, it seems like everyone wants to stick it to us.'

'Why do you think that is?' I ask.

'It's the profile, I guess,' he replies. 'Drugs are a high profile business. Every cent you make is scrutinised. And people are very quick to criticise.'

'You don't think you deserve any criticism?'

'Perhaps. There could have been mistakes in the past. But when I talk to my friends in other industries it seems the drugs industry is different. We can do something and get hammered for it, but it wouldn't turn a hair in some other industry. We seem to get judged by different standards.'

'And is that bad or good?'

'It makes life very difficult.'

I watch him wander back into the hall in sombre mood; his face seems fallen. In the afternoon, however, a contrast takes over. Wheeling into view comes a man called James Molt. Neat and well tuned, he is the director of regulatory affairs at Merck. The company's name has a Germanic sound to it, unsurprisingly, since it is a German company transplanted to America. But it has a crispness to it as well. It sounds square jawed and clean cut, which is right, because Merck is square jawed and clean cut. It is also the largest drugs company in the world, and, with a market capitalisation of over $30 billion, a member of an elite, exclusive band – that of the biggest twenty-five industrial groups doing anything, anywhere.

It has something else as well, something less definable, and something more challenging: a mystery perhaps, or a dream or a vision. Wherever Merck goes, wherever it swanks and swerves, it carries with it a question: can nice guys win? And it brings an answer in its baggage as well: of course they can – just look at us.

Merck is not just big. Under the guidance of its president Roy Vagelos, a man who dragged the company out of a slump in its fortunes in the mid seventies, it has become a force throughout the industrial world. For the second half of the eighties, a vicious and savage decade in business, Merck was consistently voted the most admired company in the United States. It won a host of other awards: best for working women; best for black employees; most innovative; best managed; and so on. It made a name for itself with startling schemes to donate drugs to the Third World and to cut its product prices for the poor and needy. At a time when greed was triumphing, Merck seemed to have found a different way, a better way even. And, to the dismay of the greedmongers, it combined benevolence with a string of exhilarating financial results that lifted it into the top ten American corporations, behind IBM and Exxon but ahead of such traditional standard-bearers of American capitalism as General Motors and Du Pont.

The delegates have perked up now, their interest captured. In the drugs industry, Merck merits the kind of respect that only outlandish success can bring. People listen because they want to learn: to discover how the thing is done, and to imitate it. Molt is dwelling this afternoon on the nature of chemical drugs. 'These powerful compounds, taken in relatively minute quantities, have the power to cure or hold at bay life-threatening illnesses,' he starts out. 'And because of their power they also have the ability to cause potentially serious side effects. Where life and death may ride on the quality and effectiveness of a drug, it's no wonder that the public demands that the safety and efficacy of these compounds be assured by their government agencies.'

The relationship between the drugs industry and governments is a web of complexity. It is a highly controlled business. All its products have to run through a battery of tests before they can be marketed. Outside the United States, prices are set by negotiation between governments and companies. Yet, at the same time, the industry is strangely out of control, running with its own pack, and often ending up in bruising confrontations with the governments that have such power to control it.

The industry is not supine, it is not cowed by authority. More often, the reverse is true – government is cowed by the industry. The reason lies in the very power of the chemical compounds Molt draws attention to. We have the pills, the industry seems to be saying constantly. So don't mess with us, or it will hurt. That is a pretty powerful message. But Molt is spelling out a different message. He suggests a more conciliatory approach, a recognition of the destructive as well as the beneficial power of the compounds. The approach of an active citizen within a community rather than a marauding commercial adventurer. For most of his audience, it is a novel and daring idea. As the second day winds away, the delegates disappear – wondering, perhaps, if they have wholly misunderstood the nature of their industry.

Time is drawing on now. Delegates are into the third and last day of the conference and tiredness and boredom are setting in. This is just a morning session: by lunchtime everyone will be gone. Yet, as the end draws closer, the clouds of neuroticism and uncertainty still hang heavily over the event. They seem about to break in the presentation of Professor Walter von Wartburg, an expert in health policy, and member of the management committee at the Swiss drugs and chemical combine Ciba-Geigy. Wartburg has the professorial act finely honed. He looks older than the universe and his head has only wisps of neatly combed grey hair. He wears glasses, and stands looking down as he speaks, as if in deep introspection. His voice is clipped and Germanic, suggesting a knowledge that is both precise and slightly sinister. His is not a warm presence: a chill has quietly descended since he came into view.

Wartburg has peered into the darkness afflicting his audience and found its edge. He starts by rehearsing the difficulties they are all familiar with: finding new drugs, the elixirs of profit, is becoming ever harder, a fact witnessed by the ever-declining rate of innovation; the hurdles placed in front of a new drug grow ever higher, a legacy of the wild and lethal potions marketed by these people in the past; price levels – the source of the industry's wealth – are being eroded; patents, the guardians of corporate strength, are slipping and sliding away; and competition from the manufacturers of cheap, unpatented copies intensifies every day.

But none of that is too bad. Nothing really, remarks the professor. There are worse things on the horizon. And having warned his audience, he starts to take a tour. There is the steadily rising cost of health care, up now to around ten per cent of gross national product in the advanced economies, and nearing what many fear are critical limits. And this at a time when the drugs industry is experiencing a gradual but relentless decline in its profitability – not a happy combination.

Still he hasn't reached the real nut of the problem, which comes in two parts, related but not identical. One part is a growing ambivalence, a rising sense of uncertainty, over the connection between science and progress. The other a growing revulsion against risk of any sort, a rising demand for total and complete safety. Mixed in with this is a change in the political forces, the balance of power governing the chemical manipulation of the body. In the past, doctors, drugs companies and governments played in this game, making the rules, and making the results. Now, new and unruly groups have pitched for a slice of the power; consumer organisations, patient groups, the media, political parties, environmentalists. These people have edged in from the distant fringe to the mainstream. They don't know the rules too well, but it doesn't matter much, since they don't intend to play by them.

But there is more to come. The concepts of science and progress, once so strongly bound together, have been drifting apart for some time. The decoupling could be dated back to the explosion of the first nuclear weapons but, closer to the druggies' hearts, it might just as well stem from the thalidomide scandal of the early sixties. Until then, drugs had enjoyed a good ride. But the sight of monstrously deformed babies peering pathetically out of magazine pages was enough to shake the average person's faith in the meaning of pretty much everything, let alone something so relatively fragile as the kindly nature of the drugs industry. Reactions are delayed, naturally, but the men in the casino sense they may be approaching the end of their lucky run.

Yet, the professor goes on, this is still ambivalence. The public's faith may be eroded, but the desire for progress endures. Faced with an illness, be it AIDS or cancer or heart failure, there is still a tremendous clamour for cures. A growing clamour, even, as the pressure groups organised by AIDS victims make clear. A contradiction, perhaps: people will the ends, but reject the means. If nothing else, it is certainly a tangle.

The nub of this is the question of risk. The professor points out how, among most people in most places, there is now a 'zero risk desire'. In his academic way, he means that nobody is taking any chances. Mostly, drugs have been perceived as relatively risk-free. Certainly, people don't worry about taking pills in the way they worry about getting on aeroplanes. Yet the drugs are not particularly safe. Part of the problem is secrecy. Both the drugs industry and the medical profession have kept very quiet about the possible side effects of ordinary medicines. So, when damaging side effects (even dead bodies) start turning up, there is shock and outrage. The effect is intensified by the fact that the side effects were so unexpected.

But then the secrecy was part of the mix, part of the illusion that made the drugs industry so successful. Without secrecy, it would have been difficult to deliver its promise to abolish disease. It is as if Toyota or Ford were to confess that motor cars were a slow, difficult and dangerous way of getting around. Some of the magic would be lost. Again, it is a nasty and depressing tangle. 'We clearly have a problem with what society expects from us, and with what society grants us,' intones the professor in his clipped voice.

This a challenge that industrial organisations have traditionally been ill equipped to deal with: problems of faith haven't normally been their bag. That much is clear from the reactions of the delegates: they are not so much in disagreement with these ideas as simply bemused by them. The professor goes on to offer some hints towards a remedy. He suggests the ethics of the business need to be redefined – that its research and development processes need to be opened up to the new players in the game, and that the risks and benefits of drugs need to be better explained, not just to the traditional regulators and physicians, but to the wider public as well. He suggests new social contracts between the industry and society. And he suggests that the drugs companies have to come to see themselves more as public utilities, less as gamblers in the games room of the molecular casino.

This is the way they have played in the past, however, and these are conservative men. There is really only one thing anyone needs to know about gamblers: they are optimists, incurable and hopeless. One more roll of the dice, they invariably think, and everything will be fine. When the going gets tough in the drugs industry, one thought rattles around the minds of industry executives: one more roll of the pill, that's all we need. Just one more roll.

Up on the stage is a man called Christopher Adam, the head of marketing at Glaxo. As soon as he appears, I can sense the rapt attention in the audience: a visible leaning forward, a palpable air of expectancy. Adam is a man in his fifties and he wears a grey suit and has grey hair, but there is nothing grey about his manner. He bounces and swivels as he speaks, grinning, and pumping the air with his hands. The audience is enthralled, captured. The hall is packed, and the drug executives listen intently to every word. Not surprisingly, since Glaxo is a company on a ten-year roll.

In the last decade, under the leadership of its masterful chairman, Sir Paul Girolami, Glaxo has been a runaway success. From being a very ordinary, very medium sized, English pharmaceutical company, Glaxo has turned itself into the major world player in the industry. It rose to a spot only a whisker behind Merck in global market share, and it terrified its rivals in a series of frantic mergers. From a lowly status it has progressed to become the UK's fourth largest company, and Europe's tenth biggest; with a market capitalisation of over twenty billion dollars it trails only such ancient British heavyweights as Shell and British Petroleum. For consistent progress over the decade it has emerged as Europe's most successful company, a competition won on a continent that has the heaviest concentration of big business anywhere. Glaxo's is, as everyone in the hall is aware, the most dramatic business success of the decade. In this congregation of gamblers, Glaxo seems to possess the one thing everyone wants; a system.

'We are moving into the mega-product age,' starts out Adam, beginning a talk constantly pepped up with the smooth, competitive lingo of big-time business.

He talks about the system. A drug, he remarks, is only one-third hardware, by which he means the chemicals encapsulated in a pill and swallowed by a sick person. This is news to people who thought, foolishly, that a drug was three thirds hardware. The rest, he explains, is software, or communications, made up of the knowledge about the drug which persuades doctors to prescribe it, and the monitoring and pushing of the drug which persuade the patients to keep taking it. It is a salesman's definition, created by a salesman for other salesmen.

'As two thirds of our products are based on communication, a hypothesis must be created, indicating which type of activity in his field will give the best return on investment. Over the twenty-five years I have been involved in drug marketing, I have come to be convinced about the following principles: concepts sell drugs; their effectiveness resells them; their profile of side effects resells them definitively,' he says.

For all the jargon, there is genuine insight here. Adam realises, more precisely and more acutely than most of his rivals in the industry, that the drugs business prospers because of its artfully created omnipotence in the fight against disease. 'Concepts sell drugs' was his way of putting it, and it is a powerful and incisive notion. Glaxo is a company that has achieved great wealth and success by creating a series of such powerful and incisive notions, and by testing them to the limit.

'My vision of the future of the pharmaceutical industry is extremely optimistic,' he continues. He supports this view with some demographics. The ageing of populations in all the rich industrial countries is one factor, and since the average sixty-year-old consumes four times as much health care as the average forty-year-old, this can only be good news. The number of doctors is also rising fast, and past statistics show that the more doctors there are, the more drugs are prescribed. Thirdly, there are new population groups joining the rich, industrialised world, from the fast-growing economies of East Asia to the newly liberated countries of Eastern Europe. And lastly, there are new drugs to cure both new and old diseases, drugs which will create their own demand. 'The fundamental tendency is inflationist,' he concludes.

All this is very upbeat, but it has another side to it. There is a tendency, within entrepreneurial corporations, for the people all the way down the line to resemble the one inspiring individual within the company. This principle is certainly at work inside Glaxo. Adam, with his combination of sharp intelligence and keen salesmanship, is a Girolami clone. So are most of the Glaxo people. Yet there are only so many clones in the world.

But Adam, I can sense from the expressions lining the smiling faces of the delegates, has had a telling effect. The magic of his salesmanship has momentarily dispelled the gloom. The druggies are back to dreaming. Their disquiet has been calmed, and their thoughts have turned back to their normal track: just one more roll.

His is the last of the big presentations; the last item on the agenda anyone really wants to hear. As the chairman sweeps up the remaining points, there are a few seconds to reflect. Darkness has hovered over this hall, though it has lifted from time to time. It hung over the delegates gathered here as they contemplated their possible future. A future of declining profitability, of declining influence, of declining public acceptance, of decline full stop. It gripped them as they contemplated the possibility of becoming the servants of health systems, of losing their position as masters. It held them as they witnessed the hideous spectacle of Roche, fallen from arrogant mastery of everything it saw, now reduced to whingeing pointlessly about Japanese competition.

The darkness receded with the teasing mystery of Merck, a company which, through its own size and strength, and through its own sense of destiny, seems able to glide effortlessly through the market, picking up prizes and profits along the way. It receded further with the evangelical power of Glaxo. Here is a company that seems to have found a way through the night, a route that involves a return to the old truths of confidence and hardnosed salesmanship. A company which pays little attention to changing trends, preferring to shape the world itself, as the entire industry did in its heyday.

Both these companies, the two dominant powers in the industry, seem to have found a way. Yet then the darkness loomed again, because Merck and Glaxo seem to represent sharply contrasting styles. Merck succeeds because it finds some relationship with the societies and markets in which it operates. It compromises and contributes and strikes a deal. Within the framework of the deal, it prospers. Glaxo is another story. It struggles, summoning up great and ingenious reserves of cunning and skill, to impose itself on the market. It doesn't contribute or compromise. Eventually, it too makes a deal but – and here is the difference – it makes the deal on its own terms.

To the people gathered in this room, the two companies present a choice and a dilemma. Through this window the darkness and anxiety creep back into their minds. Which way should they go? With the light and airy genius of Roy Vagelos? Or with the dark and brooding genius of Sir Paul Girolami?

The question itself provokes deep anxiety: it is difficult even to pose because the answer is so uncertain. Which way works? There is no way of knowing for sure. Only one thing is straightforward and clear: the logic of competition means that both ways can't work at the same time. One of the two companies will prove itself more consistently successful – its way, its method, its style and its attitude will triumph. It will become the role model for others to follow. But which one?

That is the drama of the drugs industry, a drama played out every day in countless different markets around the world. A drama of crucial importance, since the drugs industry has long been established as a test of the marriage between science and business, a marriage which more and more dominates the most advanced and richest sectors of the industrial economies. A drama, also, of human ambition, since both Merck and Glaxo are companies created in the image of their powerful leaders.

And so the conference ends. The delegates in their grey suits file away. They pause on their way out to take one more drink, chatting among themselves, before drifting away to London, Frankfurt, Milan, Tokyo, New York or Los Angeles. They take with them their papers, their notes and their questions. Which way is best? Which model to follow? Which method will win? Behind them the hall is deserted and empty. The lights go out. It is truly dark now. The battle, the clash, the drama moves out into

PART ONE

The Originator: Hoffmann - La Roche

1 The industrialists of Basle

Basle has the feel of a place where things are finished off. A place where ideas or projects or lives are terminated, not begun. It has that spooky atmosphere to it: an air of certainty, an air of seriousness, an air of finality. After here, it seems to be saying, there isn't anything else. This is it.

The town itself is pretty. Straddling the banks of the Rhine, it has a fine old university and a cathedral nestling in the centre of a medieval town. It has old cobbled streets, licked perfectly clean, and lined with trim bistros, discreet banks and gaudy chocolate shops. It is tucked into a far corner of Switzerland, within spitting distance of both the French and German borders. Despite that, it is an overwhelmingly German town; orderly and fastidious and charming in a way, though a little dry and dull. A town where even the police station looks like a computer consultancy.

Yet it has a brittleness to it also. Its deeply Germanic feel, so close to Germany proper, suggests a community of people who have just slipped over the border, probably under cover of darkness, and probably for tax reasons. Along its neat roadways scuttle bankers and industrialists, each kitted out in blue or grey suits, carrying attache cases with combination locks, and hiding their faces behind dark glasses. The windows of the chocolate box houses are covered by stained wooden shutters, usually closed, hiding the inside of the homes. The town is not welcoming. It is furtive and sly, as if it harboured some dark secret: a secret likely to corrupt and destroy all those who come close to it.

For anyone interested in the drugs business, this is the place to come. This is where it started. By some strange and quirky historical coincidence, the two pivotal events in the development of the industry, though separated by some four hundred years, happened in the same small town. In the sixteenth century, a man by the name of Paracelsus merged medicine and chemistry and made the bond that was to produce such miracles in the twentieth century. And in the late nineteenth century, a man called Fritz Hoffmann was to set up a drugs company which, more than any other, was to turn that bond into something even more alluring: money and power.

Paracelsus has been called the Luther of Medicine. Whether that is justified or not, he certainly had the Protestant's trick of combining an intellectual revolution with great and startling showmanship. In 1527 Paracelsus was newly installed as the professor of medicine at the University of Basle. Confronting his students with a display of pyrotechnics, he assembled on his podium the works of Galen, Hippocrates, Avicenna and other traditional masters of medicine and, speaking in German instead of the traditional Latin used for lectures, he torched the old authorities, speaking to his audience through the smoke, summoning up through the flames his vision of a new order.

'Follow me,' he cried. 'Not I you, Avicenna, Galen, Rhazes, Montagnand, Mesue, and ye others. Ye of Paris, of Montpellier, of Swabia, of Cologne, of Vienna; from the banks of the Danube, of the Rhine, from the islands of the seas, from Italy, Dalmatia, Sarmatia, and Athens; Greeks, Arabs, Israelites, I shall be the monarch and mine shall be the monarchy.'

It was a tough sounding lecture, delivered by a man who had lived a tough life. The one surviving portrait of Paracelsus, a copper engraving made towards the end of his life, shows a rugged, wild looking man. His nose is long and thick, hooking outwards from his solid face. His forehead is bald and large, rising up over slender eyebrows, and running back over a head pitted and bumpy. His eyes are large and sad, and his mouth tapers downwards in a deep, sullen expression. His shoulders are frayed and slumped, as if weighed down by some unseen burden.

The engraving, reportedly, is taken from his own sketches, which suggests that is how Paracelsus saw himself: as a man who, having discovered some great knowledge, found it too great a weight to bear. He doesn't look happy.

Judging by the portrait, were he to be seen around today he would be taken for some kind of hobo or tramp. It would be a reasonably accurate assessment. Paracelsus was born at Einseideln in Switzerland on 10 November 1493. His father was a physician, who christened his son Theophrastus, after a disciple of Aristotle, of whom he was an admirer. His mother died while he was still a boy, and the child was raised by his father alone, and taught the basics of alchemy, pharmacy, surgery and medicine.

Arrogance came early to the young man. At the age of sixteen he went to the university of Basle, where he took up the alias Paracelsus. He chose the nickname to demonstrate his intention of becoming more knowledgeable than the Roman physician Celsus, a man still considered an authority on the human body some fifteen centuries after his death. Paracelsus studied medicine at the university, then magic under Johannes Trithemius, the Abbot of Spanheim, and then alchemy, while working in the silver mines and laboratories at Schwarz.

An appetite for discovery came early as well. At the age of twenty-three, Paracelsus ventured on a trip around the known world. He journeyed around central Europe, went south to Granada and Lisbon, north to England and Sweden, and east, to Russia and Constantinople. According to legend, he was captured by the Tartars, and was for a time a favourite at the court of the Grand Khan.

Along the way he learnt what he could of the traditional remedies for sickness. In 1526 he settled in Wurtemberg as a practising physician and surgeon, collecting around himself a group of young followers. He began experimenting with the type of medicine that made him famous, using simple remedies and condemning the elaborate and painful concoctions used at the time. It didn't make him popular with the profession – Paracelsus eventually fled Wurtemburg after threats on his life from his fellow doctors and pharmacists, which was how he ended up in Basle, as a professor, declaring himself monarch. 'Experience must verify what can be accepted or not accepted,' he wrote of his travels in one of his books. 'Knowledge is experience.'

It may seem an ordinary enough thought to twentieth-century eyes, but in his time it was a novel and dangerous idea; knowledge was the received, ancient wisdom, not something to be gleaned through close observation of the ordinary world. Paracelsus merits a special place in the history of the drugs business, not for discovering any specific medicines, but for a more central insight: for describing the body as a chemical laboratory, which could be influenced and cured by chemical compounds. He fiercely rejected the prevailing notion of the body, stemming from Galen but still around today in some of the theories of alternative medicine, as a system in which illness is the result of a disequilibrium that needs to be restored to peace. His point was that illness had to be treated within a specific organ, and chemical compounds needed to be devised to treat just that organ. He also emphasised that experimentation was the only possible authority, not the texts of the old masters. 'There will be no reference to complexions and humours,' he told his students in Basle, 'which, while thought to be the cause of diseases, have widely prohibited the understanding of them, their origin, and their critical course.'

The result of Paracelsus's lectures was to shatter the cosy and ignorant cocoon of medicine as it had been practised since classical times. After he had spoken, the old consensus could never be restored. He and his followers began to study the internal uses of chemical remedies, including mineral salts and acids, and substances obtained by processes such as distillation and extraction, and made the chemicals a matter for systematic study and experimentation. By attempting to extract what he saw as the healing virtue from inert substances, rejecting the powerful notion that only plants and herbs could have any medicinal use, Paracelsus set medical chemistry along its modern path.

None of which made him a popular man. The trade of apothecary was a profitable corner of the medieval economy, and the pharmacists did not look kindly on his attacks on the business. 'They can compose only insipid syrups and repulsive concoctions and they overlook many of the valuable extracts and dyes in the stills,' he said of the apothecaries in Basle.

As now, so it was then. Basle isn't the sort of place where you attack a profitable line of business and get away with it lightly. Paracelsus was threatened with imprisonment, was run out of town, and found himself hoofing it on the road again. He went for a time to Alsace, still working as a doctor; then to Esslingen, where he worked on constructing a laboratory for alchemical and astrological studies; and then to Nuremberg, Ratisbon, Innsbruck, Ulm, Vienna and, lastly, Salzburg, where he died in 1541.

Along the way he continued to be hounded, his work condemned, and his books banned. Such is the way it goes for intellectual revolutionaries. There are stories from his time that tell of how he was thrown to his death by rivals, or secretly poisoned on their orders. None of them are in any way verified, and are most likely untrue. The rumours, however, might well have amused Paracelsus himself. For a man who so enjoyed stirring, it would have been a neat way to go. 'I pleased no one except the sick, whom I healed,' was his own final, and surprisingly modest, epitaph on his life and achievements.

As befits a man who lived at the disjointed junction of two intellectual eras, Paracelsus was part genius and part madman. His ideas on medicine were part of a larger religious and mystical framework. He was a devout believer. To him the concept of a benevolent God could not be questioned. This led him to the idea that within nature's store of materials would be found many substances to cure the sick, which was a very perceptive and accurate idea. But his conviction that there was a unity in the universe, which also stemmed from religious conviction, led him to the notion that the movement of the stars and planets could influence the parts of the body and set in motion the remedies to be used against sickness.

Some of his doctrines were plain silly, by the standards of our times, if not by the standards of his. One cure he advocated was the use of the hellebore root against epilepsy, but he strictly cautioned that the root must be gathered on a Friday, during the waning of the moon, to be of any use against the disease. Another of his medicines for use against epilepsy was plain gross: he advised using an oil, obtained by distillation from the fluid in the skull of a man who had never been buried. In the case of wounds, he was also keen on applying medicine, not to the wound, but to the weapon that had caused the wound, in the belief that this would cure the person it had struck – a standard but very dumb idea of the time.

There is not much in the way of monuments to Paracelsus in Basle. The university where he taught and burnt books is still there, and the cathedral where he no doubt worshipped is still there as well. In the backstreets of the medieval part of town, on a hill leading away from the Rhine and up to the university, there is a small museum of pharmacy, in a three-storey building off a courtyard. Inside there is a bust of the man, taken from the engraving, and immortalising his bull-like face and harsh expression in cold stone. The inscription at its side mentions that he worked at Basle, but that's about it. It isn't much of a memorial to one of the most significant tutorials in the history of medicinal science, but then Basle is an unforgiving place, and the Swiss are an unforgiving people. They ran him out of town once, and they aren't about to have him back.

In another way, however, the town is full of monuments to Paracelsus. As you stand on the bridge that crosses the river at the centre of Basle, you gaze out on one of those striking middle European views: the river winding through the countryside, crossing into the town, with the buildings rising on either side, each looking as if it were designed just for this spot, and each looking perfectly and lovingly preserved. The imprint of Paracelsus is evident everywhere. On one side of the bridge, about a mile away, you can see the towers of Sandoz and Ciba-Geigy, two lofty giants of the drugs industry, peering at each other over the river with watchful suspicion. Turning your back on them, and on the other side, also about a mile distant, you can make out the Roche building, laid out along the banks of the river on the edge of the town.

These three buildings, and the companies they harbour, are a more accurate and telling memorial to their legendary forerunner. In his rantings and ravings, and in his delvings into the ancient and mysterious arts of alchemy, Paracelsus came up with one gem of a quotation. 'It is not the task of alchemy to make gold, to make silver,' he said, 'but to prepare medicines.' Nowhere was that message – that chemicals could be turned into gold via the medium of medicine – to be better understood than among the industrialists of Basle.

Among those sober and profit-minded industrialists, none grasped the elemental and forceful truth of what Paracelsus was saying better than Fritz Hoffmann. He was, from the few contemporary accounts, a sod of a man. Yet he was also a genius of sorts, one of the visionary entrepreneurs of the late nineteenth century who understood instinctively that the future lay with the great industrial combine: with the companies which could bring together large-scale science and large-scale organisation; and who, with others of his type, turned the German-speaking territories into the prosperous heartland of the European continent. His was quite a story.

Hoffmann was born on 24 October 1868. His father, Friedrich Hoffmann-Merian, came from a distinguished Basle family, and made a living as a wholesaler of raw silk. He was a respected member of the town's provincial community. His son, however, seemed likely to be a disappointment to him. Fritz was a rotten student, failing miserably at a succession of schools. Eventually his father, despairing of finding any worth in him, dumped young Fritz into an apprenticeship with the bankers A. Piguet & Cie in Yverdon. That, too, didn't work out, and at the age of twenty-one he was moved on to a less respectable apprenticeship with Bohney, Hollinger & Cie, a Basle firm of druggists and grocers.

It was a climbdown, even for a boy with such limited qualifications and achievements. Grocery was not much of a trade for an ambitious young man. Drugs, however, though still strictly small-time, had possibilities: possibilities which he was soon to sense. The last decade of the nineteenth century was a time of boundless opportunity in the drugs industry, and there were boundless opportunities for the men in it.

For three centuries after the death of Paracelsus, the man might as well not have lived. Few of his ground-breaking theories were taken up. But in the early years of the nineteenth century two significant discoveries were made: in 1806 morphine was first isolated, and in 1828 urea, a chemical compound found mainly in urine, was first synthesised. The result was to create an explosion in chemistry during the first thirty years of the century. In the next few years, numerous natural compounds were isolated for the first time: quinine, caffeine, nicotine, codeine, strychnine, and many others.

The powers of these compounds stimulated the first, fledgling steps towards a manufacturing pharmaceutical industry. The apothecaries and pharmacists whom Paracelsus had railed against were strictly corner-shop operations, preparing their strange potions on the premises and dispensing them to the sick. New compounds opened the way to the first glimmers of industrial production. Quinine, isolated from bark in 1820, was one of the early runners. Pelletier and Caventou, the two French pharmacists who made the discovery, set up a factory in Neuilly which produced sixty thousand ounces of the drug a year, a huge amount by the standards of the time.

Other pharmacists began producing for the emerging mass market, and many of the major companies today both in the United States and Europe can be traced back, ultimately, to some ambitious apothecary in a small town somewhere. At the same time the discovery of synthetic dyestuffs had deep consequences for the emerging drugs business: it proved the existence of bacteria despite widespread disbelief in the scientific community, and it created the giant industrial chemical combines, in particular Bayer and Hoechst in Germany, that were later to take a leading role in creating the drugs industry.

It was into this world, a world on the edge of new discoveries, that Fritz Hoffmann stepped when he joined the grocers and druggists in 1889. He lasted two years at the company before leaving for London where he found work with Ferd, Krohn & Co., a chemicals trading company. He stayed there for a few months, travelling on to Hamburg where he found another apprenticeship, this time with the druggists G. Lipmann & Geffcken.

In truth, not much was going right for young Fritz. He was wandering about Europe, flitting from job to job, and making no progress in any of them. He still looked like a failure, unable to stick at anything. But in 1893 his father intervened again, this time more decisively. He bought a share, which cost him two hundred thousand Swiss francs, in Bohney, Hollinger & Cie. This allowed Hoffmann to return to his old firm in some style, now as a senior manager at the company. Sticking to his upswing, the following year he married the daughter of an important Basle trading family, Adèle La Roche.

In 1889 Bohney, Hollinger & Cie had taken over a small chemical laboratory, manufacturing tinctures and extracts, potions, linseed oil, floor waxes, and any other junk it could find a market for. The laboratory was sited on the Grenzacherstrasse, a street which is still there today. It runs out of the centre of Basle, on the opposite bank of the Rhine from the university and the cathedral and is lined with trim houses and sturdy beer halls. A visitor walking down it today, however, would feel only one presence: the massive Bauhaus buildings of F. Hoffmann - La Roche rising up on both sides of the street.

The laboratory was run by a Munich chemist, Max Carl Traub. Bohney, Hollinger & Cie had bought the thing, but they did not take a great deal of interest in it, regarding it as no more than an insignificant sideline. Fritz Hoffmann, however, was fascinated, devoting all his time and attention to the tiny unit. It soon seemed logical to break the laboratory away from the rest of the trading firm, and on 3 March 1894, Hoffmann, Traub & Co. was created as a separate company, with Fritz Hoffmann as the senior partner. Drugs were to be the main business of the new operation – the linseed oils and floor waxes were quickly dropped from the lines. Hoffmann - La Roche, as it was later to be called, had been created.

Right from the start, Fritz Hoffmann had one firm idea fixed in his mind. If he could manufacture industrially produced drugs of a consistent quality and stamped with a well known brand name, and if he could, in addition, sell those drugs around the world, he could create a commercial giant. The idea was based on trends visible at the time, yet, in the way of trends, only barely discernible through the fog of conventional wisdom and habit. Although the huge majority of drugs was still mixed and prepared by hand at the corner-shop pharmacy stores from ingredients supplied elsewhere, there were signs that a new type of organis-ation would eventually triumph. In France some branded drugs were beginning to make progress in the market, in Germany the chemicals companies were starting to turn their attention to drugs, and other businesses, particularly the food industry – which was not unlike the pharmaceutical industry in those days – provided clear evidence of the power and reach of mass-produced goods manufactured and distributed for mass consumption. This was a time when the age of the mass consumer was just starting, emerging slowly from the old ways of local shops and local manufacturers. And, sensing the trend, Hoffmann had realised that consumers would buy and take medicines in the same way as they bought foods, alcohol and cigarettes.

The rest of Fritz Hoffmann's life was to be consumed by that one idea. To most outside observers, and particularly to the conservative financial and business community in Basle, it seemed a wild and wacked-out scheme. Even to many of his employees and colleagues it seemed too ambitious, and many left over the years. Max Carl Traub, for one, quit the company in 1896. Hoffmann had two loyal allies in his quest, however. In particular he had Emil Christoph Barrell, who took over the running of the business after Hoffmann's death, and who created much of its uniquely cold and steely character.

Barrell brought to the company a good knowledge of

chemistry, but, more important, he brought a ruthless sense of discipline and organisation. He appears, from the accounts left of his character, to have been a bitter and cranky soul. Yet with his Germanic passion for technical efficiency he was to become the perfect partner for Hoffmann's entrepreneurial flair.

The first hit the two men had was a cough syrup called Sirolin, a product which, in the way it was invented, manufactured and marketed, set the tone of Hoffmann - La Roche's operation, as well as eventually laying the financial base for the future success of the firm. It is an instructive and illuminating story, revealing much of the strange ways of the drugs business in its pre-modern form. And, just as significantly, it was to shape the character and attitudes of the company which, many years later, was to stumble across a much more lucrative and exciting medicine when it discovered the tranquilliser Valium.

In 1887 a Berne clinician, Dr Hermann Sahli, had recommended a substance called guaiacol for the treatment of tuberculosis, an infectious, wasting disease that was both widespread and terrifying at the time. Any sort of medicine for the illness promised great profits. Sahli's suggestion was jumped on by the team of Hoffmann - La Roche. A decade of tests proved disappointing, however. Guaiacol did not do much good as a cure, but it did have the important benefit of making the patient feel better. This was useful, since there were no available cures; but guaiacol also had nasty side effects. Barrell, who was still employed by Hoffmann primarily as a chemist, laboured long and hard on the drug, eventually producing a pure form of the compound, which was finally patented by the company and introduced as a therapy under the trade name Thirocol in 1898. It was not in itself a great triumph: it turned out that the drug could not be used to combat tuberculosis as intended and later investigation found it to have little or no therapeutic value at all.

But these were not the sort of setbacks to deter Fritz Hoffmann. Carl Schaerges, one of the more experienced chemists employed by the company, was instructed to look for a more pleasant form of Thirocol. Hoffmann was a great believer in nice tasting drugs, and laced one of the company's earlier preparations with chocolate in an optimistic attempt to improve its sales if not its medical effectiveness. For Thirocol, Hoffmann drew on his experiences in Hamburg. There had been a cholera epidemic during the time he was living in the city, and he recalled how sufferers from the disease took to drinking cognac flavoured with orange peel as a palliative for the ailment. He suggested they spiced up the drug with some orange, commissioning another Basle company, the Golden Pharmacy, to make an orange syrup. It worked. Thirocol plus orange syrup became the cough syrup Sirolin, which, although it never lived up to any of its therapeutic promises, was a tremendously popular remedy over many years.

The tale of its invention is instructive. This was quirky and accidental, and also designed to generate a product that would sell, regardless of any likely value to the consumer. Yet the style of its marketing is just as illuminating. Fritz Hoffmann was obsessed by two notions: mass markets and world markets. He intended to create both. But his was still a small and insignificant business, without the resources even to enter, let alone create, world markets. He had the ideas, but he had no money.

In 1898 the company had been restructured and recapitalised after coming close to bankruptcy, and after its bankers had withdrawn all credit, a calamity which had prompted Hoffmann senior to insist his son give up his adventures in pharmaceuticals. Fritz refused. He was saved by his father's death, and by the arrival in Basle of Carl Meerwein, a man who had been dealing in drugs in London, but had returned to the town with money and was looking for a new enterprise. He was introduced to Hoffmann by the local banking house La Roche & Co., and the company was reformed with Hoffmann and Meerwein as the partners, backed by investments from Hoffmann's mother and from his father-in-law, Alfred La Roche Passavant. A year later, 1899, on the brink of the new century, the company for the first time recorded a small profit for the year. Now Hoffmann had the money to finance his adventures.

The multinational corporation is often thought to be a twentieth-century invention. It wasn't. Its elements were created in the late nineteenth century, and Hoffmann and Meerwein were typical of the entrepreneurs that first began to criss-cross the globe with their lines of business. A branch in Milan had been established as early as 1896, and a French branch of the company followed soon afterwards. In the United States, import agents had been used at first, but in 1905 the Hoffmann - La Roche Chemical Works was founded in downtown Manhattan with a capital of $25,000. New branches were set up in Vienna in 1907 and in London in 1909. In the next year an office was set up in St Petersburg, after both Thirocol and Sirolin had proved themselves popular in the Russian market. In 1911 a branch was set up in Yokohama to crack the emerging Japanese market.

The developing Roche network, its offices and agents around the world, were not just traders, however, nor were they just a way of winning export orders. Hoffmann had grasped the essence of the multinational early. The world company existed to create world brands, and the trick with world brands is to push down costs through economies of scale, and to push up prices through customer awareness and loyalty. The net result is to leave a fatter profit margin between the cost and the price. Fritz Hoffman was well aware of this lucrative line of logic, and chased it to his death.

Sirolin was his first experience in creating a brand. One key element, obvious now but novel for its time, was for the product to have the same name in every country in the world. Early into its development, the Paris agent for the syrup, a firm called Herrmann & Barrière, complained about the name, suggesting in its place the French title Sirop Roche. Hoffmann was angered by this, since it contradicted his strategy for the product. He yielded, eventually, but quickly added the word Roche to the Sirolin name around the world to give the product the consistency he sought. The Roche name was subsequently added to every product that came out of the company.

Just as novel was Roche's promotion of the cough syrup. Newspaper advertisements were already common for medicinal drugs, quack or well founded. Hoffmann's were typical of the period. One showed a young boy, about five or six, dressed up in formal dinner dress, with a top hat planted on his head, and with frazzled, ragamuffin blond hair tumbling out from beneath his hat. He is holding a giant bottle of Sirolin about half his size. Clutching his arm is his sister, about four, wearing a white dress, white socks and white shoes, and looking as sweet as sugar. She too is holding a giant bottle of Sirolin. There is no copy line, nothing singing the praises of the medicine. Just a cute image. It is a very basic piece of eye-catching and 'feel-good' advertising.

Other, more imaginative, marketing ploys were strung in to promote the brand. Early experiments with junk mail were tried out – the company mailed out thousands of postcards (and sometimes pictures of saints) with puff lines attached. More radical, and more instructive for the future, were attempts to broaden the constituency of consumers. Hoffmann had realised that a drugs company's fortunes would soon be bound up with its relations with the medical and scientific worlds. Scientific reports on the effects of its medicines, invariably glowing, were written by the company laboratory and published in medical and scientific journals. As early as 1903 the French branch began publishing its own scientific journal, which was presumably friendlier to its products than independent publications. This was a departure. At the turn of the century there was little contact between the medical doctors and the drugs industry. The two communities were often in open conflict, not surprisingly since they were fighting for the same dollar or franc. Over the years this was to change as the two professions developed a close and highly dependent partnership. Hoffmann was one of the first entrepreneurs of the industry to see that its future lay with the doctors, and not in opposition to them.

Sirolin and Fritz Hoffmann, in combination, were the man and the product that created Hoffmann - La Roche. With the Sirolin campaign the essentials of the company's style were established. Its products were to be conjured up through accident and error, through diversions and misplaced trails, and through an exaggerated enthusiasm for their potential as medical cures. The products would be marketed with a mastery and invention that was missing from the laboratory. And, through it all, the angles would be played with a precision that made sure maximum revenue would be milked from minimal resources. It was a combination of tricks and talents which, many decades later, was to make Hoffmann - La Roche the largest drugs company in the world. And which was to ensure that the firm and its products secured a slug of any social history of the post-war world. Before any of that could happen, however, the company had to survive two knocks: the disruption and near disaster of the First World War, and the untimely death of its founder.

Early in the company's history, Hoffmann had sited a factory over the border in Germany, in Grenzach. He had done it because the patent protection on medicine was better in Germany than it was in Switzerland. With the outbreak of war, however, it proved to be a disastrous move. In 1915 German police raided the Grenzach factory after a sacked and embittered employee accused the company of supplying the French army with medicines from the plant. Barrell was arrested and locked up in Berlin, though he was eventually released and returned to Basle.

From there, its troubles just mounted. Even though Hoffmann - La Roche was a Swiss company, and Switzerland was neutral during the war, it was widely believed to be a German business. In Paris, the company's headquarters was continually raided by the police, who, even when they had discovered it was Swiss, suspected it of having pro-German sympathies. Pharmacists and doctors, harbouring the same suspicions, boycotted Hoffmann - La Roche products. In England it was the same. Wild rumours swirled around the company: that it was producing poison gas for the German army; that it was a haven for German spies; that munitions were stockpiled in its London office, and so on. A blockade was slapped on the company's imports, a ban which was lifted only after British officials had inspected the Basle premises. Meanwhile, back in Germany, Hoffmann - La Roche was winning no friends despite its rumoured pro-German sympathies. Instead, attempts by the company to disprove its German links and ingratiate itself with the British and French governments angered the authorities in Berlin. They put the company on their blacklist, and secretly issued orders for the army to stop using Roche medicines. The result was the company missed out on the war altogether, while the insatiable demand for medicines along the Western front was a bonanza for its rivals. It was a completely no-win situation.

But it was not as bad as the situation in Russia. In 1917 the Russian market accounted for a fifth of Hoffmann - La Roche's worldwide sales. When the revolution erupted those sales were lost in one calamitous moment. The local director of its St Petersburg office stayed in his post, struggling to keep the branch going; what happened to him was never discovered by the company, although lengthy investigations were staged. He was lost. Worse, so were a million Swiss francs in credits, a loss which was to take Hoffmann - La Roche back to the brink of bankruptcy.

The solution, the only solution, was to transform the business from a partnership into a joint-stock company. In April 1919 the new company was created, with new shareholders; Hoffmann's brother-in-law Rudolph Albert Koechlin Hoffmann, a banker, joined as president of the company, and Barrell became a shareholder and board member. Hoffmann was relegated to the role of vice-president, with day-to-day responsibility for running the company. The real management was handed over to Barrell, however. Hoffmann by this time was suffering from kidney problems, a condition which was to kill him on 18 April 1920.

Standing at Hoffmann's graveside in 1920, Barrell said of his colleague and mentor: 'To none who had dealings with him did he remain a stranger.' From the few accounts of the man, Hoffmann appears to have been a volcanic, quirky and often unreasonable character. There are stories of how the whole office would tremble each time he walked in to the room. An account from the

London office of the company, recalls how, despite a strict ban on smoking in the office, the place would reek with the thick stench of Hoffmann's cigar smoke after the founder of the company had walked through the building.

His moods swung between great optimism and great pessimism, marking the dangerous swings in the fortunes of the company. In 1946, at a celebration to mark his fifty years with the company, Barrell recalled the early days like this: 'Whoever has never had to pass sleepless nights scheming how to find the means for the next pay day, does not know the worries of the responsible businessman. And whoever does not receive blows – such as, in the history of our firm, the loss of the Russian market and the credits to the tune of a million francs we had there – without thinking of handing the loss over to the financiers or the state, knows nothing of the worries of the independent businessman.' Though not eloquently expressed, it is a poignant epitaph. Being Fritz Hoffmann was not a happy or peaceful experience.

He was not a great manager, nor was he a subtle or pleasant man. But he was a skilful entrepreneur, dashing from one project to another, and from one scheme to the next, with great gusts of energy. He was a man of considerable vision, able to see a trend coming, capture it, and ride it. Yet like most entrepreneurs he was not ultimately a great success: a talent for innovation is seldom combined with a knack for humdrum management, and many entrepreneurs end up destroying much of what they have created. Hoffmann ended his life leaving his company in almost as fragile a state as it had been when his father took a stake in the local grocers and druggists. That was the cycle, however. That was the way it went.

In the twenty-seven years he worked in the firm, Hoffmann struggled with the thing he had created. He had pushed it through a progression that was to repeat itself on a larger and more dramatic scale decades later. He had grown the company from nothing, and turned it, with a hit product, into a multinational corporation. And then he had seen it being torn apart by politics and war, while he sat on the sidelines, unable to do anything, and powerless to escape from the predicament. He had set the pattern. It was a pattern of growth and destruction that was to remain deeply embedded within Hoffmann - La Roche.

2 Valiumania

In the mid 1950s Leo Sternbach was working at the Hoffmann - La Roche laboratories in Nutley, New Jersey, the company's United States headquarters a few miles from New York. Sternbach was a Polish Jew, a former professor at the University of Cracow, who fled the country to escape persecution by the Nazis. He had come to America looking for work and had found it at Roche. But while he was there he found something else; something more shattering than he or his employers could have conceived of – a drug that was to change America.

Those were exciting years to be working in the drugs industry. The era of the wonder drugs had started with penicillin. Coming into production during the war, the drug had already changed people's perception of their vulnerability to disease. A host of other challenging compounds were launched through the fifties: the polio vaccine and the contraceptive pill were two that made a wide impact. Another was a drug called Milltown, launched by Wallace Laboratories in 1955.

Milltown was the New Jersey home town of Frank Berger, the man who discovered the first of the minor tranquillisers. The drug was a tremendous hit, both financially – the market was worth around forty million dollars a year – and culturally; Milltown was regularly covered in the press as the pharmacological symbol of a nervous, edgy, cold-war decade. Back in Basle, Hoffmann - La Roche executives scented the appetite for tranquillisers. Orders were sent down to the laboratories: we want our own tranquilliser.

The task of discovering a drug was shunted along to Sternbach. He didn't have much idea where to look, however. His knowledge of the chemical workings of the brain was limited and, try as he might, he could not think of any scientific hypothesis to point him in the right direction. Instead, he had to fall back on the traditional stand-by of drug discoverers in a fix: pot luck and crossed fingers. It was roulette time.

Sternbach recalled a group of compounds he had worked on while studying dyestuff chemistry at Cracow University. He figured they might throw up something useful, and gave them a try. He synthesised about twenty-four versions of the compound, sending them along one by one for testing. One by one they came back as duds. Eventually, harassed by his bosses to come up with something useful, Sternbach put the trials to one side. His search had been a failure.

A year later, in April 1957, the pace of work in his laboratory was filling the place to overflowing: beakers and test tubes were stacked in disorderly piles around the room. Space to work was fast running out. Tired of the mess, Sternbach's co-worker Earl Reeder told him it was about time he threw some of the rubbish away. Sternbach, however, did not like throwing things away. Among the junk were two other versions of the compound he had been testing a year earlier. He decided there was nothing to lose by sending them along to be tested: if nothing else, the results might yield a small paper in one of the scientific journals.

Only days later, Sternbach had a wildly excited phone call from the doctor in charge of testing, Lowell Randell. The first test had indicated strong muscle relaxation and sedation in mice; the second a taming effect in cats; the third a muscle relaxation in cats. More tests revealed the compound was more effective than Milltown. It was perfect. Sternbach had stumbled across a winner.

Later, more detailed tests were to reveal just how effective the compound was. One which made a big impact on Randell was called the 'fighting mouse' test. It was carried out by provoking a pair of mice into a fight by delivering electric shocks to their feet. Tranquillisers would then be pumped into the mice. Most of the other compounds already on the market would stop them fighting, but only this one would do so at below the muscle-relaxant dose, and without any hypnotic effects. More tests showed it had a unique taming effect on monkeys; later the researchers were to show it could even tame dogs, lions and tigers.

The compound Sternbach had discovered was Librium, the first of a class of drugs called the benzodiazepines. Sternbach did not have much idea what he had discovered. However, that was not uncommon at the time. Little was known about how drugs worked. All that counted was that they worked. A patent application for the new compound was filed in May 1958 and the patent was granted in July 1959. Tests were quickly carried out to prove its safety, and the drug won marketing approval from the United States regulators in record time. Two and a half years after its discovery, Librium was on the market. Almost immediately, work started on a successor. Another compound was discovered, within the same class, which was five times as powerful. By 1963 it was on the market as Valium. Together, the two drugs were to become the biggest-selling and best-known drugs ever produced.

In Basle, executives were delighted. This was the product they had been waiting for. Hoffmann-La Roche had prospered since its founder had died. The firm had established world markets for itself in speciality chemicals and vitamins, expanding on the back of the growth in vitamin additives for mass-produced foods from the 1930s onwards. It had been led by Hoffmann's sidekick Emil Barrell, who had forged the company in the image of his own personality. It was not, however, an attractive personality, as one anecdote makes clear. One time Barrell hired a Basle local for the job of chief storeman at the factory. But he had a reservation about the appointment: he thought the man was too fat, and told him so. The man was offered the job anyway, but only on one condition: that he agree to lose weight and bring Barrell a stamped weight card every week so his progress could be checked. It was an austere and autocratic organisation, rigid, unbending and unsympathetic. Barrell had died in 1953. His job had been taken over by Dr Albert Caflisch, a shy and secretive man who rarely ventured out of his office. It still lacked a major drug of its own. Librium would fill in that gap.

The company was immediately convinced the tranquilliser would be a success. 'We were pretty confident about it. You could afford to joke about it, because everyone knew it was going to be a hit,' recalls John Ward, an Englishman who worked in the marketing department of Basle from 1955 onwards. 'There was a story about a director who was in the US during the pre-launch period and he was very keen on clay-pigeon shooting. So somebody from Roche Nutley said, "If you are at all nervous about shooting, we have a new drug," so he took a capsule. And when he came back to Basle he went around saying, "There is this wonderful new drug. I've had personal experience of it and it's an absolute winner." Anyway, it turned out he had just been given a placebo. That story was bandied around and around, and it indicated how confident everyone was about it.'

More than ten years later, legal proceedings in Canada were to reveal another reason for Hoffmann-La Roche's joy over its new discovery. Patent hearings initiated by the Attorney General of Canada delved into the production costs and margins on Valium. It was revealed that the raw materials for the drug cost $87 a kilo. Transforming the raw materials into its final dosage form, and manufacturing the labels and packages, took the cost up to a final figure of $487. That amount of money, working with the initial kilo of raw material, was enough to produce a hundred thousand ten-milligram pills. And the retail price in Canada for a hundred thousand Valium pills was $11,000. So the final selling price for Hoffmann-La Roche was over a hundred and twenty-six times the cost of the raw materials, and well over twenty times the total production costs. The company had cracked the secret Paracelsus had searched for in Basle four hundred years earlier: the secret of turning base chemicals into medicine, and, through the medicine, into gold.

But the drug still had to be sold. To mint its fortune from the alchemical concoction Sternbach had delivered, Hoffmann-La Roche first had to create a market for the drug, and deliver it to the possible patients. It did so by dreaming up the first of the great modern pharmaceutical marketing campaigns.

The key figure was an American named Paul Hacker, a phycology and marketing graduate who joined Roche in Basle just before the worldwide launch of Librium. 'He sorted out the managerial problems at the company, and then he was in charge of marketing,' recalls his former colleague, John Ward. 'He was very formative. He had brilliant ideas, he would throw them out, and if anyone else came up with an idea he would weigh it very carefully. He was a born marketeer and he was in his prime.'

Drugs marketing in the late 1950s was still simple stuff. The product came out of the laboratory, and there were salesmen to tramp round the physicians hassling them to start prescribing the medicine. But that was it: a basic manufacturing and distribution system. Hacker, with his background in marketing, realised more was needed: that drugs, although uniquely different from other consumer goods, still needed to be marketed. He came closest to realising Fritz Hoffmann's ideal of medicines branded and marketed and sold with the same campaign around the world. Hacker died young, in 1963. But by that time the essential techniques of Librium and Valium salesmanship had been mapped out and had proved effective.

In Boston in 1959 a symposium was held for America's leading psychiatrists – its aim was to introduce them to Librium. The symposium was a wild success, according to later recollections. At the same time, the testing of Librium – it was tested on one thousand six hundred people before it was approved for use – was carefully spread out across the United States. There was no scientific need for the spread: it could just as well have been tested in one small town. The idea was to give as many physicians as possible some experience of the drug before its launch. Both these ideas, the symposia and the testing, were clever innovations. The tactic was to involve physicians in the development and the launch of the drug, to let them feel the potency of the new compound in treating their patients, and to create a shared sense of power between the drugs company and the physicians in their control of the new drug. The same technique was employed around Western Europe. Details varied according to local culture – in Switzerland the symposia were given the genteel description of 'coffee mornings' – but the idea of introducing the drug to the doctors in groups and in a scientific style was successfully transplanted everywhere. In Europe there was a greater reluctance to acknowledge anxiety as a disease. It was overcome, as in the United States, by getting doctors to speak about their experiences with the drug.

Another smart idea was the films. Part of the initial testing of Librium had been to try it out on leopards, lions and tigers at San Diego Zoo. The drug had powerful and visible effects on the animals and these were captured on film for their dramatic impact. Sometimes the idea backfired. One American marketing man for the drug recalls how a salesman would take the short movie round to a physician's office, set up a projector and show it right there. Usually the physicians were interested enough to watch, but would turn round after it was over, saying, 'Very good, fella, but I don't treat animals.' Yet, if it was sometimes too populist a trick for physicians, the films had a great impact on the general public. In the United States, *Life* ran a story on Librium's power to tame wild animals. And in the United Kingdom, after Hoffmann - La Roche had called a press conference to show the film, one popular newspaper ran a story with the headline 'The Drug that Tames Tigers – What will it do for Nervous Women?'

The two key elements in the marketing campaign were established right away. Roche created a rapport with the doctors and an immediate, widespread awareness of the drug. And there was an awareness, also, among the ordinary public – not the same detailed knowledge as the physicians had, but an impression of Librium as an immensely powerful, almost magical, compound. Those two effects were soon translated into sales. Librium took off on a steep, forty-five degree sales curve, and soon established itself as one of the best-selling drugs in the world. Once launched, it never slowed down.

Work on Valium – both marketing and development work –

started even before Librium was launched. It was a similar drug to Librium, only more powerful. It combined a tranquillising action with a muscle relaxant and also an hypnotic effect; it was the only drug to combine all three actions. And there was, as a marketing man was later to recall, 'almost nothing you couldn't use it for'. There is a story within the company that the president of Roche Nutley tried the drug out on his mother-in-law, and was so impressed by its calming influence he backed it to the hilt.

Executives at Hoffmann - La Roche had a feeling Valium could have a greater impact even than Librium, but could not be quite sure. 'In the drugs business, you don't really see a role, you deal with the data you collect,' recalls one marketing executive who worked on the drug in the United States. 'Librium was going straight up at the time. In 1960 it quickly overtook meprobanate [the earlier class of tranquillisers, and the one Roche had set out to imitate], and we were riding on a real winner with Librium, so we had a fairly large portfolio of two thousand compounds we were looking at because they were all interesting drugs. Valium was the only one with indications in all three areas. So as we got closer to the market place it was clear to us that the anxiety effect was the most profound, because of the potential market. But we didn't really know what the market was for some of these other areas. To predict the market was difficult for us. We put the same horsepower behind Librium and Valium at the same time. And Valium just took off.'

The name was a stroke of genius. Naming drugs has since become a small art form all of its own, but Hoffmann - La Roche was again ahead of the pack in realising the marketing significance of the name. It needed to combine a scientific air, while at the same time generating good feelings about the effects of the drug. Valium fitted the bill perfectly: taken from a Latin stem, it implied 'to be well and strong'.

Real genius, however, was devoted to the advertising of the drug. Marketing policy at Hoffmann - La Roche in the 1960s was heavily directed to advertising directly to the physicians, through pages paid for in the medical journals, and through direct mail.

The advertisements for Valium – largely created by the New York agency William Douglas McAdams – were to be brilliantly conceived and brilliantly executed.

One advertisement, a classic, shows a grainy, black and white picture of a housewife sitting back in an armchair stirring a cup of tea. Her coffee table dominates the front of the picture. It has an ashtray on it with a couple of cigarettes stubbed out, and a glass which looks as though it might contain alcohol. A magazine is lying half-open on the housewife's lap, and her position is listless and lifeless. Her head is askew, and on her face there is an expression of acute misery and depression. Below the picture is the headline: 'Psychic support for the "always weary".' The rest of the copy reads: 'When psychic tension is the reason for chronic fatigue, Valium can help provide the right kind of support. That's because, in proper dosage, Valium calms the tense, tired patient while seldom dulling the senses or interfering with function. In this way, the patient may be better.'

The image is carefully created. The bored, tired, exhausted housewife was a familiar figure at most physicians' surgeries, and was one the physician rarely had much idea how to deal with. The Valium advert plays on the theme: it holds out the promise of instant relief for a person clearly depressed with the condition of her life.

Similar themes and messages were to appear and reappear. One advertisement showed an attractive young college student carrying her books around the campus. At the top the legend ran: 'A whole new world of anxiety', while the copy went on to suggest starting college was a stressful experience for a young woman; Valium would be the cure for that experience. Another suggested playfully that Valium was the best way of clearing troublesome patients out of the physician's office.

Behind the advertisements was a highly developed sense of the potential for drug advertising. Hoffmann-La Roche had won regulatory approval for Librium and Valium as treatments for acute anxiety, a medical condition defined as a state where anxiety has reached a level where a patient is no longer able to function normally. Starting from that point, the company gradually managed to widen the prescribing of the drug. Ultimately it was recommending the drug be prescribed for anyone who was just feeling mildly fed up with things in general.

It was clever marketing. The product, the name, the advertisements and the stunts came together to capture the mood of the decade; as early as 1964 *Newsweek* coined the term 'The tranquilliser decade'. Once the mood was created, the company could hold it and ride it. The campaign was to make Hoffmann-La Roche the most successful drugs company in the world. In 1965, in the United States, Librium was the top selling drug, ringing up sales of $59 million a year. Valium, two years after its launch, was the seventh largest pharmaceutical product, with sales of $27 million. By the end of the decade, Hoffmann-La Roche had moved comfortably into the top spot in the world industry. Its global drug sales came to $840 million, well past the number two company, Merck, with $670 million. By 1970, Valium in the United States alone was a product worth $200 million, making it the biggest-selling and most profitable drug ever created.

Yet the drug had done something more than just spout money. In the thirteen years since Leo Sternbach had stumbled across the compound in the laboratory at Nutley, Hoffmann-La Roche had created the modern drugs industry. It had built its form and structure. From here on, as the rest of the industry was quickly to learn, it was all very obvious. The trick was to find a compound for a common, and preferably loosely-defined, illness and to prove the effectiveness of the drug. Then place a patent on it and go to work on the marketing, weaving an image for the drug as a solution to the problems of contemporary life. Make it so well known that the drug becomes a household word, a word on everyone's lips, and increase the pressure on physicians to keep up prescriptions to demanding patients. And, most important of all, keep on widening the possible range of conditions it can be used to treat. Then sit back and watch the money roll in.

The strategy was one of endless expansion, of boundless opportunities. There seemed no limit to how successful this product could be. Moreover, it was a monopoly, with monopoly profits to match. Yet, as Hoffmann - La Roche was soon to discover, expansion is seldom infinite, and opportunities are seldom without boundaries. At the same time as discovering the secrets and riches of the drugs industry, the company was to discover its surprises and traps as well. And it was to discover them very soon.

3 The hunted men

On 9 September 1979, Senator Edward Kennedy opened a meeting of the United States Senate Subcommittee on Health and Scientific Research by announcing the committee would be studying the use of the benzodiazepines, the clinical name for the class of drugs pioneered by Librium and Valium. Their purpose, the Senator went on, was 'to try to understand the reasons for their use and misuse, to try to alert the American people to the consequences of misuse and abuse, and to see what can be done to assure appropriate use.'

Kennedy was flanked that morning by Senators Schweiker and Metzenbaum. Also present were Robert Clark, the president of Hoffmann - La Roche in the United States, and Bruce Medd, the company's marketing physician. The meeting opened in a hostile and unfriendly atmosphere for the two drug company men. Before them were paraded a procession of men and women, each one giving testimony before the committee, telling their stories of use and abuse. Each one was styled as a victim of Valium.

The first up was William Thomas, a physician from Long Beach, California, who admitted developing a regular Valium habit, swallowing more than fifty tablets a day. Next in line was William Ryan, a Catholic priest, who confessed to a combined Valium and alcohol addiction that made 'emptying a waste basket a week-long project'. He was followed by Joan Hinton, a housewife from Delaware, who described how she had been given separate prescriptions for Valium from the four different psychiatrists she was seeing at the same time. And so it went on.

There was another housewife from Delaware who claimed her psychiatrist had told her she needed Valium in the same way a diabetic needs insulin. A woman bank officer from California told how she had realised she was addicted to Valium after watching a television show on the drug. And lastly there was another physician from North Carolina who provided the parade with its most memorable and wittiest line of testimony. 'While all the other doctors in Boston were reading their mail I was eating mine,' he said.

For the two drug company men it was a uniquely depressing session: a modern form of public flogging. Clark opened his defence in combative style. 'The first panel of witnesses unquestionably involved the most classic disobeyance of the package insert that I have ever heard in my life,' he countered. His defence did him little good; the flogging was to continue. The Senators turned their fire to the Cornell Stress Program, a three-year study into stress which was funded by Hoffmann - La Roche to the tune of over four million dollars. The implication was that the company had paid for the programme on the understanding that it would recommend Valium as a treatment.

Senator Metzenbaum certainly saw it that way. He read out a transcript of a cassette recording of an interview between two of the academics leading the study, eighty thousand of which had been sent out by Cornell Medical School. 'You could not have read anything that was more of a push for Valium than the statements that are made in that particular transcript of the cassette. I find nowhere that any other medicines are mentioned,' he started. Metzenbaum went on: 'Now, what concerns me, Mr Clark, is that you head up a very responsible and respected company; you have a good reputation in the industry. Is there not some sense of impropriety in spending over four million dollars to fund a programme at Cornell, which, in essence, winds up being nothing more than a kind of medical approval [for a product] merchandised and marketed by your company? Is there not something wrong with that kind of procedure? You give four million dollars and you get all this extra push for your product.'

'Let me reiterate again that we have no control over what that doctor [one of the two academics] says,' answered Robert Clark.

'Mr Clark,' continued the Senator. 'Do you not think that when you give somebody four million dollars to head up a programme and they wind up saying all the right things about your product, you do not have to say: "Now doctor, you have to remember to say it this way." It's obvious. He said it that way for four million dollars.'

'Senator Metzenbaum, you are a terrible cynic, I am afraid,' replied Clark. 'I know that doctor and I think he is a very reliable, honest man. He happens to mention Valium, because that is what everyone talks about when they are talking about tranquillisers.'

'And Valium just happens to be the one funding the programme,' said Metzenbaum.

And so it went on. The Kennedy hearings were the high point of a ten-year campaign against Valium: a campaign waged by pressure groups, by feminists, by doctors, by the media, by everyone; and a campaign waged with a bitterness and ferocity as yet unseen in attacks on corporate behaviour. Hoffmann-La Roche had discovered the price of wealth and fame.

It started, say former company executives, sporadically in the mid sixties. There was one attack in Denmark by a psychiatrist in 1965, and more followed. Valium by that time had become more than just a drug. It was a fashion item: no smart handbag in the United States or Western Europe was without a few capsules. And it had become a symbol: it was as much a part of the swinging sixties as mini skirts, Martinis and the Vietnam war. The hype, once it started, just rolled and rolled. Rock bands sang about it – 'Mother's Little Helper' by the Rolling Stones; authors wrote about it – *Valley of the Dolls* by Jacqueline Susanne; and comedians told jokes about it – there is a scene in a Woody Allen movie where he asks if anyone has a Valium, and everyone in the room dips their hands into their pockets. The drug by now had moved out of the closed triangle of drugs companies, regulators and physicians, and it had entered the stormy world of mass media and mass markets. It had become a cultural as much as a medical commodity: it had broken its boundaries. And Hoffmann-La Roche had surrendered control of its most profitable product.

Control of the drug, in truth, had moved away from the company some time earlier. Unwittingly, it had given up the drug through its own policies and plans. Although the early publicity for Librium was stimulated by Hoffmann-La Roche, marketing executives, after the early tiger films, had done little to create an awareness of the drug among the general public. The fame of Valium had been created by its own success as the most widely prescribed medicine in the world. But the company had done everything it could think of to popularise the drug among physicians, and to portray it as the solution to their problematic and difficult patients. By doing so it had lost all ability to keep control of how and why Valium was being prescribed. It had surrendered control as part of a deliberate marketing campaign.

Hoffmann-La Roche executives were constantly surprised throughout the sixties by the different uses of Valium that kept cropping up. 'I don't think we were really aware of how widely Valium was used until it started turning up in things like novels,' is how John Ward remembers the attitude in Basle in the late sixties. It is a revealing comment. When a marketing department needs to flick through the pages of pulp bestsellers on the station bookstalls to find out what is happening to their product, it is not hard to figure out there has been little monitoring of the usage of the drug in the market place.

'Valiumania' was a term coined by the *New York Times* magazine in the seventies to characterise the rise and rise of the drug. The phrase caught the popularity of the drug in physicians' surgeries; and it caught as well its emerging status as a modern demon. The attacks started for real with the publication of a book by a woman television executive, Barbara Gordon, describing how she was put on Valium and became addicted to the drug – both Hoffmann-La Roche and the prescribing doctors were criticised heavily. From then on, attacks on the drug were to start turning serious.

By the turn of the decade they were in full swing. In 1969,

during Senate hearings on the drugs industry, Senator Gaylord Nelson examined the growth of tranquillisers, posing in his opening address a question common in America at the time. 'When Aldous Huxley wrote his fantasy concept of the world of the future in *Brave New World*, he created an uncomfortable, emotionless culture of escapism dependent upon tiny tablets of tranquillity called soma. It was chillingly disconserting to read in Huxley's book of figures frantically hiding from reality. It was comforting, however, that the book was, after all, only science fiction. But in the nearly forty years since Huxley created his classic, the fiction has started to read like reality. It became a prophetic insight into the kind of society we seem to be moving towards today.

'In our complex society, we have our soma to escape the frustrations. We find psychotropic drugs to escape in, barbiturates and tranquillisers. Over the past few years, if we can believe only a small part of what has been written, Americans have been insulating themselves from the pressures of modern life by using tranquillising drugs in rapidly increasing numbers. Our problem is that we don't really know very much about the tranquillising drugs or what they are doing to us as individuals and to our society as a whole.'

Those same questions and fears were stated in a starker form by the first of the witnesses before the hearings, Dr Stanley Yolles, the director of the National Institutes of Medical Health: 'To what extent would Western culture be altered by the widespread use of tranquillisers?' he asked. 'Would Yankee initiative disappear?'

Here was something quite unexpected for Hoffmann-La Roche. The company stood accused – not by wide-eyed fanatics but by Senators – of destroying the American Way of Life. And accused, to make it worse, of finishing off two thousand years of Western civilisation. This was serious stuff.

It was to get worse. In a related set of hearings held in 1971, Senator Nelson turned his guns directly on Hoffmann-La Roche and its marketing techniques. Appearing before him was Dr Charles Edwards, then Commissioner of the Food and Drug

Administration, the American regulatory agency. The Senator cross-examined the Commissioner on Librium and Valium advertising.

'For example, let us take this ad for Librium,' he started out. 'At the top it says "A whole new world of anxiety" and it says "The new college student may be afflicted by a sense of lost identity in a strange environment. Today's changing morality and the possible consequences of her 'new freedom' may provoke acute feelings of insecurity. She may be excessively concerned over competition, both male and female, for top grades. Unrealistic parental expectation may further increase her emotional tension. Her newly stimulated intellectual curiosity' – get this – 'may make her more sensitive to an apprehension about unstable national and world conditions. Exposure to new friends and other influences may make her re-evaluate herself and her goals . . . Take Librium."

'Then there is a page of warnings, precautions and so forth, which is not very conspicuous. Now, what proof, what controlled clinical trials have been filed with the FDA to demonstrate that this drug is efficacious for treating these conditions?'

It was a good question. Dr Edwards replied like this: 'Well, we have none. I think it is important to point out that when these drugs were approved by the Food and Drug Administration, these particular symptoms that you indicated – anxiety, tension, neurosis, and so forth – were part of a medical condition, a medical disorder. They were not approved for treating an everyday situation or ordinary life problem. What has happened is the advertisers, the promoters of these drugs, have taken them out of context and applied them to day-to-day situations that we are all confronted with. As a result they have developed this totally misleading advertising. The original approval of these drugs by the Food and Drug Administration was legitimate. We were thinking of these drugs in terms of medical conditions and not for use in ordinary life situations.'

'So, in other words, what you are saying is that when the drug company filed the New Drug Application and proof of efficacy is required', questioned Nelson, 'the controlled clinical trials were for medical conditions only?'

'That is exactly correct,' answered Edwards.

Nelson continued: 'Then are you saying that since that time they have expanded the definition of their use, so to speak, to go beyond what would be classified as a medical condition?'

And Edwards replied: 'That is exactly correct, yes.'

The corporation had been rumbled; its precise and carefully executed marketing plans had been laid open, and condemned. Now, with the Senate's blessing, it was open season on Hoffmann - La Roche. And the vultures and scavengers were about to descend.

There were three main lines of attack developed against the drug. One was medical: it argued that Valium was addictive, particularly when taken regularly for months or even years, and it also noted how Valium was often included among the pills taken by people who killed themselves through drug overdoses. The second was feminist: women's rights activists argued the drug was prescribed by a male-dominated medical profession as a way of controlling and supressing women – the argument was supported by statistics showing clearly how Valium was taken more by women than men. The third attack pitched itself somewhere between sociology and morality, developing an attitude later termed Pharmacological Calvinism. It argued that Valium was a form of escapism from the everyday stresses that are part of the experience of humanity: it suggested, in other words, that people suffering from anxiety should just grin and bear it, and not seek their salvation in a bottle of pills.

The heat of the attacks was intensified by the changing temperature of the times. In the late fifties, when Hoffmann - La Roche had asked Leo Sternbach to look for a tranquilliser, technology, and drugs in particular, was seen a universal solution. Few then would have thought to question its benefits, or to suggest technology could be bad as well as good. By the late sixties the climate was different. Technology was no longer universally regarded as a good. And neither was the system that produced it.

Between the late sixties and the early seventies a drug counter-culture emerged: a kind of warped mirror-image of the staid monoliths of the pharmaceuticals business. Like the drugs barons of the big companies, the drugs radicals of the campuses held out the promise of a social transformation through the chemical manipulation of the human mind. Theirs, however, was a very different agenda from that of the industrialists. 'Tune in, turn on, drop out', was the motto of the guru Timothy Leary. Dope and acid were the preferred drugs; and the movement speculated that a better and more peaceful world could be created by the use of mind-expanding drugs. In this picture Hoffmann - La Roche emerged clearly as the enemy. Valium was not a mind-expanding drug; it was a mind-closing drug. It was not the drug of the campuses or the city centre; it was the drug of the suburbs. And it was not the drug of the hipsters or the radicals; it was a drug for the squares – a drug for making people fit into the system, a capitalist drug, and a capitalist tool. Or so it went, anyway, in the paranoid fantasies popular in radical circles at the time.

The company had painted itself into a corner. If you were looking for an example of big, bad business to carve into, it didn't take too long to discover Hoffmann - La Roche. Nor did it take long to realise it was the perfect bad guy. It was almost a self-parody: it was Swiss, it was monopolist, it was multinational, it made wild and absurd profits, it was fantastically secretive, and its products could be classed as extremely dangerous. It was as if the company had studied left-wing tracts on the wicked corporation and said, 'All right! Let's do it.' And to make it even better, with every twist, and with every turn, the company only spun itself into a harder tangle.

Back at Basle they were starting to sweat. Trapped and baited, the company was confused and directionless in its own response. 'We made considerable efforts to persuade doctors that these drugs were really to be used for a period when the patient was really ill and to make patients more responsive to a doctor's advice on how to correct a failing lifestyle so that anxiety wouldn't occur,' recalls Ward. 'But by then Valium had its own reputation, and its own life. The doctors blamed the patient for demanding a prescription, and the patient blamed the doctors for giving them Valium.'

Everyone, meantime, blamed Hoffmann - La Roche for continuing to churn the stuff out of its factories. High up in the company there was a solid policy of never responding to press enquiries, or rising to any form of attack. Secrecy was inbred in the Basle headquarters: in those days, using the always-helpful small print of Swiss company law, financial figures – beyond crude turnover totals – were not even published. Any sort of response to the attacks, felt the corpracrats in Basle, would only inflame the controversy, feed it, and worsen it. By the early seventies, however, it became painfully obvious that the situation couldn't get any worse. The company needed to start muscling its way out of the corner.

A committee was set up within Basle, bringing together all the senior marketing men from the major markets to co-ordinate a response to the attacks. There were arguments within the company: some executives, the to-hell-with-it school, said they should keep pushing the drug; others, the conciliators and pacifiers, figured they should turn down the level of promotion. It was a tough battle: years of astounding success had created an air of invulnerability within the company, and had bred a sense of mastery. But the pacifiers won and some of the heat was taken out of the marketing campaign. 'There were fewer people, as time went on, saying low-key is not the answer, we should go out and sell as much as we can. That very quickly disappeared,' recalls Ward. 'But I think it is true that there was over-confidence. In general, in marketing, I think we were somewhat over-confident.'

In the United States new types of advertisements started appearing. One, using a cutsie-pie personalised approach, appeared under the headline 'Examine Me'. The copy started out: 'During the past several years, I have heard my name mentioned in movies, on televison and radio talk shows, and even at Senate subcommittee sessions. And I have seen it repeatedly in newspapers, magazines and, yes, bestsellers. Lately, whenever I see or hear the phrases "over-medicated society", "over-use", "misuse" and "abuse", my name is one of the reference points. Sometimes even *the* reference point . . . Amid all this controversy, I ask you to reflect on and re-examine my merits.' The advertisement then went on to restate the uses of Valium in treating anxiety and stress, although with nothing of the overt hard-sell of the earlier promotion.

This was the new-look, nice-guy Hoffmann - La Roche. But when you're down, you're down, and you stay down. In the late sixties the British government decided the company was abusing its monopoly on Librium and Valium by charging excessive prices for the drugs. Negotiations over the issue led to Hoffmann - La Roche agreeing to pay $1.6 million in excess profits back to the UK for the years 1967 to 1969: the company figured it was better to refund profits than cut prices in case demands for equal reductions arose in other countries. But by 1971 Hoffmann - La Roche had tired of this game. After all, making excess profits was its business. It refused to make any refunds for 1970.

In Britain the Department of Health and Social Security followed up by setting up an investigation into the company by the Monopolies Commission, the independent government agency for checking abuses of commercial power. It studied the costs of production for the drugs, and did not like what it saw; its published report recommended the price of Librium be cut to forty per cent of the 1970 level, and the price of Valium be cut to twenty-five per cent of the 1970 level. Those were the sort of figures, it concluded, where Hoffmann - La Roche would be making fair profits.

On 12 April 1973, the British government fixed the prices of the two drugs at the newly recommended level. Still in fighting mode, Hoffmann - La Roche initiated court proceedings to challenge the Monopolies Commission's findings. Eventually, the battle was settled out of court when the company agreed to repay the government $3.75 million in excess profits, and to cut the prices for Librium and Valium to half the 1970 levels.

Back in Basle they were sweating again. Britain by itself they could cope with: it was just one, medium-sized market. But the publicity given to the case around Europe, and its close monitoring by other governments, had shaken the company. Soon after the British case started, similar actions were initiated in Germany and Holland. 'There was considerable anxiety about it in Basle, partly because it was part of a price war breaking out at the time,' recalls Ward. 'We were mortally afraid of that because Roche always had very different prices in different countries. That was why we were so worried, because we were sure this was going to spill over into other countries that had been teetering on the brink.'

There was worse to come. In the early seventies a British employee named Stanley Adams revealed corrupt commercial tactics in Hoffmann-La Roche's vitamin business; the charges involved illegal fidelity payments to bulk buyers. The company did not respond generously to his allegations. Using corruption-friendly Swiss law, it managed to have Adams temporarily arrested and jailed for making the revelations. While he was in jail his wife committed suicide. Adams took his case to the European Community, which, in 1979, finally found Hoffmann-La Roche guilty of abusing its market power and posted a fine of DM732,000. It wasn't a huge fine, but the company was acquiring a reputation: offence after offence (a year later, in Canada, it was found guilty of predatory market practices with Librium and Valium). The Adams affair became a *cause célèbre* in Europe, painting the company's image blacker and blacker. Then in 1975, in Seveso, in Italy, an accident at a Roche plant released a dioxin cloud over the countryside, damaging the environment, animals and people for miles around.

The relentless attacks on its tranquillisers had started to have an effect on sales. Librium and Valium peaked in the early seventies, and sales were flat for many years after that, before starting to fall towards the end of the decade. In the meantime, the company was frantically pumping the money which was pouring in from the two drugs into research and development. It needed another winner.

Estimates suggest Hoffmann - La Roche spent between six and eight million Swiss francs through the seventies searching for a successor to its wonder drug. It never found one. Many pale imitations of Valium, tranquillisers in the same class, came out of the laboratories. But nothing novel, and nothing to match its past successes.

To add to the company's troubles, Valium was beginning to lose its patent in a succession of European countries. As soon as the patent went, so did the profits. Generic manufacturers began producing their own versions of Librium and Valium at a fraction of the cost. Sales and prices for the Hoffmann - La Roche product started slipping away. By 1978/79 the company's profits were going into decline – the overall profit margin of the company fell back from 16 per cent in 1976 to only 3.7 per cent in 1981. The money was sinking into research and once the notes went into the laboratories they never came out again. Then, in 1985, Valium went off patent in the United States, the most important market of all. The company immediately sacked one thousand workers in an attempt to trim costs. But nothing could stop the slide. In 1987, the first full financial year reflecting the loss of the US patent, Hoffmann - La Roche's total sales were down by twelve full percentage points. The price of fame was now being paid in the hard currency of dollars and francs.

Hoffmann - La Roche had metamorphosed entirely. From being a clever story of corporate success it had become a cautionary tale. In 1984, in a newspaper interview, Fritz Gerber, who took over as chairman in 1975, reflected upon its downfall. 'There was an arrogance,' he mused. 'Roche was taken by surprise [by its success] and was not ready for it. This might have created some kind of self-confidence. The company isolated itself, it became more conservative, and quite litigious. There was an I-couldn't-care-less attitude to many outsiders which gave the company completely the wrong image.'

It was more than just a wrong image. By 1984 the company had slipped from a dominating first place in the industry, the master of all it surveyed, to a lowly ninth place, one of the pack, scratching to make a living. It was a steep fall: as steep as its rise had been twenty years earlier. Hoffmann - La Roche had stepped on to a rollercoaster, climbed the curve to its peak, and then thrown away the brakes, freewheeling for the rest of the journey. It had been that kind of a trip – wild and fast and scary. And once it had started, there was no way of stopping.

One man saw it all. Bruce Medd has a way of cropping up wherever Valium is mentioned. He was there at the Kennedy hearings, accompanying the president of the company. He is there in all the press clippings, all the television debates, in the radio talk shows. It's weird: as if wherever he went people felt this compulsion to start attacking Valium. In reality, naturally, it was no accident. Medd was there on purpose. He was the man employed by Hoffmann - La Roche to take the flak: a kind of professional bullet-proof jacket, a man to be flung out when the dogs howled.

He has worked at the company since 1962, joining soon after he qualified as a medical doctor. He was given the job of marketing physician, the medical man attached to the marketing organis-ation of the corporation. Valium was the first drug he worked on, and he has been working on it ever since. Through its rise and through its fall, Medd has stuck loyally at the side of the molecule, pushing, explaining and excusing. If anybody can nail this thing, he can.

Roche Nutley, the US headquarters of the company, is sited a few miles outside New York on the edges of a small town. It is openly visible from the highway – a huge white administrative and manufacturing complex with a large Stars and Stripes fluttering in the breeze outside. Getting closer, it is an imposing building. Built in the thirties, it is constructed in a form of subdued art deco. Inside, it is a mix of the old and the new: attempts have been made to turn it into a modern, pot-planted, open-plan office, but the old, regimented, separate office style it was built for keeps getting in the way. Mostly it is dominated by long corridors and staircases.

Bruce Medd looks as though he is pushing fifty. He has grey, wispy hair, and his face has a long, slightly haggard look. When speaking, he sits back, tucking his knees up in front of his body. From time to time he slaps his hands on the table to make a point, and he sweats a little when he gets tense. But most of the time his manner is calm and relaxed – except for the eyes. His eyes have a haunted, hunted spark to them. So, Bruce, why was Valium so popular?

'I've tried to convince the various boards I've worked for that it was me,' he says with a laugh, 'but none of them have believed me. Really, I think it was the drug. I hate to admit that as a marketeer, but I think it was a better drug than we had anticipated. We used the term "psychic tension". Everybody felt Valium was different, and the way they articulated it was that there seemed to be more relaxation on the part of the patient. We were always trying to figure out if that was the muscle relaxant element, and I think it was, but we were always trying to figure it out. The patient had this relaxing feeling. It had this physical aspect to relieving emotional pain. So we tended to concentrate on that aspect. If people were impossible to live with, then they took the drug and suddenly they became reasonable, nice even, that had a great impact. People remembered the experience.'

Medd's mood begins to shift a little as he recalls the sudden change in the fortune of the drug. 'It was around 1970,' he recalls. 'It started with the idea of the over-medicated society. The over-use of drugs in general started being a battleground, and then it became focused on the tranquillisers. The argument was that these drugs are being used and there is no need for it. There was this Calvinistic belief that anxiety was not a disease, and that if you couldn't just grin and bear it then there was something wrong with you as a person.'

As the attacks grew in ferocity, the company started to move into some very weird territory. Being attacked on commercial grounds, or economic grounds, a company can expect that. But to have your product attacked for being immoral, for just exist-ing . . .

'Oh, yeah,' says Medd, his eyes quivering a little now. 'Here was something that was totally outside the medical environment. This was a sociological phenomenon. And how could we deal with that? Tied into it was not only an over-medicated society but a male-dominated society as well – a male-dominated medical profession prescribing these drugs to women. There was this harried housewife concept, that doctors were prescribing these drugs to women because they had two or three babies and the laundry and the food to make and everything. And they said we were taking advantage of the phenomenon.'

It wasn't just a moral or a sociological attack, though. There were medical reasons, weren't there? The use of Valium for committing suicide, for example. Medd looks wearied by the question, bored even: 'When you have a drug that is prescribed for emotionally distressed people, you will have some depressed patients who at some time in their therapy are likely to be prescribed Valium. Some of those people unfortunately attempt suicide. If you happen to be one of the more common medications in the medicine cabinet and somebody decides to take everything that's in there, you will, at times, be associated with successful suicides. So there was that issue of people taking the drug to kill themselves. In fact it is an extremely safe compound. It's been said that the best way to kill yourself with Valium is to be buried alive in the tablets. But when you did it with other drugs you get a cocktail, and the drug itself may have nothing to do with it, but it's there, and you get blamed.'

But here he is refuting all the criticisms made of Valium over the years. Did any of the attacks ever strike him or the company as valid? Did it learn anything from its critics?

Medd pauses, thinking, and seemingly puzzled by whether he learnt anything. 'I think the one thing we learnt is this. When we first started, if someone had said how long should someone be on this medicine, I wouldn't have known. There was no question that Valium was an extremely effective treatment for the symptoms of anxiety. But we certainly learnt that more has to be done to get to the underlying situation causing the anxiety. In many cases, once the person had the symptoms relieved they could look at their lifestyle and solve the problem. And I did a lot of meetings with physicians in the seventies trying to share some of what we had learnt with them.'

The doctors were the key. They were the people who prescribed the drug, and the people whose opinion mattered most. Yet their reactions to the attacks on Valium were a mess of confusion.

'You got a spectrum,' he says. 'If you are basically a Calvinist you are going to sympathise with the attack. The medical profession generally felt that Valium was one of its most useful tools and really did not sympathise with the attackers. The critics were saying the physicians didn't know what they were doing. But they were the ones who saw the benefits of the drug. And they would go to the critics and say, "You don't know what you're saying because you don't practise medicine."'

Those were strange times. For the men at Hoffmann - La Roche, at the centre of this storm, it must have been a strange and unnerving time.

The hunted look returns to Medd's eyes. 'I always had a very positive attitude about both the benefits and the drawbacks of these drugs. But it wasn't easy. Sometimes it seemed as if everybody who wanted to get into the press attacked Valium. I remember one year some guy in San Fransisco had shown Valium stopped muscle division or something in chickens, and the front page of the newspaper the next day said Valium destroys muscles. And that was it. He'd got his publicity and then he'd be off doing something else, but I'd still be trying to figure out what it meant. These things always seemed to happen around Christmas, so on the Friday before you'd go home you'd be trying to figure this stuff out. It was like that then. Any Woody Allen movie, any Neil Simon play, it had a Valium joke in it. For a while there you couldn't pick up a book without seeing Valium. A well known person couldn't have a problem without implicating Valium. One after the other. You know, some celebrity goes to the hospital, Elvis Presley dies, and if there is any possibility that this person had taken one Valium in their lives it becomes a Valium problem.

How could you defend against that? How could you even answer the question? If I'd known more about the cases I might have had an answer, but most of the time I just didn't know.'

The company started out by ignoring all the controversy. It pretended it was not happening, and hoped it would all go away. Then it came out and started debating all the charges made against it.

Medd's eyes flicker towards the ceiling as he thinks about the point. 'Our industry is not media-orientated. It just didn't have to be. When the media started focusing attention on us we had to decide whether to talk or not. In the sixties we didn't do much with the media, we concentrated on the physicians. But there was continued pressure to talk and to come forward, and that decision was finally made in the seventies. All hell broke loose after that. It was both good and bad. Afterwards the media would check a story with you, which was good because if someone is going to murder you, it's better to have your say.' Medd laughs. 'Better anyway than having a shot outside the company with the gate closed, and the journalist going on about this faceless, monolithic, Swiss-owned company. I mean there was nothing redeeming about us.'

Did they win?

'We're still here,' says Medd with a heavy shrug. 'The diazepam molecule is still the second most prescribed drug in its class. We have a lot of people who respect us and some who don't. And we just continue to do it. You know, it's like doctors: everybody hates doctors until they get sick, and then they can't understand why they can't get to see the doctor. And then, when they do, they hate the pills. It's just life.'

Just life? There is something curiously fatalistic about Hoffmann - La Roche. There often is about people who get beaten on continually. But there is something curiously defiant as well: we'll just continue to do it. There is an arrogance about them: the arrogance of power and the arrogance of greed.

Its story encapsulates the drugs industry. It captures its wealth of ideas and ambition and, naturally, its economic wealth. It tells of a rise from shabby beginnings to an industry of great power and influence. But it reflects its poverty as well: a poverty of ideals, humanity and humility. Hoffmann - La Roche was a flawed enterprise: the flaws, when the attacks started, brought the business to its knees.

There must be something more to the industry than this. Something that comes after; something that has learnt from the rise and fall of Valium, something different. To find it, I turn in the direction of another small New Jersey town. Measured in land, it is only a few minutes' drive away. But measured by character, it is a distance of many miles.

PART TWO
The Aristocrat: Merck

4 A different tomato in another sandwich

The drive out of New York along the New Jersey Turnpike is a journey which, in the space of an hour or so, spans continents and centuries. As you dip beneath the tunnel, the smoke and haze and steam of the city are left behind, somewhere distant, over the water. The city, with its enclaves of European communities, its cluttered buildings, its constant violence and its hard, cynical streets, is too reminiscent of the Europe which spawned it: a warped, kitsch version, perhaps, but a version all the same. It is a place of transition, dazed and confused, between the Old World and the New.

At the gates of the Turnpike America unfolds. For the price of a few dollars' toll, a journey into the vast, empty continent begins. Look back, and towering slabs of skyscrapers fade into the skyline. Turn forward, and the country lies ahead, its people and communities and workplaces scattered all around. The highway drives through the countryside like a shallow scar. America, once you get outside New York, looks like a place where the people have only just arrived, where they haven't really had time to unpack yet. It seems messy and disorganised, as if nobody particularly cared about the way things looked. Beneath the roads and the buildings, the wilderness is still there, sprouting up in the gaps between civilisations. To the right, heading west, is a sprawling docks, where massive cargo ships dump their Japanese and Korean imports. To the left are the rail tracks, lying rusty and unused; the factories, many of them boarded up and decrepit; the airport, with planes zipping down low over the automobiles and on to the runways; and the road signs, pleading and clamouring and begging for attention.

Rahway is about an hour's drive from New York, but it could be light years away. It is a small town strung out along a main street. It has banks and burger bars and supermarkets and gas stations, and it has small clusters of neat homes laid out in grids over patches of grass. It is a blue-collar town, most famous for its state prison, and a place infused with the sweaty and oily smell of the industrial worker. It is an immigrant's town as well, a place where successive waves of hopeful migrants have rolled up, worked, lived, saved and moved on west. It has that transient feel to it, the feel of a town which is really only a stop-over point.

At the far end of the town is its one major industrial site. A McDonalds on the corner marks the turning to swing off the road, and through a suburban settlement looms the headquarters of Merck, the world's largest drugs company. It is a peaceful place to site a headquarters, though also an ambiguous one: this is a place that is neither town nor country. Small wooden houses surround it. They are not homes for rich people: the paintwork is frayed and the cars outside are cheap American or Japanese standards, a few years old. But they are not poor either: there is no dereliction, and the walkways are empty and safe.

Inside Merck, past the guard house and past the no smoking signs, the world is transformed once more. Here everything is neat and orderly, and the atmosphere is calm and purposeful and prosperous. The buildings are redbrick and low – even the chairman's office is only on the fifth floor. Well tended lawns separate the administrative buildings from the factories to one side and the laboratories to the other. The blocks rise out of the lawns quite naturally; the landscaping is a natural blend of pastoral and urban forms. It doesn't seem like an industrial complex. It has none of the ragged, frenzied, imperialistic, and monied posing expected of the corporate headquarters. It is too harmonic, too gentle, and too subtle. But as I stroll through the grounds, a question plays on my mind: if this is not industrial, then what?

Visiting the complex for the first time, I make straight for the canteen. This is partly because I am hungry, but also because I want to find out more about the organisation. Heading into a corporate canteen is like checking out a person's house: it shows you the kind of person they are when they are just being themselves.

Merck's canteen is huge, covering several hundred square feet. It has windows stretching from the ceiling to the floor, allowing whatever light there is outside to fill up the room. At one end there is a serving area: you start with the salad and soup area, move on to the hot food counter, on to the sandwich counter, and end up at the drinks machine, dispensing Cokes and Seven-Ups. A full meal costs around two dollars.

I stack up my tray with a ham and cheese and tomato sandwich, plus a lettuce and tomato salad, plus some Mexican-style chips and a medium-sized Coke Classic, and head off to find somewhere to sit. I am surrounded by Merck employees. They are sitting on plastic, not very comfortable chairs, at plastic tables, some separate, some grouped together. Mostly they are with their friends or colleagues, eating lunch and chatting. Most of them are casually dressed, the men in slacks and pullovers, the women in loose skirts or pants with blouses and sweaters. It is a Friday lunchtime, and Friday at Merck is casual dress day.

There is nothing very remarkable about the canteen, but three things catch my eye. Two of them are posters. One of these is announcing how many days there are left in the company blood drive. Another has six pictures of people, men and women who include a black, an Asian, an Hispanic, an old person. Above the pictures is a question: 'Which one is a typical Merck employee?' Below is some blurb, explaining how the company has an equal opportunities programme, and how none of them are typical employees, and yet how they all are.

The next thing to catch my attention is a pair of men sitting about twenty-five yards away. They are called Ed and Al. They both look as though they are in their mid fifties. Ed is a tall man with a slight stoop who leans forward on the table, resting his face in his hands. He has brown, thinning hair, combed across his head, and he is wearing a plain shirt with a checked tie hanging loosely around his neck. He has forgotten this is casual dress day, but looks pretty casual anyway. Al is leaning back in his chair, turned away from the table with his feet up and crossed. He has greying hair, also thinning, and thick grey eyebrows that seem to sprout directly out of his intense forehead.

They look like a couple of regular guys. They could be workmen of some sort; mechanics or electricians or machine operators. And they look as if they are discussing everyday stuff; baseball or gas prices or television. Appearances are deceptive, however. They are both, in their own way, big money men, high-rollers, and Wall Street stars; 'masters of the universe', to crib a peculiarly eighties phrase. Ed is Ed Scolnick, the heard of research and development at Merck, and a man with $850 million to spend a year on drug discovery. And Al is Al Alberts, a senior Merck scientist, the man who led the discovery of Mevacor, a novel new cholesterol drug with sales confidently estimated to hit one billion dollars a year. Some workmen.

At around one thirty, they drain their cups of Coke and head off; Ed to manage his millions, Al to peer over his molecules. The two men, despite their importance to the company, operate in a low-key, mild and informal manner. Their act is homespun and small town, not chichi and big city. And their style is scientific and earnest and solid, not artsy, combative or flippant.

Much the same can be said of Merck. It is a company strangely out of tune with its times. During the 1980s, a decade when greed, savagery, risk and danger were the admired characteristics of American business, the company plodded along in its own quiet way. It stuck to what it knew, creating and selling medicines, and stuck to the old-fashioned formula of scientific and technical excellence as the route to commercial success. It resisted the sweet apples the serpents of the decade had to offer: the leverage, the debt, the junk, the restructurings, the asset swaps and all the rest of the financial paraphernalia of the decade. It had at times been sorely tempted. It had felt hunger and it saw the shine on the apple, but it resisted.

Yet it scarcely plodded. In the five years between 1985 and 1990 its sales almost doubled – rising from $3.5 billion to $6.5 billion, and its profits almost trebled – rising from $857 million pre-tax to $2.3 billion pre-tax. As a result its value grew enormously. With a market capitalisation of $32 billion it now ranks as the sixth largest corporation in the United States.

The stark figures miss the real point. Merck doubled its size while it was already the industry leader, not when it was some whippersnapper of a little company. Doubling in size is a lot harder when you are already very big. And Merck did so while carving out its own peculiar style. For the last four years, Merck has been voted the most admired company in the United States in the annual *Fortune* poll, an accolade from rivals and peers across the industrial spectrum. It has won a host of other awards as well: the best for black employees, the best for working women, the best managed, the most innovative, and so on and so on. It has launched some unusual and novel schemes; schemes for supplying free drugs to the third world; schemes for supplying drugs at lower prices to the poor people of the United States; and so on. It has squared some tricky circles: how to grow while already at the top of the business; and how to combine an exhilarating financial performance with a highly developed sense of corporate responsibility. All of which is some achievement.

From the canteen to the laboratories it is about a five-minute stroll, a walk along a neat tarmac path running through the lawns, filled with workers returning after lunch. As I walk along there is a question; is this old-fashioned or new-fashioned. It is not so much a question as a riddle. Many of the things to be witnessed here seem like flashbacks to an earlier era. There is the technical and scientific emphasis, a throwback to the latter half of the nineteenth century, when industry was about inventions and not about skilful marketing, complex organisation or tricky financial games. Here is the simple pared-to-the-bone style, the modesty, a throwback to the same distant era, when businessmen were thrifty and careful, not lavish, opulent, self-indulgent or kingly spenders of other people's money. And here is the altruism, the sense of fellowship, so reminiscent of that past era when companies grew out of a small town, and built the town and its people as they built the business, and of a time when corporate executives were not part of a small community all to themselves, living alone in corporate jets thousands of feet above the ordinary people, but lived with and among those people.

Yet it also seems so modern. It is hi-tech; the drugs Merck works with are right at the frontiers of the biological and chemical sciences, and the industrial processes are mechanised and computerised to the nth degree. Then there is the cleanliness, the informality and the egalitarianism of the workplace, with none of the grime or cruelty of the nineteenth-century corporation. That too is modern. There is the global scale and scope of the organisation, with factories and offices and sales forces strung out around the planet. Modern again. The answer to the riddle might be that it is some subtle post-modern and post-industrial blend.

Inside the swing-glass doors of the laboratories there is a clue. In the corner of the foyer there is a model, made of wood, paper and paint. It is a miniature reproduction – a sort of corporate doll's house – of a seventeenth-century German town building, all painted stone and shutters. An inscription describes it as a model of an old apothecary, set up in 1668 in the German town of Darmstadt. The name of the family which established it was Merck. So if this conundrum is not old-fashioned, it is at least very old.

5 From Darmstadt to Rahway

The business was founded by Friedrich Jacob Merck. In 1668 he took over a pharmacy on a street beside the castle moat in Darmstadt, an apothecary trading under the odd-sounding name of 'At the Sign of the Angel'. Pharmacists, though their skills were rudimentary, were respected members of their communities, and the Merck family were no exception. They were regularly elected to public offices in the town, and were on equal terms with nobles and intellectuals. Johann Heinrich Merck, born in 1741 and one of the sons who took over the business, was a close friend of the German writer Goethe, the author of *Doctor Faustus*, and Goethe was later to praise Merck as one of the critical influences on his intellectual and spiritual development.

It is an unusually literary touch to find in any company history. But Merck is an unusual company. A business of its size is seldom made up of a single stream; instead it is a river fed by many tributaries. The Merck family gave it its name, and much of its character as well. Yet Darmstadt is only a starting point. Like many immigrant families in the United States, in crossing the Atlantic, it has entered the melting pot of European and American cultures. Though it has German roots, Merck's is a very American story: a story which tracks both the development of the American drugs industry and the development of American capitalism.

Darmstadt was where it began, however, and the place, also, where the family began to lay down deep scientific roots.

Heinrich Emmanuel Merck, born in 1794 and another of the

sons who took over the pharmacy, was a close friend of Justus von Liebig, also a resident of Darmstadt and one of the founders of modern organic chemistry. Liebig was one of the scientists who began isolating therapeutic compounds in the early part of the nineteenth century, and Heinrich Merck was one of the industrialists who first observed their work and then began exploiting its commercial potential. In 1824 he set up a small chemical laboratory next to the family apothecary, then still run by his father, and in 1827 he set up a small factory on the outskirts of the town. Here the chemical company E. Merck was established, with the intention, according to its founder, of manufacturing the highest quality medicines anywhere in the world.

His first product was morphine, a powerful drug made from opium and still used as a pain killer today. Other drugs followed: veratrine in 1828, codeine, another drug made from opium and used as a pain reliever and sleeping tablet, in 1832; andatrophine, and quinine, a bitter-tasting drug used to treat malaria. Each of those preparations paved the way for an enduring E. Merck speciality, the manufacture of alkaloids, substances containing nitrogen and derived from plants, many of which are used in medicines. The company even added to the range – George Franz Merck, a son of Heinrich, discovered papaverine, a muscle relaxant also derived from the ubiquitous and always popular poppy plant.

By the time Heinrich Emmanuel died in 1855, the chemical company he had established was known and respected worldwide. It was an example of the extraordinary flowering of entrepreneurial skill in Germany in the middle of the nineteenth century, skill built on technical excellence, and which was soon to make the country a rival to Britain and the United States for industrial leadership of the world. E. Merck still exists as a company today: it hovers along somewhere near the bottom of the worldwide league tables for the industry, although it is still a force in Germany. But Heinrich Emmanuel's real and lasting legacy was to be in the United States, where his real inheritors were to prosper a long way from their original location.

In the 1880s, America, then bursting suddenly into great wealth and prosperity, became a major customer for the Merck chemicals and medicines. Like many of the European drugs companies at that time, the company was set on international expansion, and in 1887 the market across the Atlantic was significant enough for a Darmstadt-bred chemist, Theodore Weicker, to be sent over to head up the operation in New York. Four years later, in 1891, he was joined at the New York office by George Merck, the grandson of Heinrich Emmanuel, and then only twenty-four years old.

They made a potent pair. Weicker, an earnest looking man with a goatee beard, was a brilliant chemist, who also had a personal stake in the American business, and George Merck had inherited his grandfather's drive, energy and entrepreneurial gifts. George Merck was sent over as part of his training in the ways of the business; he was meant only to watch and learn how it worked. But he liked Manhattan more than Darmstadt and stayed, gradually increasing his involvement in the American subsidiary.

In 1899 he bought a tract of land in Rahway – then, as now, a small immigrant town close by the main Pennsylvania rail line. A factory was set up at the site – Merck products had previously been mostly imported from Germany – to manufacture a range of pharmaceutical preparations: iodides, bismuth salts, narcotics, alkaloids, disinfectants, plus a range of photographic and speciality chemicals that were to become the mainstay of Merck America for the first decades of the twentieth century.

But the progress of the company, despite the solidity of its German name and backing, was at times turbulent and rocky. Both Weicker and George Merck were tough, opinionated and strong-willed individuals. Both had the resources to refuse to budge: Merck had the family fortune and control to back him and Weicker had money from his father-in-law, a mid-Westerner called Lowell E. Palmer, who had minted his fortune in typically rumbustious American style, first by setting up factories to make barrels, and then by starting sugar refineries to buy the barrels.

In 1904 they split; George Merck bought out Weicker's share. He continued to build the business, and established himself as a classic turn-of-the-century American gentleman. With his German wife he bought a house in Llewelyn Park, in New Jersey, and raised five children. The firm prospered, and by 1914 was selling chemicals worth some four million dollars a year. Weicker did just as well. With the help of his father-in-law he bought control of E. R. Squibb & Sons, a drug company which merged with Bristol-Myers in 1989 to create the second largest business in the industry, just behind Merck.

The next decade, however, was to hold some tough challenges for George Merck. Nineteen fourteen was a poor year to be a German-owned company in the American drugs business. By the time the United States entered the First World War, its position, particularly as a supplier of drugs to the US army, became untenable, and George Merck made the smart move of volunteering to hand over the eighty per cent of the company still in the hands of the German branch of the family to the Alien Property Custodian, a government body set up to manage German commercial operations in the United States. Otherwise, the war, as it generally is for drugs companies, was a blessing; sales doubled. When the war ended, the shareholding was sold for three million dollars to a group of investors led by Goldman Sachs and Shearson Lehman. The German connections had been severed, with George Merck still owning twenty per cent of the company and in effective control over its future. (Though there is still an agreement between E. Merck and Merck which prevents Merck using the name in Europe – the American company calls itself Merck, Sharp & Dohme instead.)

George Merck died in 1926, a year after he had surrendered control of the company to his son, George W. Merck. George junior had been raised as an all-American boy, part of the generation of monied, almost aristocratic Americans who emerged in the 1920s and 1930s. Six feet five inches tall, with broad shoulders and blond hair and blue eyes, he graduated in chemistry from Harvard in 1915 with ideas of public service already drilled into his head. He went straight to work with his father, along with his brother-in-law George Perkins, who had married his sister Linn. But unlike his father, who had concentrated on establishing the business and on keeping it alive, the second George Merck concentrated on making the company great.

He was helped by the terrible condition of the German economy after the war. E. Merck had suffered, and the American offshoot was able to move into the world markets it had vacated by the 1920s, and capitalise on its reputation; a case of the boy devouring the father. But although the company itself may have had a good reputation, it was still operating on the fringes of an industry that was considered, in the United States more than anywhere, to be the natural territory of scumbags and swindlers.

In his novel *Martin Arrowsmith*, published in 1925, Sinclair Lewis, the author of *Main Street* and the first American writer to win the Nobel Prize for Literature, has an immunologist called Max Gottlieb as a character. He joins the Hunziker Company, a drugs house, as a researcher, and is condemned by his colleagues as having 'gone over to that damned pill peddlar', and described by the novel's hero as 'falling for those crooks'. It was a harsh judgement but one which reflected the popular mood of its time. In the same decade, most medical schools prevented their members from working with the drugs firms; and the American Society for Pharmacology and Experimental Therapeutics, the main professional association, had a rule explicitly preventing members from working with the drugs companies.

That antagonism lay deeply rooted in the haphazard development of the American drugs industry. The colonial states had pharmacies modelled on the European industry from their earliest creation; one of the first manufacturing drugs houses was opened in Carlisle, Pennsylvania, in 1778 to supply medicine to Washington's revolutionary army. But the American story was different from the European. In Europe the physicians, though often incompetent, were an established profession, with established rules of conduct. The pharmacists, also, had established associations and rules. Equally significant, the pecking order was clear: the pharmacists occupied a secondary role, in terms of economic and social status, to the physicians.

In the United States it was not so simple. The intensely democratic nature of the country, particularly in the first half of the nineteenth century, created a suspicion of experts. The waves of European immigrants who populated America harboured a resentment of physicians carried over from their home countries: there they had been upper-class men who charged expensive fees and did very little good. In the New World they were not going to have the same status. Populist writers argued, with great success, that there was nothing to the medical profession but the creation of mystery and mystique, cleverly created and sustained to protect the earnings of the practitioners. In the days before modern scientific medicine, it was a compelling argument. It created, however, the explosion of patent medicine and snake-oil peddlars that were such a strong feature of nineteenth-century American culture. These men, with their insipid and noxious potions, their sharp, streetwise sales patter, and their gaudy and fictitious newspaper advertisements, were the forerunners of the American drugs industry. They were also the creators of its low public esteem.

Between the physicians and the peddlars of patent medicines (very few of which actually had patents) there was a long-running battle for control over the patient. Dim echoes of the conflict can still be heard today in debates on over-the-counter medicines, yet, in the early part of the nineteenth century, the battle was won by the physicians. The most important blow was struck by a series of revelations by muck-raking journalists. In October 1905 the magazine *Collier's Weekly* began a series by reporter Samuel Hopkins Adams on the patent medicine companies, detailing the frauds and deceptions that provided the basis of the industry. He detailed laboratory reports showing the medicines to be worthless, and reprinted death certificates of people who had given testimonials to the wondrous nature of the cure, but who had in fact died of the disease it was meant to heal. 'Printer's ink, when it spells out a doctor's promise to cure, is one of the subtlest and most dangerous of poisons,' Adams famously concluded.

The impact of his work, and the muck-raking that followed in its trail, was tremendous. The American Medical Association, the physicians' professional grouping, distributed a hundred and fifty thousand copies of his work in a booklet entitled *The Great American Fraud*. Coupled with Upton Sinclair's novel *The Jungle* which revealed the horrors of the meat-packing industry, public pressure for action intensified. Congress responded in 1906 by passing the Pure Food and Drug Act, the beginning of drug regulation on a federal level, and an Act which led to the creation of the Food and Drug Administration. At the same time the AMA, by now a stronger and better financed body, stepped up its battle against the snake-oil merchants, eventually forcing most of the drugs houses to choose between manufacturing medicines for prescription by physicians, or manufacturing remedies to be sold via newspaper advertising or street-corner hucksters. Although many of the companies which preferred huckstering became rich, only the companies working through the physicians survived. Despite their ultimate demise, the odour of the hucksters' snake-oil lingered over the industry for many years after the muckrakers had moved on to fresh scandals.

It was in this turbulent and hostile environment that George W. Merck set about building up his company. He did not have much to play with. In the years before the Second World War, the size of the drugs business was tiny compared with other major industries, and it was financially insecure. During the Depression years of 1932 to 1934 more than three thousand five hundred drugs companies collapsed. And as late as 1939, the entire American industry had a combined turnover of only $150 million, spread between over a thousand businesses. Even the largest of them did not have a turnover to match the takings of a big city department store.

Even so, Merck did what he could to strengthen the firm. In 1933, he and Perkins established the Merck Institute for Therapeutic Research, and constructed the company's first modern set of laboratories on the Rahway site. The purpose, according to the ponderous blurb of the company at the time, was to create a place where brilliant minds could be 'so protected that their mental powers of thought, study and imagination can concentrate on problems of great difficulty'. Two distinguished scientists – Dr Randolph Major from Princeton and Dr Hans Molitor from the University of Vienna – were hired to run the Institute.

The research team established an early lead in the production of vitamins. Merck was the first pre-war patent holder on Vitamin B1, which it manufactured and sold to packagers and to food manufacturers. But the real development of the company was to come with the arrival of the era of the wonder drugs, an era sparked by the discovery of penicillin, a discovery in which Merck was partly involved.

Penicillin was first discovered by the British scientist Alexander Fleming in 1928, but it was only developed, with the encouragement of the British government, during the Second World War. Two of the British scientists working on the drug – Florey and Heatley – brought it to America in 1941; the two governments wanted to make sure work on it continued even if Britain were invaded. Merck was one of a number of American drugs companies working on the development and production of penicillin, a task for which George Merck, in a high-minded move typical of the man, turned down government financial assistance. The company's efforts did not bear fruit, however. Merck scientists were convinced the drug could be synthesised, and laboured to find a synthetic production process. That idea, however, eventually proved wrong, and Merck paid for its stubbornness by losing a potential lead in the commercial production of the drug.

It had other successes to fall back on. In 1943 Dr Selman Waksman, who worked at nearby Rutgers University and was supported by a Merck grant, discovered a compound called streptomycin. Waksman, who later won a Nobel Prize for his work on the drug, had been working on it in association with

Merck scientists since 1938, screening thousands of soil compounds in search of an antibiotic. Once he struck it, the Merck laboratories worked for fourteen months on developing the compound and bringing it through clinical trials. It turned out to be a potent antibiotic, as effective in its own way as penicillin. It was an effective treatment for meningitis, influenza and types of pneumonia. These days, however, it is best known as the drug which defeated tuberculosis.

Its creation was the first major scientific triumph for Merck: Waksman was later to credit its invention to the company 'having created a university-like atmosphere where basic research was understood and pursued'. But commercially the story was even stranger.

The funding agreement between Waksman and Merck gave the company the sole development and marketing rights to any product discovered by his research. When the potential money-spinner was struck, however, Waksman was unhappy with the deal. He argued that the drug was too important a contribution to human health to be the sole property of any one company. George Merck agreed with him. The deal was renegotiated. Instead of Merck owning the patent, it was handed over free of charge to the Rutgers Research and Endowment Foundation. In return Merck only received an exception on the first $500,000 in royalties it would have had to pay the Foundation for its own production of streptomycin. It did gain a small advantage; it was the first of the eight licensed manufacturers to go into commercial production. But by 1950 there was a surplus of the drug and the price fell drastically.

This almost unworldly disregard for the normal commercial rules of engagement was to characterise the company for as long as George Merck remained in command. In 1944 the company had its second great success with the discovery of cortisone, the first of the steroid anti-inflammatory drugs used in the treatment of arthritis. The compound was isolated after painstaking research by Dr Edward Kendell of the Mayo Clinic, with which Merck had a research agreement, and by the Dutch-born Merck senior chemist, Jacob van de Kemp. Once cortisone had been isolated, the then president of the company, James Kerrigan (who had worked his way up from office boy), put the firm's entire scientific and commercial resources behind it. But he did not chase maximum profits on the discovery. Since Merck still did not then sell its products directly, either to the public or to the pharmacists, the drug was licensed out to a number of other companies. Merck, however, insisted that the price of the new drug be continually cut to bring it into the price range of ordinary sufferers, and in the early days of short supply and massive demand from arthritics it even published the list price in the newspapers in an attempt to stifle the black market.

Throughout his involvement in three of the major drug discoveries of the century, George Merck stuck to his lordly, aristocratic disdain for making a maximum return from his business. The company continued to regard itself as a wholesale, speciality chemical manufacturer, and it left to others the sordid business of making and selling its products. There was no regular sales force and no regular marketing: as late as the 1950s its idea of an advertisement was the snappy but innocent-sounding slogan 'Merck's the standard and it costs no more'. It was cheerful, but hardly a corporate hard-sell.

George Merck himself had no need of the money: he had plenty of it already. Nor was there any great pressure from the shareholders. In 1946 the company was listed on the New York Stock Exchange when Goldman Sachs sold nine million dollars' worth of shares, yet the Merck family remained in control with over a third of the voting stock. As long as George Merck was there, the aristocratic attitude of the firm was unlikely to change. 'Medicine is for patients. It is not for profits,' he insisted once. 'The profits follow and if we've remembered that, they have never failed to appear. The better we have remembered it, the larger they have been.'

But that disdain for commercial realities was easier to sustain in a small and static industry than in a big and fast-growing one. As the wonder drugs exploded the size of the market, rougher minds and harder characters entered the fray. Other drugs houses, which had earlier been happy to license or buy in Merck products, began inventing and developing their own medicines, gradually squeezing Merck out of the market. Between 1948 and 1951 it made profits from a new line of hormone products. But by 1952, with new competition from Upjohn and Schering in steroids, with Swiss, German, Italian and Japanese companies shipping in vitamins at low prices, and with new antibiotics from Lederle, Pfizer and Parke-Davis, the profits had faded away. For the first time Merck's future looked clouded and bleak.

It responded in 1953 by merging with Sharp & Dohme, a company with a different, more natively American, tradition. It had been founded as an apothecary in 1845 in Baltimore by Alpheus Phineas Sharp, the first graduate of the Maryland College of Pharmacy, and became Sharp & Dohme when Louis Dohme, another graduate of the Maryland school, joined as a partner in 1860. It grew quickly by manufacturing medicines for the Union Army during the Civil War, a boost for many of the emerging American drugs companies of that time. Sharp & Dohme was mainly a processor and wholesaler of the standard preparations of its day, and it was primarily a regional company during the nineteenth century – it competed fiercely with its near neighbour SmithKline, now a part of SmithKline Beecham.

In 1929 it merged with H. K. Mulford & Co., a firm with a more interesting history. It was an early pioneer of the adoption of advanced science by the drugs industry. The firm was founded in 1891 by Henry Mulford as a small manufacturing pharmacy employing twelve people in Philadelphia, specialising in lozenges, antiseptics and syrups. It grew quickly: by 1893 it had a range of five hundred products, and over two thousand by the end of the century. Its real breakthrough, however, was the invention of a tableting machine for making soluble pills, a vast improvement on the hard and indigestible pills and the powders sold by other pharmacies at the time.

The business was run by Milton Campbell, its president, part-owner, and all-round visionary. Campbell, who would have sympathised with Fritz Hoffmann had he ever met him, saw two important trends early: that drugs companies needed to be first national and then international in their operations, and that they needed to have close and warm relations with the scientific and medical communities.

National and international expansion was easy: offices were opened up around the United States, and later in Canada, Argentina, New Zealand and South Africa. The scientific side was harder. Campbell increased the size and standing of his laboratory and gave it three tasks: to standardise the production of existing products; to invent new products; and to give the company a scientific image. Although it made some progress with the first two, it was most successful with the third. Campbell pushed this line, stressing his distaste for crass advertising and for the lax to non-existent ethical standards reigning in the drugs industry at the time. His concern was partly showmanship. Although he employed some good scientists (Selman Waksman worked there during his holidays while a student at the University of California) the diphtheria antitoxin that became one of the company's biggest products was later shown to have no effect on the disease, and the firm made no significant medical breakthroughs.

Mulford merged with Sharp & Dohme just before the Wall Street Crash of 1929, one of a number of drug company mergers that took place in the 1920s. The idea was to create a marriage of a leading science-based manufacturer with a leading wholesaler and distributor, and the deal was hailed by the financiers and stock pushers of the time. Mulford may not have ultimately contributed much to science, but neither had its competitors. Yet it had achieved three things; it had helped create a different image for the drugs industry; it had helped find a role for the industry once it was pushed under the thumb of the physicians; and it had contributed to a raising of ethical standards. All of which were substantial achievements.

By 1953, however, the company was not in good shape. It had suffered from falling prices in two of its main product lines – sulphas and antibiotics – and from low margins on sales of blood plasma to the US government. And it had over-extended itself financially: it had built a new four-million-dollar research laboratory at West Point, Pennsylvania and was carrying heavy debts.

At the time of the merger, Merck had assets of over $112 million compared with assets of $46 million at Sharp & Dohme. Merck was the bigger and better respected company, and it took over the running of the merged corporation. George W. Merck became chairman of the board, and Kerrigan president, while Sharp & Dohme's John Zinsser became vice-president. But Sharp & Dohme had the sales and marketing techniques and the distribution network that Merck had preferred not to build up for itself. It delivered a way for Merck to sell as well as to discover and manufacture its own products. The Pennsylvania company also had some useful products: it was a leader in vaccines and blood plasma, and had an over-the-counter medicines business which included such well known American brand names as Sucrets.

In 1957, more than thirty years after he took over the running of the company, George Merck died. He had by that time been succeeded by professional managers: John Connor, a lawyer, had become president, and Henry Gadsden, a Sharp & Dohme man, had become executive vice-president. They had pared down the company, shifting it out of a mass of unprofitable lines, and focusing on human drugs, with smaller sidelines in animal healthcare, speciality chemicals and over-the-counter medicines. They had also established the central line, from the laboratory through the factory to the physician, that was characteristic of the post-war drugs industry. Later than most of its rivals, Merck had joined the modern world.

George Merck had no blood successors: no more Mercks were to be involved in the day-to-day running of the company, although the family trust still holds an important stake in the business. In another sense, however, he did have successors. The company was never to recapture his peculiar queasiness over the profit motive; it is unlikely it could have survived had it done so. Yet throughout its later history, the attitudes of their famous forerunner were to linger in the minds of its senior managers; they

6 A host of crocks and cruds

Jerry Jackson is a short man, no more than five feet five inches tall. He is slimmish and smartly, though not flashily, dressed; he sticks to one-tone suits and shirts, and simple striped ties. He has a bob of grey hair, most probably originally styled as a Beatles mop-top but now longer and thinner. And he has a long face, with a high forehead and round, droopy jowls, which make him look like the old cartoon character Deputy Dawg.

Jackson has worked at Merck for twenty-five years. He graduated from the University of New Mexico in 1963, after studying biology, and went to work as a school teacher in the same state. He taught seventh and eighth graders maths and speed reading, but didn't like the place much. He found it bureaucratic and slow moving, the teachers apathetic and the standards low; he felt himself becoming trapped in a culture that suffered from a poverty of expectations. It didn't suit him. After a year he quit and set about finding himself a new job.

The University of New Mexico had a scheme for finding graduates work. Jackson signed up, figuring he would find work as a salesman. He started exploring the drugs business as one of the possibilities, although he knew little about it, and had not done any research. He recalls his first contact with Merck like this: 'One day I had signed up to be interviewed by two pharmaceutical companies. One of them was Lederle Laboratories and the other was Merck. The first I had to go to was Lederle. It was a hot day and they were holding the interviews in this old World War Two barracks-overflow building with no air conditioning. When I arrived to see the district sales manager from Lederle, I walked in and saw him there, with his feet up, his coat off and his tie loose. I came through the door and he looked up at me and said: "Hi, sonny. Do you have any sales experience?" I said, "No." Now he knew that already because he had my resumé, and I didn't have any sales experience. Then he said: "Are you a pharmacist?" And I said, "No." And then he said: "For Christ's sake, you're wasting my time!" I was astonished, and I retreated back into the lobby. And I remember thinking to myself: the pharmaceutical business must be a tough, negative sort of business. I thought that I wouldn't have anything to do with it. And I certainly didn't want to go and see the Merck guy, who I was scheduled to see thirty minutes later.'

The university scheme had a rule, however: you had to go along to the interviews you had signed up for, otherwise you were off their list. So Jackson went along, although only as a formality.

'I went to see the Merck guy with a chip on my shoulder, because I had been treated so rudely,' he recalls. 'When I got there I found the complete, one hundred and eighty degree opposite of what had happened earlier – a sharply dressed professional who shook my hand. It was a real lucky escape. Then later when I was assigned a territory as a professional sales representative the district sales manager I had seen at Lederle had been demoted and worked exactly the same territory as I did. I can tell you, I was very pleased to beat him in the areas where we had competitive products. Eventually, however, we became reasonably good friends, and we even had lunch together occasionally.'

Jackson was hired by Merck as a drug salesman and sent to its West Point offices for training courses. His teacher there was a man called Bill Rait, a salesman of the old, evangelical school, who preached that salesmanship was about confidence in oneself and confidence in the product. It was about belief. His first job was as a 'spare', a salesman assigned to a region, but without a territory, who filled in when other salesmen were away. Jackson's region was the west of the United States, headquartered in

Denver, covering the country all the way from Washington State on the Canadian border to the Mexican border in the south. His first territory was in his home town of Albuquerque, covering the whole of the Rio Grande valley, all the way down to El Paso. It was back-breaking work, even for a young man. Over a year he would clock up fifty thousand miles in his car, leaving home often before dawn on Monday morning and travelling over three hundred miles to the first of the day's appointments; often he wouldn't finish until after midnight, as the hours between 11 p.m. and 12 p.m. were a useful time to catch physicians after their surgeries had closed for the day.

Jackson worked that strung-out route for three years, pounding away at physicians with the company's latest products. The working routine, the lifestyle, the mileage, each was typical of the work of a drug salesman both then and now.

He describes a typical sale as an exercise in persistence. 'I remember round about the first year I had been out there I called on a doctor. He was about seventy years old. He was called Dr Ballinger. I was trying to introduce him to Indocin, so I talked to him about it, and while I was talking he would pull out his desk drawer and play with the paper clips and so on. This went on for several months. I would talk about Indocin and he would play with his paper clips. And then I would go to the pharmacist in the town and ask if Dr Ballinger was prescribing Indocin and he would tell me no. So one day I couldn't contain myself any longer and I said to him: "What do I have to do to get you to prescribe Indocin?" And he looked back at me and said: "Oh, young man, you're doing fine." "Well," I replied, "I get the feeling I'm not doing so good." "Well," he answered, "I've been using the other drugs for many years, and you keep talking to me about Indocin, and when I know as much about Indocin as I do about the others, then perhaps. I'm not objecting to you sitting here month after month talking to me about Indocin, and when you have my confidence at the right level then I'll use it. I don't necessarily use the best drug, I use the drug that I know best." And I kept on until he became a good user of Indocin, when he really understood how to use it,' concludes Jackson.

It is a cute story and a good demonstration of the commitment Merck tried to encourage in its salesmen in the 1960s. Here, however, is another piece of documentary evidence from the same decade which puts a different twist on the story.

'It is obvious that Indocin will work in that whole host of crocks and cruds which every general practitioner, internist, and orthopaedic surgeon sees every day in his practice . . . Tell 'em again, and again, and again . . . Tell 'em until they are sold and stay sold . . . You've told him this story now, probably a hundred and thirty times. The physician, however, has only heard it once. So, go back, and tell it again and again and again, until it is indelibly impressed in his mind and he starts – and continues – to prescribe Indocin. Let's go . . . Take off the kid gloves. If he wants to use aspirin as a base-line therapy, let him use it. Chances are the patient is already taking aspirin. He has come to the physician because aspirin alone is not affording satisfactory, optimal effects . . . Now every extra bottle of one thousand Indocin that you sell is worth an extra two dollars eighty in incentive payments. Go get it. Pile it in.'

That extract comes from a US Senate inquiry into drug promotion carried out in 1968; the investigators had unearthed details of instructions Merck had given to salesmen working the highways with its drugs. Indocin, an anti-arthritic drug that followed on from the discovery of cortisone, was one of Merck's biggest selling products throughout the 1960s. When it was introduced in 1963 it had only been proven effective against four types of arthritic disease; the company, however, promoted it for treatments in other types of arthritis against which it had no proven effect. At the same time, it was alleged that Merck covered up the possibility of the drug increasing susceptibility to infection; and that it had also covered up the fact that the drug had caused the death of several young children.

When the Senate inquiry invited the then Merck president

Henry Gadsden to explain the manic, almost crazed, hard-sell of the drug, he attempted to cover the company's embarrassment with this reply: 'Language is not a perfect method of communication and it may well be that the words and phrases that are used in the belief that they mean one thing may have been interpreted by some physicians to mean something else.'

Much had changed at the company since the death of George Merck eleven years earlier. It was to carry on changing. In the mid seventies, in the wake of the Lockheed bribery scandal, the Securities and Exchange Commission in New York set about monitoring the level of bribery at major American corporations. It did not, however, have the resources nor the many months or years of international legwork needed to uncover routine corruption. Instead, it set up a scheme which allowed companies to disclose examples of bribery. In return, the Commission agreed that none of the acts disclosed could be used as criminal evidence against the company. And the company would agree to make reforms in its own internal procedures to prevent corruption. The deal created incentives for companies to identify themselves and reveal information. What proportion of bribery was revealed it is impossible to judge; it is unlikely the companies revealed everything they were up to. Even so, a wealth of day-to-day corruption was exposed by the scheme.

The drugs business ranked as one of the most consistent payers of back-handers, when the results were analysed: it ranked alongside oil and aircraft, two other industries notorious for their sleaze and greed. Merck, despite its clean image both within the industry and without, emerged as one of the guiltiest of the guilty.

Bribery has been common in the drugs business. The industry is heavily regulated, and its products everywhere require government approval before they can be sold. That creates a temptation to bribe, and where bribery is a way of life, it is almost a necessity. In underdeveloped or developing countries it is not even particularly expensive: reportedly a few hundred dollars is often enough to get a drug on the market.

In its disclosures, Merck revealed that it had paid out $3.6

million in 'questionable payments' in a total of thirty-nine foreign countries; $2.3 million of that was paid to unidentified third parties who might or might not have passed the money on to government officials. Among the disclosures, Merck admitted to having paid out money to a cabinet-level official; neither the person nor the country were revealed. The company had claimed the 'questionable payments' as tax deductions, which was adding injury to insult: it later agreed to pay the US Internal Revenue Service an additional tax payment of $264,000 as a result of the disclosures.

The corruption league was not a table the company wanted to lead. Stung by the evidence, it set up a committee of outsiders to investigate. But when its investigations were completed, Henry Gadsden came in for some more heavy flak.

The investigators' report concluded: 'Mr Gadsden said that payments of the kind under discussion were rather common in the conduct of business in some foreign countries, but stated that prior to the investigation he did not believe that the company or its employees were involved in any such payments, except for minor gratuities . . . The Committee was advised, however, that in two instances possible warning signals may have been sounded in Mr Gadsden's presence which could have prompted him to probe into the matters now in question. Mr Gadsden did not recall one of these incidents. He did not pursue the second which occurred in April 1975; however, he was informed at the time that line executives had given assurances that there would be no problems of this sort at Merck.'

Another senior executive, Raymond Snyder, then the executive vice-president (administration), was also criticised for possible collusion with corruption. Overall, the committee drew three damning conclusions about Merck's management. It said an atmosphere of passive acceptance of bribery had been created by the senior managers. It said that middle-ranking managers made efforts to prevent details of corruption coming to the attention of the top executives, on the tacit understanding that the senior men did not want to know what was happening out in the field; and that there was a consistent absence of investigation by top management, despite plenty of evidence that investigation was needed.

In a response to the SEC, following the investigation, Merck argued that payments were made because its employees were put under pressure by foreign government officials to hand over money; because managers knew the payments were necessary to hit sales targets in particular countries; and because the managers in those countries believed they were acting in the best interests of the company. Once again the senior Merck managers, caught and cornered, were offering limp excuses for blatantly unethical behaviour. It was another indication of how much the company had slipped since the death of George Merck. It had been attempting to match the commercial firepower of its competitors, but, in doing so, was gradually becoming indistinguishable from them.

It was not only the moral fibre of the firm that had changed. In 1970 Merck ranked in second place in the industry, just behind Hoffmann - La Roche, with drugs sales amounting to some $670 million. The 1960s had seen some important innovations coming out of the laboratory: Indocin, despite its problems, was a big-selling drug; Aldomet was launched in 1962 for high blood pressure; and novel vaccines were created for mumps, measles and rubella. But as the sixties gave way to the seventies, and after Max Tishler was replaced as head of research by Lewis Sarret, the rate of innovation at the company steadily slowed down to a trickle.

Merck was not alone. The new decade, a gloomy decade anyway as it turned out, was marked by a general sense of pessimism among the druggies. In the era of the wonder drugs, the industry had grown accustomed to supercharged growth, a growth based on the products that seemed to stagger regularly out of the laboratories, often through sheer chance and good fortune. In those days, however, research had been much simpler: with medical and chemical knowledge working from a low base line, there were many vital compounds waiting around to be discovered by hard-working and patient scientists. But as diseases relatively susceptible to chemical warfare were tackled one by one, the scientific and medical problems involved in each innovation became deeper and more intractable. And the rate of innovation, measured by the numbers of new chemical entities registered for patents each year, began to grind worryingly towards a halt. From a peak of sixty-five new entities introduced to the US market in 1959, the number had fallen to a low of only nine by 1969. At the same time, the cost of each innovation was rising year by year: one calculation, by the OECD, says that in constant dollars the research and development cost of each new drug put on the market rose from $6.5 million in 1962 to $45 million in 1980. It was becoming clear that the old formula of molecular roulette that had served the industry so well during the wonder drug era was drawing to a close. But what to replace it with, nobody yet knew.

The industry had become used to fast growth and had difficulty adjusting its expectations downwards. Mergers became a wild fad – the two Basle firms of Ciba and Geigy merged, and in the US Warner merged with Lambert – as companies sought the temporary fix of fast growth provided by combination. It was one way out of the dilemma. Another was diversification. Working on the always popular theory that if you can't manage your own business perhaps you'll be able to manage somebody else's, the drugs companies began scratching around other areas in an attempt to recapture the fast growth that had slipped from its grasp.

Merck was unable to stand aside from the general malaise. If anything, with its own particular problems, it was feeling it even more intensely than its rivals. 'We were in the pits,' recalls one senior executive, a finance man during the early to mid seventies. 'On any measure, whether it was sales gains or earnings gains, we were doing lousy.'

Merck had its own thoughts on diversification. In 1967, already feeling fretful about the squeeze, it had bought a company called Calgon, and had concentrated its consumer products in that division, which included such products as Cling-Free, an anti-static fabric softener, and Sucrets, the lozenges it had inherited from the merger with Sharp & Dohme. Its adventures away from drugs were not successful, however. Calgon had a turnover of $100 million, and in 1975 made a profit of $8.4 million. In that year Merck spent $10 million on promotion, a spend which yielded only $12 million in extra sales; it was about as complete a disaster as can strike in consumer goods marketing. The next year it made a loss of $400,000, and Merck sold the division to Beecham of the UK for $84 million.

Even so, the senior management at Merck was not deterred by the catastrophe of its experiences outside pharmaceuticals. Throughout the mid seventies they toyed with the idea of moving away from the drugs industry; cosmetics was one of the businesses they thought they might have more success in. They saw little future in drugs. They had little stomach for carrying on, and they wanted to duck the challenge.

'I'd say it was eighty twenty, that decision,' recalls one senior manager of the time. 'Eighty per cent of the people here wanted to diversify, twenty per cent wanted to stay in pharmaceuticals.'

It was that close: an almost universal demoralisation within the company, a demoralisation so great it looked as if Merck would abandon its basic business, the business in which it had been so triumphant only twenty years earlier, and the business which George Merck had striven to create and had made so special. The company had already fallen far from the ideals he had set for it and it now looked set to confirm its decline with an undignified exit from the drugs business, creeping out by the back door.

A few voices within the company spoke up, however. They argued that Merck should stay in the drugs business, and they argued it with all the soul and passion they could muster. One of those few voices, and one of the loudest, was the new head of Research and Development, a young and distinguished scientist brimming with ideas and commitment. His name was Roy P. Vagelos. Within a few years he was to change everything.

7 The rational man

Roy Vagelos was born and raised in Rahway, New Jersey. The story, and it is the stuff of legend at Merck, goes like this. The Vagelos family were Greek immigrants, who came to the United States in the early 1920s. They settled in Rahway, where Roy's father opened some small, local businesses. One of them was a diner. It was sited just around the corner from the Merck headquarters and, at night, the scientists who had been working on their molecules all day would come round to the diner to get a bite to eat. As they were eating the scientists would talk about their work with each other. As they were chattering away, a lanky teenage boy, the son of the owner, would be helping out at the diner; he would be taking orders and wiping tables and listening to every word. He heard the scientists talk, and found their conversation fascinating, and as he worked an ambition within him grew. He too would become a scientist and work in a laboratory, just like the men he was serving. And so it turned out. The lanky, teenage boy grew up and went to college and became a scientist and became head of research at Merck and then became president of the company.

It is the stuff of movies or fairytales, but in Roy Vagelos's case it happened for real. After graduating from Rahway High School he went to the University of Pennsylvania, where he completed his course in three years instead of the normal four, taking time out in the vacations to work as an intern at Merck alongside the scientists he had worshipped a few years earlier. After college he went to medical school, and from there he worked at the

Massachusetts General Hospital for two years. He owed the government two years' draft service so from there he went to work at the National Institutes of Health, doing research work on cardiology and heart patients. He stayed there for ten years, and then became professor of biochemistry at Washington University in St Louis. That took up another nine years, during which he became the head of the department. And then, all of a sudden, at the age of forty-five, he was appointed head of research at Merck.

Vagelos is a tall man, well over six feet. He is thin, too, in an angular way that exaggerates his slender shape. He has grey hair and a narrow, lined face. And he has large, peering brown eyes which dominate his face. He has long arms, with large hands and long fingers: he uses the fingers to stab sharply downwards every time he makes a point.

When he joined the company, there was much finger-jabbing to be done. The Merck research laboratories, despite their fine reputation, were at a low ebb: there was little original thinking coming through. Vagelos's first task was to bring in new people. Men such as Ed Scolnick, now the head of research, and Al Alberts, the discoverer of Mevacor, came with Vagelos from Washington University; scores of other were recruited from colleges around the country.

But more important than the new faces were the new ideas. Vagelos and the men who came with him brought with them an infusion of biochemical thinking. Quietly, in the universities, a revolution in biochemical theory had occurred. It was a revolution, however, which had not yet filtered through to the commercial research laboratories.

The old game of molecular roulette, the technique that had been developed in the 1890s and had yielded the first generation of wonder drugs, was dead. In its place men such as Vagelos brought in the notion of 'rational drug discovery' – sometimes mistakenly called 'drug design', although design is too precise a word to describe the process.

Rational drug discovery follows on from advances in the understanding of the role of enzymes, proteins formed within living cells which act as catalysts for the many thousands of chemical reactions occurring with the human body. By understanding first how the enzymes and the chemical within a reaction worked in detail, drug researchers can then move on to finding an agent to influence the reaction one way or another. By changing a chemical reaction within the body, its health can be quickly changed.

The rational approach is a game of skill rather than a game of chance. In the past, researchers would discover a drug, if they were lucky, but even then had little or no idea how it worked. With this new approach, understanding first how the disease worked, drug researchers could narrow the range of potential agents to act against it, and, if they found an agent, could have a surer idea of the effects it was having on the body. It was enough of a change to hold out the promise of a second era of wonder drugs, and Merck was in the lead.

Almost immediately, Vagelos's new-look laboratory had a success with Vasotec, a drug for reducing high blood pressure and relieving congestive heart failure. The drug joined Capoten, a similar medicine manufactured by Bristol-Myers Squibb, and made a tremendous impact on the market. It is now the third biggest selling drug in the world, with sales of $1.2 billion. It passed the one billion dollar mark in annual sales in 1988, and became the most successful product Merck had ever made.

However, the greatest success during the ten years Vagelos spent as head of research was Mevacor, a novel compound for reducing cholesterol levels. It is a drug in which he and his close colleagues were intimately involved, and it is a story which captures the way the laboratories work, and how modern hi-tech drugs are discovered.

High levels of cholesterol are a major threat to health. It has been known for decades that high levels of cholesterol in the bloodstream create atherosclerosis, a form of hardening of the arteries. Cholesterol itself is a wax-like substance found naturally in all living cells, and the body needs a modest supply of it to sustain life – it is created naturally within the body from acetic acid, through the actions of enzymes. But too much cholesterol is a bad thing: it causes heart attacks, strokes and chronic kidney ailments. In the United States alone, heart attacks are estimated to cause five hundred thousand deaths a year, many of them resulting from high cholesterol levels. Yet there is little those half million people can do to save themselves. Research has shown that only a small proportion of the cholesterol in the body is there because of diet; the great bulk of it is produced naturally. This provided a role for a drug; if an agent could be found to slow down the rate at which the body creates cholesterol, then a significant blow could be struck against heart disease.

The story of that quest starts in 1956, naturally enough at Merck in Rahway. There researchers investigating vitamins isolated melvonic acid, a key substance in the body's production of cholesterol. It was later discovered that the body uses a specific enzyme to form melvonic acid. Altogether there are a series of twenty-five reactions in the chain that creates cholesterol. But the reaction which makes melvonic acid is the slowest of those twenty-five. Because it is the slowest – the bottleneck in the process – it can be used to regulate the whole process; slow down the rate at which melvonic acid is formed and the whole process slows down, reducing the amount of cholesterol released into the body. Find the melvonic acid enzyme, and you can make a cholesterol-reducing drug.

Enough had been discovered about the internal processes of the body to map out the path towards making a drug. The thing still had to be done, however. Vagelos became interested in the cholesterol process while he was working at the National Heart Institute within the National Institutes of Health in 1959; he was joined by Al Alberts as his laboratory assistant. The work they did together on enzymology was to lead directly to Vagelos's chair at Washington University. Alberts went with him, becoming an associate professor.

Meanwhile, between 1972 and 1974, Michael Brown and Joseph Goldstein at the University of Texas identified the key biochemical steps in the regulation of cholesterol – work for which they were to receive a Nobel Prize for Medicine in 1985. Again there were connections back to Vagelos; the two men had trained together at the National Institutes of Health.

In Japan, meantime, a scientist called Akira Endo was working for the drugs company Sankyo. Endo figured a natural substance could be found to control the production of cholesterol, inspired, he said, by the fact that micro-organisms had led to the discovery of penicillin. Endo worked the old roulette wheel: over a two-year period he laboriously tested six thousand micro-organisms, eventually striking a compound derived from an organism called *Penicillium citrinum*, found in abundance in soil. Sankyo slapped a patent on the compound in 1974; by 1976 articles about its ability to lower cholesterol levels had started to appear in the scientific journals. The struggle to control cholesterol was not only coming closer: it was also turning into a race.

Endo's work, coupled with the work of Brown and Goldstein, had rekindled Vagelos's interest in cholesterol. Soon after taking over the research department at Merck, he hired Alberts to work with him. Alberts was put in charge of finding a cholesterol drug for Merck (people with such leading roles are called 'product champions' around the laboratories).

Alberts set up his laboratory in a building known obliquely as '80 N' on the Rahway site. He already knew what he was looking for: enzyme HMG CoA reductase, the enzyme that creates melvonic acid. The problem was to find an agent to control it. He knew Sankyo had found something, and, he figured, if they could find an agent, then so could he. Alberts's main colleague in the search was a young lab assistant called Julie Chen. Together they started work on the crucial round of experiments in September 1978. Chen would put a chemical mixture containing radioactive HMG CoA into a row of test tubes. She then injected particles of the compounds they were investigating into the test tubes. If the compound had any effect on inhibiting the enzyme then there should be little or no radioactivity after the experiment was finished. When that happened, they would know they had it.

The experiments, one after another, dragged on through

September and October, and into November. On 16 November Chen walked into Alberts's room in the lab. She had good news: a test tube showing almost no radioactivity. It could be they had a compound; or it could be they had a false reading. Alberts, tingling with excitement, anticipation and anxiety now, told her to go away and try the experiment again. Years of research, he knew, and millions of dollars were riding on the levels of radioactivity in that one small tube. He waited and waited. Twenty-four nervous hours later, they had their answer. There had been no mistake. They had found the compound.

There was relief all around the laboratory: the breakthrough had arrived. Yet the real work was just about to begin. First a pure form of the compound had to be isolated. That took several more weeks, and when it was found it was given the chemical name lovasatin. By February the next year, the structure of the compound had been unravelled, and work was due to begin on testing its effectiveness in animals to find out whether it really worked.

A shock interrupted the process. In February, Sankyo, still working on its own product, filed a patent in Japan on a compound similar to lovasatin. The race was heating up. Alberts mobilised the laboratory's pilot production plant to begin manufacturing enough lovasatin to start testing the drug on a wide scale. 'The more we found,' he was later to recall, 'the more excitement, enthusiasm and pressure we felt. It's something most people don't realise. The competition starts at the lab bench.'

The testing began on rats and dogs in late 1979. The first indications were good: Mevacor proved to be highly potent at reducing cholestorol levels. The programme was speeded up and trials in humans started in 1980. Then, in September 1980, the prospects for the drug darkened as suddenly as they had shone two years earlier. A message came through from the Merck people in Japan that Sankyo had stopped all work on its own compound, compacten: there were rumours circulating through the industry that the company had discovered it caused cancerous tumours in dogs. If so, the drug was dead. It would not have been entirely unexpected: as many as nine out of every ten drugs discovered fail at the testing stage. But it was a disappointment. All testing work on Mevacor was brought to an abrupt stop, while the scientists tried to work out where they should go next.

They were still trying to figure it out in 1982, when a group of doctors came to Merck asking if they could have the drug on an experimental basis. They wanted to use it on patients suffering from familial hypercholesterolemia, an hereditary disease creating very high cholesterol levels. They had read about Mevacor, and wanted desperately to try it. Vagelos pondered the request. Eventually he gave it the go ahead. The doctors applied to the Food and Drug Administration for an investigative licence to try out the drug, and got it. The drug was tried out on the patients and it worked: cholesterol levels dropped by thirty per cent and there were very few side effects.

Those results jump-started the project back into life. In the laboratories, work was going ahead furiously to finish the drug. One team was working on back-up compounds to try out if Mevacor eventually failed. Another was testing. Drugs are tested in animals by delivering ever-increasing doses until eventually they reach toxicity. With a drug like Mevacor, toxicity is inevitable at some stage; cholesterol formation is a vital process and once enough of it is shut off, the effects will be harmful. The question is one of degree: what dosage is safe?

As the scientists tested, they found they kept getting different toxicities for different animals. That made their task doubly difficult. It was hard for them to discover whether the toxicity was caused by the compound itself, or by the dosage they were delivering. If it was the compound, they would have to go all the way back to the laboratory bench and start altering its molecular structure. If it was only the dosage, they could go ahead: although the results in humans can never be entirely predicted from results in animals, the scientists could be reasonably confident that if low doses were not toxic in animals, a similar low dosage could be delivered safely to people.

Over the next few years, they delivered hundreds of different doses to different animals, enough to decide whether the toxicity was just due to the dosage. 'We were confident that it was not basically an unsafe drug,' recalled one of the scientists later. 'And the big question was whether we could find a dosage of Mevacor that would lower the cholesterol and which would not produce the toxicity. And that, really, is just the luck of how the body works.' By 1984, four years after the cancer scare had set back their work, the researchers were confident enough of their product to restart large-scale clinical testing. There were other problems to sort out; about two per cent of the dogs tested had developed cataracts; others had developed liver abnormalities. But the scientists felt the side effects were not severe enough to hold up further progress on the drug.

The team that had begun as just Alberts and Chen had by now grown to more than a hundred people. As it progressed, different specialists within the laboratory network had been called on board: chemists, pharmacologists, toxicologists, microbiologists, safety assessors, and others. The marketing people – first told about the potential of the drug in 1979 – were also brought aboard. They were none too impressed by what they saw. The marketeers had already carried out studies showing the existing market for cholesterol drugs was only about a hundred million dollars: not much of a return for all this work. The scientists had their own arguments. This is a novel drug, they pointed out: it will create a brand new market because it is a brand new treatment.

Despite marketing doubts, the project went ahead, consuming more and more money as it moved into the final lap of development. At its last stages, Mevacor was devouring a quarter of the research and development budget – at that time around five hundred million dollars a year. There were still a few problems. The drug design staff had sketched in a yellowy colour for the Mevacor tablet. But the scientists didn't like that: yellow reminded them of the colour of butter, quite the wrong image for a cholesterol-lowering drug. Eventually it was changed to a pale blue.

On 14 November 1986 Merck sent a van loaded with a hundred

and four volumes, each one weighing in at four hundred pages, to the Food and Drug Administration. The regulatory affairs unit within the company had been monitoring the drug constantly since 1978, preparing their submission, and keeping the FDA officials updated on the progress of the medicine. This was their big moment. A speedy approval by the FDA is a vital part of the process: the sooner a drug is approved the longer there is left on the patent already filed on the product. Lose a year in the application and you lose a potential year of sales; that can mean several hundred dollars is washed down the tubes.

The regulatory affairs department consists of over a hundred people who outline every last detail of a drug, laboriously completing the forty-one thousand pages of information the FDA needs to make a decision. Even after the application goes in, the work only becomes harder and faster: on Mevacor there were some six thousand individual questions and target dates for information from the regulators to be answered and met. One piece of good news came early: Merck won a date for a public hearing on the drug only three months after filing its application. The meeting was set for 19 February 1987.

The day before the hearing, Dr Ed Scolnick, Vagelos's successor as the head of research and development, took a group of fifty people down to Washington on the train. That night, they practised their respective roles, running through and rehearsing their lines. The hearing took place in one of the auditoria at the National Institutes of Health in Bethesda, Maryland. The hall was packed first thing in the morning with people hanging on the result: on the floor were the regulators and the Merck people, in the gallery were share analysts, ready to rush the news back to Wall Street, and representatives of rival drug companies, anxious to discover what Merck was about to release.

The hearing dragged on all day. By its end, the FDA panel voted unanimously in favour of Mevacor. 'We were literally estactic,' Scolnick said later. 'It's what you see when a baseball team wins the World Series. It was a tremendous feeling of camaraderie.' There was still a long wait to clear the final hurdle:

full approval of the drug. It came on 31 August, at 6 p.m., a couple of hours after the FDA had called Merck asking for some minor changes in the labelling of the drug. The wait was over. Mevacor, nine years after the trail had first been scented, and after $125 million had been spent on development, was at long last ready to be sold to patients.

Now the story was close to its end. The drug still had to be priced, and the price turned out to be high: a single two-milligram pill costs $1.64 in the United States, an amount that would bring the bill for a year's treatment to $3,000. And the drug still had to be marketed. That was another tale altogether. It was, however, a success. In its first full year on the market, 1988, it sold to the tune of $250 million; by 1989 that total had doubled to $500 million, making it the fourteenth best-selling drug in the world; and it was confidently predicted within the industry that it would easily top the one-billion mark. The scientists had been proved right and the marketeers wrong; evidence, to their minds at least, that the industry was still driven by innovative products and not by skilful salesmen.

Vagelos's term of office as head of research and development was rapidly turning into a triumph. He had overseen the development and launch of Vasotec, an anti-hypertension drug which had become a billion-dollar product; and he had inspired and instigated the discovery of Mevacor, which was also set to become a billion-dollar product. There were other significant advances. Pepcid, a drug for petic ulcers was licensed in from Yamanouchi of Japan, and launched in the US, to become a $100 million product. The first ever vaccine for hepatitis-B was launched, and called Recombivax HB.

Work had also been started on a drug to cure benign prostatic hypertrophy or enlarged prostate, a painful and common condition; a third of men over fifty suffer from it, and half of men over seventy. Currently it can only be cured by surgery, a tricky operation carrying with it a six-per-cent risk of losing the sexual functions. This research project, starting from the mid seventies, had been led by a scientist called Eugene Cordiss. He had been studying a class of men called pseudo-hermaphrodites – men who, because of an enzyme deficiency at birth, physically resemble women when they are born.

Cordiss noticed something very odd about this group of men: they never get acne, they never go bald, and they never develop prostate glands. He figured it was the enzyme deficiency stopping the prostates developing, from which, he deduced, there must be an enzyme in there somewhere creating the condition. Find it and block it, and there would be a drug. They found it, and successfully located an agent to block the enzyme. The drug was christened Proscar, and by 1990 had moved into phase three of clinical trials, the last leg of the testing process before filing an FDA application. It holds out the promise of being an even greater money-spinner than Mevacor.

The rational approach had worked. By discarding the roulette wheel and switching the research laboratories on to modern molecular biology, Vagelos had succeeded in bringing six new drugs through the development process, three of them major ones. Drugs companies live or die by the productivity of their research and this was an unprecedented level of innovation. It was to have an electrifying effect on the company.

In 1986 sales, pushed onwards by the launch of Vasotec, had started climbing: they were up by $600 million in that year alone. In the next year another $900 million was added to the previous total. From there, sales have mushroomed, almost doubling over the five-year period.

Something else was happening during those years as well, however, less profitable, but in its own way as significant for the character of the company as the transformation of its financial results. That something was a disease called onchocerciasis and a drug called ivermectin. In the leafy suburbs of Rahway, neither word has much meaning, nor do they summon up much emotion anywhere in the developed world. But in the wide open savanna of West Africa, they are words that conjure up a world of infinite darkness, terror, and despair.

Onchocerciasis is the medical term for a disease also known as 'river blindness'. Around eighteen million people, mostly in sub-Saharan Africa, suffer from the devastating condition. It is caused by parasitic worms, sometimes up to two feet long, which invade the body. The worms live inside the human carrier for up to ten years, producing during that time tens of millions of offspring called microfilariae, tiny worms too small to be seen by the naked eye but clearly visible through a microscope. These creatures migrate around the body, travelling around the skin forming knotted tangles. The effects on the body carrying them are endlessly destructive: skin rash, a softening of body tissue and, because the worms enter the eye, eventual blindness. An incurable itching is another consequence: suicides are regularly recorded because of the suffering created by the parasites.

In areas of West Africa, from Guinea through the Ivory Coast, Mali and Ghana to Benin, river blindness has destroyed rural villages. The parasites multiply as people become older, so in many villages around sixty per cent of the men and women over fifty-five have already been blinded. Their fate is to sit around the villages, no longer able to work on the land, simply waiting to die. Black flies, which carry the parasites, breed in abundance on fast-moving streams, carrying the disease from person to person. Alert to the danger flowing with the streams, villagers have moved away from the riverbanks, and headed towards less fertile areas further from the water. Here, although the danger of river blindness may diminish, the danger of starvation and malnutrition rapidly escalates.

Until recently, there were two drugs used to combat river blindness. But both had serious side effects, requiring intensive medical supervision and often hospitalisation, and making the treatment useless for a widespread disease in poor countries. Another weapon is to spray insecticide on the rivers to kill off the black flies, a programme carried out by the World Health Organisation. That has had modest success in slowing the spread of the disease; but the flies return, carried on the wind from other areas, and they have started to become immune to the poisons.

Back in the leafy suburbs of Rahway, however, a solution was soon to emerge. As well as its larger human healthcare division, Merck also has a smaller section developing and manufacturing animal medicines. Starting in the early seventies, scientists there began working on a drug to eliminate a host of tough parasites common in ordinary livestock. They worked through the conventional route, testing thousands upon thousands of micro-organisms until, in 1975, they struck with a soil bacteria from Japan. In small doses, this new compound killed the parasites, with relatively minor side effects for the animal. The drug was named Invectamin, and went on to become the largest-selling animal health product in the world.

In 1978 development work on the compound showed that it killed a worm in horses, similar to the one causing river blindness. By chance, one of the scientists working on the drugs, Mohammed Aziz, had spent time in Africa working with the World Health Organisation. Aziz had a first-hand knowledge both of the medical details of river blindness and of the misery it creates. The results in horses sparked a thought in his mind. In 1980 he and the project leader, Dr William Campbell, approached Roy Vagelos and suggested the drug be tried out for possible human uses.

Vagelos said okay: a significant decision in itself, since the cost of investigating and developing the drug would be huge, and the likely payback minimal. Within a year the drug had been tried out on victims of river blindness in Africa. The results were astounding. Although the drug does not kill the adult parasites, it kills the offspring which do most of the damage. It also inhibits the parasites' reproduction. The side effects were mild, creating only a minor swelling for a few days. And the dosages needed were low; one shot of Mectizan, the name Merck gave to the human form of the drug, turned out to be enough to protect the patient from the disease for a year.

Mectizan held out the promise of ridding Africa of this scourge. The path between Rahway and the savanna was not to be smooth, however. Full-scale trials with the WHO took a long time to set up, and it was not until 1987 that the drug was finally approved for general use. But that was the least of the trouble. A greater difficulty was who would pay. Merck listed a price of three dollars a shot for anyone wanting to buy the drug, not much, in Western terms, for protection from such a terrifying disease. Such sums, however, were far beyond the budget of the villagers, far beyond the budgets of their impoverished governments, and, for widespread use, beyond the resources of the WHO. That left Merck with a crucifying dilemma. It had developed this drug, a compound with the power to create tremendous good, and yet the tragic economics of sub-Saharan Africa could prevent the drug reaching the people who needed it.

In 1987 Roy Vagelos, by then the president of Merck, took the decision that the company would break the deadlock by giving the drug away, and by funding the development and manufacturing costs from its own pocket. The drug is now freely available to any medical agency that can deliver it to the men and women who need it, and has since been administered to over a million victims.

It was a momentous decision: significant not just for its financial or human consequences, but also for marking out the type of company Merck had become. It was, in a subtle way, reminiscent of George Merck's decision to give up the rights to streptomycin: a declaration that for a drugs company the relief of human suffering was as important a goal as the pursuit of financial gain.

The Mectizan story was the third part of a three-stage transformation of the company: a transformation of its scientific standing; a transformation of its financial standing; and a transformation of its ethical standing. The results for its reputation among American businesses were deep and rapid. From being regarded as a washed-out has-been by the stock analysts, by 1986 and 1987 Merck was being lionised by Wall Street. Its stock price began climbing, taking its market capitalisation ever upwards. In 1986 it entered the list of America's ten largest corporations, ranked by market capitalisation. By the end of the decade it had moved into the number six slot in the United States. And it had toppled IBM, the mightiest of the country's heavyweights, as the nation's most

8 What kind of fools?

The corridors of Merck's West Point research centre seem drab and, in some ways, soulless. The corridors have that pale, lifeless, institutional colour scheme. And they are very quiet. Many doors lead off the corridors. Each has a pane of glass, at around chest height. Looking through, you see a room, roughly ten foot square, and benches cluttered with test tubes, microscopes, and tubing running from flasks to test tubes. Each room has a couple of smaller rooms attached to it, more like boxes than rooms. Here you can see a man or woman sitting looking at some papers or peering into one of the microscopes, with a quizzical expression. There is no sound.

The only difference between any of these rooms, to the uninformed eye, is the *Far Side* cartoon pinned to the glass windows. Scientists, as a breed, are keen on *The Far Side*, particularly the cartoons featuring the geeky boffins; which appeal to their sense of the strange, the mysterious, the unexplained. One of the cartoons seems particularly appropriate, somehow. It shows a plain room, with a bunch of ordinary sweatshirted people hanging around, hands in pockets, shoulders hunched, dumb expressions on their faces. Behind a glass panel there are four of those geeky boffins with white coats, wild eyes and single-strand-of-hair heads. The boffins are pointing down at the ordinary people, and one of them is exclaiming: 'Of course they're fools! The question is what *kind* of fools?' Placed in that context it seems not so much a comic as a good question: what kind of fools?

Try another room. This time there are harsh, bright lights, and an acrid smell to the air. To the right is a man sitting at a desk studying some papers. And all around there are benches and test tubes and flasks. Some of the tubes are filled with a pale, colourless, odourless liquid.

The scientist's name is Mike Cordingly. He is twenty-eight years old, an Englishman with a beard. He is wearing grey cotton pants, and a checked shirt. He has been working here, in this room, for two years. 'I am in the trenches of drug discovery,' he tells me.

Is that a nice place to be?

He shrugs and smiles: 'It's all right.'

It's a living, anyway. Mike, a friendly and softly-spoken soul, came here from Cambridge University, where he took his doctorate. His job is to find a cure for AIDS. He is one of many people whose job it is to find a cure for AIDS. There are four other scientists who work with Cordingly in this room. They are working their way through the genes that make up the HIV virus, studying their structure and trying to find a particular gene that regulates the virus. If they can find that, then it might, indeed probably would, be possible to find a way of knocking it out. But that is a long way off, and he has already been working on the project for two years. His work is about as close to pure, basic, scientific research as a drugs company ever gets.

'I came here to work on AIDS,' he explains. 'It's close to basic research, but we have a very clear mandate in what we do. We have to have a clear focus, and that's to discover something, because if you haven't discovered anything then you haven't really succeeded.'

Does that happen much?

'Sure,' he answers. 'People can spend a whole career here and never work on a drug that ends up on the shelf.'

Mike heads back to his desk and starts studying his papers again. I step back out into the corridor, and amble onwards. It goes on and on, unchanging. I try another door. This one is more complicated. Inside, I am confronted by another door, and by a red light. Behind me there is a green light. I shut the first door: the green light goes out but the red light stays on.

To my left is a small office, with a man inside, sitting at a desk reading a newsaper; everyone is reading something here. His name, it turns out, is Bill. He gets up and opens the second door to let me inside the lab. 'Airlock security,' explains Bill, a tall casually dressed man. 'We don't want the air in here mixing with the air in the rest of the building.'

Really? Why's that?

'This is where we keep the AIDS virus.'

No kidding!

'Sure we do,' says Bill. 'Come and have a look.'

The room is empty right now. The lights are dim, giving the place a suitably gothic feel, spot on for a room warehousing a cargo so loaded with an atmosphere of plague and terror. There is a bench running alongside one side of the room, and along the other side there is a row of test tubes. It's in there. From a distance it doesn't look like much; just a test tube with some fluid in it. Close up it doesn't look any different. It is only at a molecular level, under the microscope that it starts to become interesting.

Hanging up are a couple of all-over body suits, spaceman-type suits, that the scientists use when they come in here to perform their experiments. The security is intense. Anybody coming in needs a special security card. Even the air and the water in here have their own security checks, with separate air-conditioning and plumbing, to prevent any possibility of contamination.

'So where do you get the virus?' I ask. 'Where does it come from?'

'We breed it here,' answers Bill. 'And we like to keep it nice and healthy and infectious.'

I suppose you would.

'Yup.'

Get many visitors?

'Ed Scolnick brought the board around here a little while back,' he answers. 'They stayed for a few minutes, but they all kept their hands in their pockets.'

Bill laughs at the recollection of such a bunch of tame chickens and heads back to his newspaper. Another day at the office. I, meantime, put my hands back in my pockets, and head out into the corridors. Things are starting to make more sense now. There is the cost: the latest industry estimates are that it cost $250 million to develop each new drug. Set in this vast complex that figure makes more sense. There is the cost of the scientists' salaries, plus pay for their assistants; there is the cost of the equipment, $600,000 in Cordingly's laboratory alone; there is the cost of the support staff. And then there is the cost of development; the cost of all those thousands of animals, the costs of monitoring the animals, and so on and so on.

But then there is also the mystery of this place. The laboratories are the heart of a drugs company; the organ within the corporate body that pumps its lifeblood. Yet how would anyone run a laboratory in the traditional corporate sense of manage and control? For a start there is very little in the way of hierarchies here. There are few bosses or workers, just individuals or teams working on different parts of problems. There are product champions, senior scientists like Al Alberts who lead a drug's development, assembling *ad hoc* coalitions of experts who come together to solve a problem, but then, just as quickly, dissolve back in to the general mass. If that is management, it is very different from the way it is usually understood.

Then there is the question of creativity. It too is a puzzle. Everyone agrees drug discovery, alongside patience and hard work, takes moments of pure inspiration and brilliance. How can you make that happen? Of course, you can't; the point about hiring creative people is precisely that you bring them aboard to do things you wouldn't be able to do; things you wouldn't even think of doing. So how can America's sixth largest corporation have an $850-million department, the most important in the corporation, which it can neither manage or control?

Still puzzled, I head off to see Ed Scolnick. He works back at the Rahway head office, in a large, plushly carpeted and well furnished room within the lab complex. He is a broad, tall man, with a slight stoop, brown to greying hair and a relaxed, almost detached manner. He is wearing a casual jacket and pants, and sits sideways in his chair as he speaks. He talks in a languid way, chewing slowly through his sentences, thinking each one over before he completes it. So Ed, I ask, how do you manage a research lab?

'The key thing is the quality of the people. That is the key ingredient. The better the people, the less you have to do. So we try to recruit the best possible people and let them assimilate the Merck research process. The process is focused on finding innovative drugs to treat illnesses that are not yet treatable: within that broad mandate anything is fair game – any field, any approach, any style. All that is required is that you do your work carefully and productively and with intensity.

'The people have to be smart, and dedicated. They have to be willing to work hard and to have persistence because any research enterprise has any number of ups and downs, whether it is academic basic research or pharmaceutical research. People have to be willing to stick to their ideas and have the conviction that they can eventually be successful. Most projects fail several times before they emerge.'

The recruitment issue is taken very seriously at Merck: Vagelos likes to wander round the organisation asking people who they've hired recently. It as an obsession than runs right through the organisation; all the managers have to keep their senior men updated on who their successors will be, and prepare regular reports on each of their employees. Yet it is not simply a matter of picking the best people and letting them run with it. Managers have to guide them, motivate them, or manipulate them, to some degree.

'It's a mixture,' says Scolnick. 'Most of the people we recruit come from an academic training, so they don't know much about drugs. You have to teach them. You can't just leave them alone in that sense. What you can hope to do is leave them alone to pick good projects to work on, and when you get very good people, that's just what happens. They do it themselves. They pick their areas, they pick their targets and once or twice a year you talk to them and see how it's going. But that is the best part of the process. If you've got people who aren't as good you have to stimulate them. You say: why aren't you working on something more productive, that isn't a very good problem, that has no connection with medicine, why aren't you working on something else?'

It isn't entirely haphazard. The research department has a number of senior scientists who meet regularly to review priorities, look at new opportunities, push old projects, and to discuss what is happening in the world of science. 'That is a dynamic, ongoing, constant process. Again, the best people do it for themselves. People who aren't as good need nudging.'

So far, he figures, more than half his team is made up of the best people in the field. 'I can't say the precise number, but of the active, exciting drug discovery programmes at Merck, well over half have come from individual scientists within the laboratory in the way I have described. Some of the best ones have come from there. The process works, and that's very encouraging. So it's over half, but I'd like to see the number even higher.'

Scolnick, it seems, belongs to the school of managers who think their job consists of doing as little as possible, and is happier the less he has to do. Yet he admits that it is very tough to find the type of people he is looking for, and many of them have doubts about joining him.

'People's doubts are about how much autonomy they will have in what to work on. But as long as they understand that what they are supposed to be doing is trying to find a drug, they have tremendous autonomy in what they do. They really do. There are no barriers here. There are as few barriers here as there are in academia if they have a good idea. But they worry about that. They worry about how much we'll stick with a project if it's not working. Then there are all the questions about companies – Will there by lay-offs? It's not a steady job, there's no tenure. And you just have to tell them, that's the reality of it, that's right, but Merck has only once had lay-offs in research and that was thirty years ago.' And firings? 'A few people yes. But only for gross incompetence, absolutely gross incompetence. The people who have been fired were so obviously out to lunch that they didn't know how to do science at all. It is very rare. And I have to approve every termination.'

He himself suffered from those kinds of doubts when he moved from Washington University to Merck. 'Sure,' he says. 'I talked about them, and worried about them, and finally decided I was a good scientist and I would just take my chances.'

The method running through all the corridors is starting, slowly, to become clear. What these men, mostly refugees from the campus themselves, are engaged in is an attempt to recreate the culture of the university within a corporate organisation.

'Sure,' nods Scolnick. 'You want an academic culture but with a different focus on the objective. That is exactly right. The focus is on discovering and developing drugs, but the innovative culture we try to foster is an academic culture. It really works, as long as people keep that focus on their work. And they do, because they can see that they can do very creative science, publish it and still discover drugs.'

There are some differences; it is not a perfect simulation. People get fired for one thing. But they are also richly rewarded for their discoveries; a lab scientist working on a major drug could become a millionaire by discovering a major product.

Yet, for the scientists the money is really only a side issue. Curiosity and the quest for discovery provide the real drive. For Scolnick himself, it is the final creation of the drug that provides the stimulus and the challenge. Echoing what others have said, he explains: 'When you are asking the critical question: is it going to work in the way you think or not, then the excitement is beyond belief. And when it works it is a fantastic high.' Then there are the failures?

'Sure. You work on projects and they go in people and they don't do what you thought they would do. It's a real low. It's quite depressing. The other depressing thing is when you get something that you think you are going to be able to go with and you put it into safety tests and you find it's toxic. That doesn't kill the project but it kills that particular version, and you have to go back and get another one. In some ways that is even worse. Lots of things go into animals and they're toxic so you have to go back and refine the chemistry. That's the toughest part of the process emotionally – persisting at that point and developing your strategy. It's a big down and one of my most important jobs is to keep those people at that point from getting like that.'

Yet for all the root excitement of science, there are still kinks in the university-within-a-company concept. Here is one: the scientists have to belong to two schools. As members of a corporation, they have to advance its financial interests, but as scientists, they have to advance knowledge.

Scolnick's eyes dip a little here; he acknowledges that this is a tricky area. 'The commercial people don't prioritise the advancement of knowledge. But in a sense they do promote knowledge because they should be disseminating new information about medical therapy. If they do that well, they are going to sell their drugs. That is the basis on which Merck's marketing optimally functions, and in that sense they are fostering science. Obviously there are commercial reasons for that, but that's when they do their best.'

So how do the two sides connect?

'At the basic research level there are very few linkages. People interact, they see marketing people, they see them at meetings, but they don't really have much linkage. We rarely, if ever, talk to marketing about what we're going to work on in basic research. But projects which go into development are followed jointly by the clinical group, the marketing group and the group dealing with drug regulators. The data is discussed, marketing's points of view are discussed, and attempts are made to make sure that the studies we are doing take account of their needs. But Merck is very careful about what it promotes. The research labs in the end always have the final call over the direction of a programme from a medical point of view or an ethical point of view. Marketing is obviously always looking for its commercial edge, but if that involves something that is not good medicine, we never let them do it. And I mean never.'

Do they ask?

'Sure they do. They always have their perspective. They don't see it the same way we do.'

From what Scolnick is saying, he appears very much in command; he is aware of being at the centre of the corporate wheel, and the rest of the business spins around his department. He agrees that the research arm is clearly the dominant group within the company. 'It was that way even before Roy Vagelos was head of the company, but it is even more so now. We give them some data for commercial purposes, but all the research, we have to approve to make sure the science is right.'

Looking at this another way around, marketing people might say they know what the public wants from drug therapy. Scolnick admits he is unsure how concerned he should be about what the public expects from his laboratories.

'It depends on the level of the question. The public expects treatment for everything. You know, they ask why there isn't a treatment for breast cancer. Well, breast cancer is not as feasible a project for the pharmaceutical industry as AIDS. It's just a more complicated process and the biochemistry is not as easy to get hold of as the biochemistry of the AIDS virus. So that part of public expectation is not bothersome to me. From my perspective, what the public expects of the pharmaceutical industry is that it should develop novel, useful new therapies. I think the biggest criticism of the industry is when companies develop "me too" drugs [drugs which imitate other successful compounds] and price them too high. Drugs often do not have as much value as their price implies. So I think the best companies have to work in areas that really don't have good therapy to justify the returns that they make. We have not worked in research on a "me too" drug. We just would not do that.'

This research department is already one of the largest in the world. Size and achievement, however, are often distant strangers to one another. Scolnick is acutely aware of the risk of running into diminishing returns the larger his laboratories become. 'What we try to do with each new field that we enter is to get each little group operating as its own little company,' he says. 'We tell them they are competing with all the other companies worldwide, and that the future of their company depends on getting that product out. Merck's goal is to remain a growth company no matter how big it gets. Not many companies do that. So how do you do it? How you do it is by developing big, new, important drugs in new fields. The more new fields you're in, the greater the possibility of hitting something and keeping that process going. The danger is that you've got to keep your quality up while doing that, otherwise things are just never going to pay off and you're just throwing money away.'

Just throwing money away is a fine description of pharmaceutical research: it is never planned that way but, all the same, that is the way it works out. It happens less at Merck than at its rivals, however, and that is the closest I get to an explanation for its success. Risk is the nub of drugs research, and risk has not been eliminated along these corridors: plenty of chances are still taken. It has been minimised, however, by modelling the company on the one institution where creativity has flourished in the past: the university. By making itself attractive to scientists, the company heightens its chances of success. But this a double-edged policy. While it lowers the risk of lousy research, it heightens the financial risks by tethering its marketing department.

9 Detail men

'Our great secret is that we have been able to rise above the university.' This secret is divulged by John Zabriskie, head of the Merck, Sharp & Dohme division of the company, the division that handles selling the drugs in North America. Zabriskie looks like the man to harbour this sort of secret. From his head to his toes, he is a corporate animal. None of this casual, laid-back, pseudo-academic style for him. He has the look and the manner of a dedicated, ladder-climbing company man. He has broad shoulders, broadened by a touch of padding on his sharply-tailored suit. He has brown hair, parted at one side and slicked back, coming to an abruptly trimmed stop just past the back of his ears. And he has a square jaw, and square, sharply-pronounced vowels, and a firm handshake. Slick, slick, slick. And so on.

Zabriskie has worked at Merck all his life. After graduating from Dartmouth College and the University of Rochester, where he took a doctorate in organic chemistry, he came to Merck to work in manufacturing research. Since then he has worked in most sections of the business: research, sales, production and marketing. He was president of Merck Frosst, the company's Canadian division. From there, in 1988, he was promoted by Vagelos to head MSD.

His job is to sell drugs. Selling drugs, however, is a complicated task, and one shot through with contradictions. One is that the people who consume the product, the patients, are different from the people who select it, the doctors. Then there is another group of people who pay for it – sometimes the patient, sometimes the government, sometimes an employer, sometimes an insurer. Another is the relationship between the customer and the company. In most capitalist enterprises, marketing people are meant to find out what the customer wants, and get the production people to make it. In drugs, it is the other way around. The researchers find out what the customer needs and then the marketing people go out and make sure they take it. But there is a more central dilemma: isn't there something weird about marketing drugs? It isn't, after all, quite like Coke or hamburgers: either the person needs it or they don't. Why the salesmanship?

In part, the salesmanship is part of the idea about lifting the organisation above the university. 'We are able to take basic ideas and commercialise them,' Zabriskie goes on to explain. Marketing at Merck starts early, at the research level. Marketing teams will, from time to time, outline product areas they want to get into. More often research sets those. But once a drug comes out of the research stage and into the long development chain, marketeers are assigned to the project. 'Marketing people go into development and actually become members of the research team,' says Zabriskie. 'And that is very important because marketing then has a fundamental understanding, early on, of exactly where the development is and at that point we can influence the critical studies that are going to be done, and we can ask for claims over and above the claims that were originally going to be developed.'

There are two stages to this. One is for the marketing people to determine whether a compound is worth the $100 million to $200 million it is likely to cost to develop. They do that by looking at the existing drugs on the market, how widespread the disease is, what the price is likely to be and so on. The other is to scientifically carve out a place for the compound in the market. That means giving it an edge over rivals by demonstrating effects on the body that the others don't have. All of this goes beyond what is scientifically or medically necessary: for example, doing clinical tests against a market leader, an idea that would occur to a marketing man but not necessarily to a scientist; another example is the spreading of clinical trials across a wide geographic spread, so that the drug becomes well known to physicians across the country.

Next is the launch. The marketing campaign starts up to three years before a drug comes out. It starts with market research, to determine where and to whom it is likely to be prescribed. Then the market has to be softened up. Doctors have first to be made more aware of the illness, an approach used for Mevacor. 'We are spending a great deal of time and effort trying to educate physicians about the dangers of high cholesterol,' says Zabriskie. 'This was not well known. So we are running up to a hundred physician symposia a year addressing the need to treat. And the next message is to tell them about Mevacor.'

Symposia and medical journal advertising create an awareness among physicians, but the conventional wisdom within the drugs business is that medicines, like encyclopedias, need to be sold door-to-door. In the United States, Merck has 2,700 reps, split into four groups: three in separate product areas, and another group selling to major buyers such as hospitals. As a rough guide, each physician in the US will get eight calls a year from each Merck product group, meaning the company sends someone to see each physician every two weeks. By the standards of the industry, that is not high. It is common for many companies to send a rep to talk to a doctor about the same product up to twenty times a year.

For Merck, marketing is not just a US business, however. It is international, and one of the keys to making money from drugs is to roll out each product around the world as fast as possible to get a return on the vast sums ploughed into research, and to maximise revenues within the limited patent life of the product. The man in charge of international marketing is Jerry Jackson, who twenty years ago was selling Indocin. Jackson has lost none of his enthusiasm in the intervening years.

Speed is the essence: 'The product life cycles are shorter now than they used to be,' explains Jackson, 'because not only do you have the limited patent life, but it used to be that when you lost the patent the product didn't decline so quickly. Now we try to do as much as we can to accelerate the launch, to get as much area under the sales curve as possible. But in doing that there is a risk, because the investment in pre-launch marketing is benefiting the other products on the market.'

Merck treats drugs as standardised products, which means it thinks they are more like Coca Cola than beer; the same Coke can be sold everywhere in the world, whereas each country and region has its own tastes in beer. It seem obvious enough – the body and the diseases that afflict it are the same everywhere – yet prescription rates for drugs differ widely from country to country. Drugs can also differ widely from the expectations of their manufacturers.

For all the precision marketing, a drug's success is directed as much by the winds of chance as by careful positioning. Jackson offers two examples. One was the hepatitis-B vaccine, a drug aimed at health workers and at the gay community, the two groups most at risk. It was launched at the time AIDS was breaking, and since it was made from human blood plasma, health workers were afraid to take it. Gays, also, were hard to reach: they turned out to be too diffuse a group to target. The result was that the vaccine only hit a quarter of its sales target. The flip side is a story about Clinoril, an anti-inflammatory drug. A modest press release put out on a slow news day was picked up by Walter Cronkite and broadcast on the television network news. The result was sales in the first four months at four times the expected level. 'Despite all the sophisticated technology, if we are plus or minus twenty-five per cent in the first year we consider ourselves lucky,' says Jackson.

Through men like Zabriskie and Jackson, Merck comes closer to operating as a typical corporation: marketing strategies, sales projections, and market shares are the concepts they trade in. Yet both men are also Vagelos appointments, put into their jobs at a time when he was reshaping the commercial side of the organisation to fit his own vision of what a drugs company should be.

They are men who must be worried, acutely worried, about the ethics of what they do. 'Back in those days I thought that working for a pharmaceutical company you were working for a company that . . . well . . . produced products on a higher plane,' recalls Zabriskie of his decision to join Merck in the mid sixties. It is a streak of idealism that has stuck with him.

The marketing men have to trouble themselves with ethics in three areas: in selling, in employment policies, and in pricing. Marketing is considered acceptable at the company insofar as it distributes products it believes to be beneficial to a wide range of people who might need them. But any notion of pushing drugs is treated with grave suspicion. At Merck there is a panel of physicians and lawyers to review and approve every single piece of information going out to the field sales force. Salesmen are allowed to say good morning and so on to the doctor, but beyond that every word they utter has to be approved by the panel. 'The panel reports to the corporation, it doesn't report to this division,' says Zabriskie. 'Even if the product manager wants to do something desperately, if the panel says no – and it says no a lot – then it doesn't happen.'

For the past twenty years, since the first women were recruited as sales representatives, the company has followed a strict affirmative action programme to integrate women and minorities into its workforce. 'We made a decision and we've gone out and recruited women and minorities – of the seven hundred representatives we hired a year ago over half were women and twenty per cent were minorities. What we've done is build a great base of women and minorities and therefore they've risen to all levels in the company,' says Zabriskie. Each and every department has targets set based on relevant demographics – the numbers in each group graduating with the relevant qualifications and so on.

The same ideal extends to the international organisation. 'We try to be a fair employer,' explains Jackson. 'The implementation varies from country to country, but the spirit is the same.' Other countries, naturally, are not as sympathetic to the idea of equality as the United States. In Japan, for example, it is unheard of to have female medical sales representatives; the medical profession is a closed male-dominated world. All the same Merck has resolved to start hiring women, as part of an effort to break the pattern of prejudice. 'I feel so strongly that we should have female representatives that we have set an objective to have them at least experimentally next year,' explains Jackson. 'We have tried to be cautious and to fit into the local culture but we have also tried to change it.'

The issue of pricing is the one that creates the most heart searching. Roy Vagelos insists on approving every price that the company sets: the commercial people recommend a price, but he decides whether it is reasonable or not. The company is acutely sensitive to accusations of over-charging. 'There is a great perception that a little bottle of pills costing fifty dollars is too expensive,' says Zabriskie. 'But if you compare it with other things at the same price it is not terribly expensive. Our leading anti-hypertensive, Vasotec, costs about seventy-five cents a day to take. That is less than a cup of coffee. Mevacor is about the same as a hamburger. My view is the pharmaceutical industry's prices are very fair in relation to other things that people buy.'

Merck's concern about pricing is shown in three ways. One is a commitment, made at the end of the last decade, not to raise its prices faster than the general rate of inflation. Another is a constant study of health economics: a large part of the marketing campaign attempts to demonstrate that the drug is not only better than existing treatment, but also cheaper. And the third is a scheme, announced early in 1990, to cut its prices to Medicaid, the US government-funded programme to supply medical treatment to poor people. The government had announced that Medicaid would not be able to supply the full range of modern drugs because the price was too high: Merck responded by offering states lower prices if they bought drugs through Medicaid.

'We were very concerned about a future in which our products would not be available to the poor people of this country,' says Zabriskie. 'So our fundamental principle was to allow full access to all our products in every state, because we believe the poor people of this country deserve our products just as much as the general public. We think that any other kind of policy is politically bad, socially unacceptable and bad medicine. Why should poor people have second-quality care? There shouldn't be two tiers of quality based on whether you are poor or rich. Again, a drug like Vasotec, at seventy-five cents a days is not terribly expensive – but that is not to say that everyone can afford seventy-five cents a day. Personally, I feel that Medicaid should be fully funded and everyone should have Vasotec. Not everyone can afford three square meals a day either, and whose responsibility is it? The manufacturers' responsibility – the food suppliers' – or is that what we have the federal government for, and food stamps, and Medicaid, and so on. We are taking on part of the problem with our own programme.'

It is certainly a tricky issue. Few other companies would go as far as Merck in taking on board some portion of responsibility for making sure its products reach people unable to pay for them. Trickier still is combining a sense of social mission with excellent commercial results. Both Zabriskie and Jackson set themselves ambitious targets. Zabriskie has to keep Merck the number one drugs company in America: it had a market share of ten per cent in 1990, but it wants to take that higher. Jackson's goal is to take Merck to number one in Europe, from its current ranking of number five, a task he believes he can accomplish with existing products. Also to take it within the top ten in Japan, the second largest drugs market in the world. Both men are keenly aware of the intense competition in the market, from the strengthened, merged companies such as Bristol-Myers Squibb, and from the upstart British challenger Glaxo; Glaxo is the one company they really rate as a rival for their own dominance of the industry. To keep Merck on top is a constant struggle. 'If you look at the graveyards of corporate America, what you find is that people didn't adapt to changes going on both within their organisation and within the market place. I believe you can manage anything so long as you understand what's going on,' says Zabriskie. 'With the Bristol-Myers Squibb merger, they now have two thousand representatives promoting their ACE-inhibitor, Capoten, and we

have seven hundred representatives promoting our ACE-inhibitor, Vasotec. That gives heightened competition. But we are still
growing, we are still taking a share from Capoten, so I think it
depends how productive you are. You can't just throw money at
things. The secret is to be very cost-conscious and to get the right
rate of return on your investment. I want us to be constantly
seeking new ways of gaining competitive advantage.'

Both productivity and competitive edge are nebulous concepts
in the drugs industry: terms borrowed from traditional manufacturing industries, and with much less meaning in this context. In
reality, there are two fairly simple objectives here: corporate
mission and corporate success. And there is little harder than
trying to do two things at the same time. So far Merck has
progressed along both tracks with remarkable ease and grace. The
circle is being squared. Somewhere in this building a host of
different objectives are being pulled together and made to work.
Chaos does not reign.

10 Courtiers

On Tuesday, 4 September 1990, a meeting took place in the boardroom on the seventh floor of Merck's Rahway headquarters. It started just before lunch and was scheduled to go on for most of the afternoon. Sitting around the long wooden table were Ed Scolnick, Jerry Jackson, John Zabriskie, Francis Spiegel, the head of strategy, John Lyons, the vice-chairman, Robert Banse, the general counsel, Douglas MacMaster, the senior vice-president, David Anstice, the vice-president for marketing, Judy Lewent, the chief financial officer and Richard Markham, the senior vice-president for marketing.

Presiding over the meeting that day was Roy Vagelos and this was his gathering: the philosopher-king and his court in session. Every week at Merck the senior managers gather in a group they call the Operating Review Committee, a body Vagelos set up after he became chief operating officer, and a body which is central to his management style.

There was a host of issues on the agenda that afternoon. Number one was a proposal from a group of scientists at Oxford University to do a study on the five-year effects of cholesterol reduction, a proposal requiring a pile of money from the company. It was discussed by everyone around the table. Next was a presentation by a couple of executives from the Japanese subsidiary on regulatory approval in the country, and why it takes so long. The participants discussed how winning Japanese approval for the next big drug, Proscar, might be speeded up. This was followed by a discussion of the company's budget for the third quarter of the year: each department reported on whether it was meeting its targets for the year, and if not, how it planned to get sales up and expenses down. And then each section head, starting from Roy Vagelos downwards, gave a five- to fifteen-minute briefing on its activities. The meeting broke up at around 4 p.m.

It was not a particularly long meeting: often the committee is in session from nine in the morning to five in the afternoon; often, also, the meeting is devoted to discussing a single issue. It is a very analytical form of decision-making; it embodies the notion that the truth will emerge through a process of debate. One regular attendant compares it with a court. Cases for and against a particular course of action are argued, sometimes for hour after hour, until eventually the judge decides. And it is within these meetings that the task of weaving together the strands of the company is achieved. It is, on the surface, an old-fashioned, autocratic style of decision-making, kingly even. But at the same time it is open, and consensual, and educative.

One of the weekly attendees is Francis Spiegel, a short, stocky man with broad shoulders, a broad face, grey hair and squinting eyes. He is a pugnacious man; argumentative and tough, but also a man who constantly interrupts himself with bursts of laughter. He spent time in the Marines, a hard training ground, and worked as an accountant after college, joining Merck after he qualified. Within the company he has worked in finance, in strategic planning, and as chief financial officer, before becoming vice-president for strategy. It is his job to figure out where the company is going and how it gets there.

Halfway through a rambling conversation he pulls out a sheet of paper and shows it to me. It is a copy of a Merck strategy document dated 1985. It shows the pharmaceutical industry as a box in the centre, and around it there are other boxes representing pressures for change in the business. They are named, and, clockwise, they read like this; competition from cheap generic copies of drugs that have gone off patent; a proliferation of R&D technology leading to greater competition from (patented) 'me too' copies; slower growth in the economy; increased costs from the escalating expense of R&D; more buying power in the hands of health organisations, leading to pressure for lower prices; new entrants into the industry; and greater international competition. It is an ugly looking picture, like a series of arrows pointing inwards on whoever happens to be in the centre; the centre in this case happens to be the established giants such as Merck. To one side of the diagram, an outcome from all this pressure is marked; it shows reduced margins on products and a lower return on capital; and it shows a consolidation of the industry as companies start to buckle under the weight of external pressure.

'What is happening with these dynamics in the industry is all these mergers,' explains Spiegel. Merck too, despite its success, has felt the same pressure. Spiegel reaches for some more research figures showing how a maximum of one in three new drugs earns a return on its investment. 'The bottom line is that this is an incredibly tough business to make profit in,' he says. 'That is contrary to what most people think. They think it is sexy because they see the returns. But they forget that it takes $231 million of investment in a new drug over twelve years before you see any return on that.'

Strategy at a drugs company always boils down to one simple issue: size. How big does a company have to be to be safe? Merck in 1990 had a five-per-cent share of the world market, and slightly less than five per cent of the world's total research and development spending. That, in the view of men like Spiegel, is not enough; there is still that element of fear that the laboratory may dry up and the company may start shrinking.

During the year of the mega-mergers, when Bristol-Myers bought Squibb and Beecham bought SmithKline, Merck examined its own merger options. There is no real opposition to mergers at Merck: in 1983 it bought fifty-five per cent of the Japanese drugs company Banyu for $313 million, one of only three Western takeovers of a listed Japanese company. None of the senior executives was opposed to a big merger on principle. But as they looked at the numbers, they couldn't work out how to make them add up.

'Bristol-Myers paid a premium of $4.4 billion for Squibb,' says Spiegel. 'That means they have to make up an extra $4.4 billion in increased efficiency before they even make a penny on the deal.' He laughs as he makes the point. Those are not the sort of numbers that appeal to him. 'That is not to say that we wouldn't make an acquisition if it weren't so expensive,' he continues. He shrugs: the point is that it is too expensive. The numbers have ruled out growing by acquisition.

'We want to increase our access to research spending and diversify our risk in what is a high-risk business. That's the reason why we went in with Du Pont. It gives us access to thirty per cent more research spending that we wouldn't have otherwise.'

Merck's route now is through alliances. In 1990 it unveiled an agreement with the chemicals giant Du Pont to form a joint venture called Du Pont Merck Pharmaceuticals. The deal came about in two stages. In September 1989 the two companies announced a drug swap agreement: Merck took over a leading role in developing a new class of anti-hypertension drugs that Du Pont researchers had discovered; in return Merck gave Du Pont the rights to its Parkinson's disease drug, Sinemet, with sales of over $100 million a year, and to one of its own anti-hypertension drugs. A party was held to celebrate the deal. There Francis Spiegel suggested to Du Pont's chief executive officer, Edgar Woolard, that they try a bigger and better deal. Woolard thought about it and came back with a positive response. The result, announced on 25 July 1990, was the joint-venture company, established as a separate entity, including the whole of Du Pont's drugs business, some Merck products and people, and Merck's expertise.

Other joint ventures have been fixed to fill gaps in Merck's product lines. As far back as 1982 it struck a deal with the Swedish drugs company Astra to take over North American licences on its drugs. The first product of that deal was Losec, a novel anti-ulcer drug with the potential to pose a challenge to Zantac, the world's best-selling medicine. When sales targets for Losec are met, the deal with Astra will be cemented into a permanent alliance between the two companies: Merck will have the North American rights to all its future products.

And in March 1989 Merck announced a joint venture with the consumer products giant Johnson & Johnson to create an over-the-counter medicines company; the pair bought the well known antacid Mylanta from Britain's ICI to start the new business. Merck had been out of over-the-counter medicine since it sold its own consumer business in the mid seventies. This deal was a way back into that sector of the market. Over-the-counter medicines are viewed by industry sages as one of the likely growth areas for the drugs business. There are two reasons. One is a trend towards self-medication; patients everywhere want to take more control over their own health. Another is that the over-the-counter business thrives on well known brands, and brands are a lot easier to protect, and survive a lot longer, than patents. As more of the big standard drugs lose their patent protection, as will happen during the nineties, drugs companies are looking for opportunities to switch prescription medicines to the non-prescription market. The joint venture combines Johnson & Johnson's experience in marketing consumer products with Merck's experience in drug development, together with its back catalogue of drugs with potential for switching. Within that back catalogue the ulcer treatment Pepcid is the drug most likely to be switched during the nineties.

Alliances are hip. If the eighties were the decade of the merger, then the nineties are the decade of the alliance; a more subtle form of combination, less of a blunderbuss, more alive to the delicate fabric of an organisation, and more concerned with building solid businesses than with smart financial trickery. That Merck should take them up so enthusiastically is unsurprising. It is what you would expect from a company run by a biochemist. Alliances fit snugly with the logic of a scientist; they are collaborative and exploratory.

Yet they are also uncharted territory for Merck, and depend crucially on individuals to make them work. All companies depend on individuals, often thousands of them. Merck depends more on one person than most; the individual who has wrought its transformation and guided it on to its current path. Size may determine how effectively it competes within its industry, but Roy Vagelos will determine its size. To understand how Merck works without understanding the background and character of its charismatic chief executive would be impossible. He is the active ingredient in this particular pill, the man who makes it work.

11 The philosopher king

On 13 May 1990, Roy Vagelos gave a speech to the graduating class at the University of Pennsylvania, his old college; his daughter Ellen was among the students, so the talk had a particular poignancy. He used his time to recall some of the episodes that had, he felt, formed his character. He recalled his father. 'From as far back as I can remember, one of my goals has been to help people. I learned that from my father,' he said. 'He was a Greek immigrant to this country, who ran a small restaurant in Rahway, New Jersey. He had four brothers and a sister. Whenever they or any members of the family faced an emergency, which was quite often, they would automatically turn to my father for help. He never let them down. Once I asked my father why he did all this. He told me, "You're not put on the earth merely to help yourself. You have to do something for others." '

Vagelos went on to recall the day he graduated from Pennsylvania in 1950. He was travelling to Europe and set off on a dormitory-style ship; his parents had bought him a ticket as a graduation gift. 'As we pulled out of the harbour that evening, everyone was excited about the wonderful adventure that lay ahead. I joined in the festivities, but at the same time I was worried. All my life I had been subject to motion sickness. However, the sea was perfectly flat the first day out.'

'But on our second day at sea I was awakened by the groans of one of my eleven cabin mates, who was obviously violently ill. I could hear the clanging of lamps, the creaking of the ship, the pounding of the waves. I knew what must be happening. We were in a storm and he was really seasick. I lay in my bunk considering the situation. I was about to begin training as a doctor in September; I was committed to helping the sick. But I knew about my susceptibility to seasickness. I made up my mind not to think about that. I had to help my friend get outside, up on deck. So I made mental preparations to face the storm. Then I lurched over to my friend's bunk, bracing myself against the edges of chairs. I leaned over the moaning patient and said. "Come on, buddy, I know what it's like to be seasick. I'll help you get outside for some air. You'll feel much better." He looked up at me miserably and sputtered, "Seasick? I'm not seasick. I've got asthma." Neverthe-less, I knew the fresh air would help. So, I hurried him up to the outside deck. To my amazement the sea was completely calm. There were no waves, there was no storm, and the ship was not creaking. I had imagined it all. But my friend was helped; the fresh air had improved his asthma. To this day I dread seasick-ness. However, I learnt never to let my own fears and preconcep-tions interfere with the impulse to help others.'

This is a strangely sentimental theme for the president of America's sixth largest corporation to choose for a talk to a group of young students. But it is also, in its way, daring. Where is the stuff about beating the Japanese to a pulp, about making America strong again; where are the ritual attacks on government and liberalism; where are the poems to greed and self-interest; and where is the pseudo-military language of strength, of control, of domination?

Roy Vagelos walks into the room and shakes me warmly by the hand. We talk. The place is a meeting room on the seventh floor of Merck's Rahway offices, a room dominated by a long wooden table and by a window looking out on the neat laboratories, offices and plant below. The room has little ornamentation, it's not showy or flash; it's functional.

Vagelos talks quickly, the words tumbling out with little natural punctuation. He has an accent like the old movie actor Jimmy Stewart, all long vowels, and pauses in the middle of words rather than between them. He peps up his conversation with phrases like 'gee', and 'I guess', rather than the 'fucks' and 'no shits' that pepper the speech of play-tough eighties' corpatalk. It adds to the Old World air about him: that of a traditional, small-town American who by some magical fluke has been transported to the president's office of a major multinational corporation at the fag end of the twentieth century.

I ask him about his family. It is a classic immigrant's story. Vagelos' grandfather was a Greek doctor who worked in Turkey. Troubles came, as troubles do. In 1922 the Turks drove the Greeks out of the country. The family – the grandfather and grandmother, the six sons and one daughter – moved back to their home in Mitilini, on the island of Lesbos. Soon afterwards the grandfather died. The children sold the family land and, one by one, moved to the United States, assembling again in the small towns of New Jersey, setting up small businesses. Like most immigrants, their attention was turned inwards, to their family and their children.

How does the son of a small-town immigrant become a professor of biological chemistry? Vagelos was not a good student at Rahway High School, not at first. He was the kid sitting at the back of the class pulling faces and fooling around. At the age of around thirteen he saw his cousins getting scholarships to good universities. And he saw them being praised to high heaven by the family. He wanted in. 'I became a very good student almost overnight. I decided it was important. From someone who was always doing everything wrong, and had terrible grades in my report card – I show them to my kids and they don't believe them – I was transmuted into something different. I went straight from the bottom of the class to the top.'

Vagelos did not like science at high school; he found it descriptive and boring. The researchers hanging out at the family diner sparked his interest. At the University of Pennsylvania, his professor fascinated him with the inner logic of chemical reactions. Even so, by the time he graduated he still had little idea what he wanted to do. 'Chemistry was number one option at the time because that was what I was interested in. Then I discovered that a lot of smart people were going to medical school. At that time it was very difficult to go to medical school, so I thought, gee, I've always liked the idea of medicine, so I thought I would apply. I applied to four, although people were applying to dozens. Of course, I was accepted everywhere so that sort of made my decision.'

Vagelos is an arrogant man. His life, at least the way he recalls it, is simply a matter of his deciding to do something and then breezing through to his selected goal. There is no hint of struggle or difficulty, or none he cares to remember. Yet his early life is strangely undirected. He is a man who waits around to see what everyone else wants to do, then resolves to do that as well, only beating everyone else along the way. He went to medical school despite a crucifying squeamishness and a terrible fear of blood; he almost dropped out in the first year because he hated anatomy classes so much. His is a competitive spirit, directed by the desire for challenges.

It was a pattern that was to repeat itself twenty-five years later. By 1975 Vagelos was forty-five years old and a successful professor at Washington University. Suddenly he left the academic life to become a drug researcher. Why would a middle-aged man do that? And why would a drugs company want him?

'I asked John Horan, the CEO who I took over from, one time, whether they realised what a terrible risk they were taking. He said: "Well, we were just banking on the fact that you had succeeded in everything else you'd done." They certainly couldn't tell whether I would be good at drug discovery, and neither could I. This was a challenge for me, and I needed a challenge. I was forty-five and I looked ahead of me at the other professors who were fifty-five and I didn't like what I saw. They were largely people who were packing their slides and that was not my bag. I needed a challenge, and it was a very tough thing to start over again in an environment which was not entirely positive. There were people in the laboratory who felt very threatened by my kind of science, were even, I would say, openly hostile. After all, this was the laboratory that had contributed Aldomet and Indocin and had synthesisied cortisone. So why should a hot-shot professor think a different approach was better?'

It turned out – naturally – that his way was better. Vagelos brought a lot of university academics into the laboratory, hiring away like crazy, networking among his old college friends, cajoling and persuading them, infecting them with his new-found enthusiasm for drug discovery.

When in 1985 Vagelos became the chief executive officer of the company, his new challenge was to infuse biochemistry through all the projects, improve the whole laboratory's rate of productivity, increasing its rate of discovery. He had a hundred senior level people in the laboratories with whom to interact and bounce around ideas.

When Vagelos left Washington University to join Merck, a cynical academic colleague commented to him, 'You know, Roy, they're going to have you selling toothbrushes and combs.' Another colleague, at Merck, recalls Vagelos saying the one thing he hated most about working for a corporation was having to wear a tie and jacket all the time (which was why he introduced casual Fridays). Why then should a man who loved science and hated the rituals of business switch from being the top scientist to being the top suit?

'I really didn't see it like that because I don't consider myself a non-scientist. I still lecture at universities. I recently turned down two centennial lectures at Stanford, one in the business school and one in the biochemistry department. I still feel I have a fair input, and I see primary data very soon after it is available, so I still feel closely knitted to it. As the head of research I was interacting, I was listening to all the business plans, and because of my technical background I was able to contribute to discussions of manufacturing and, of course, to discussions on marketing, since I knew more about the drugs than anyone in marketing did. So I was covering most of the aspects of the company. The things I knew little about are the things you learn on the fly, the legal problems, the finance all this crap that somebody's got to do. We have lawyers and financial people for that, so in a sense moving to the head of the company held very little new for me.'

That arrogance again; the arrogance of an intellectual placed among bumbling, stumbling businessmen. By the end of Vagelos' ten years with research, it was in good shape. It was the way he wanted it. But he was still not satisfied. He felt the rest of the company was not performing up to the standards he set; that it was not living up to his brilliance. Did he feel the research department was way ahead of the rest of the company?

'Yes, I think that is the case,' he says in measured, thoughtful tones. 'The company was not fully equipped, not appropriately organised to take advantage of some of the things we were doing. We've been through an evolution in practically every area. The research is different. Our marketing is different. And I have been involved in every one. I get very turned on by learning about a new area. As I said, there are two areas I don't get involved in, finance and law, everywhere else I learn about things and catalyse change. Fortunately the change is usually okay, and if it isn't we change it again. That's important. On occasion I have promoted the wrong person, and I've been known to reverse a promotion and demote the person. It's tough, but I feel it's better than allowing a mistake to propagate into the future.'

Here he is then, from the diner to the boardroom, learning away, catalysing all over the place, changing everything he sees. Despite everything he has learnt about the rest of the company, he still regards research as the most important section, the motor that drives it. 'If you look at the companies that have turned on and become paragons of marketing and sales, they're talking nonsense. They're good when they have a super product, and if they didn't have a super product they'd be the same old company they were before. To optimise a product you have to be good at everything but you can hide a lot of mistakes behind the shadow of a great product. I mean, gee, with Proscar, you don't need to be a very good marketing person to sell the idea that eliminating the need for a prostate operation with a six-per-cent loss of sex function is a good thing. People will be coming here to take the drug, you don't have to have sales people. To maximise the thing you have to have super sales and super marketing, but the motor is the drug.'

Vagelos pulls a face of pure disgust at the thought that a mediocre product with great marketing can be reasonably successful. 'It is the hardest thing to do that at Merck because we have such ethical standards. We are so tough in the way we allow promotion. We don't allow promotion people to talk about things that are not on the label, things that have not been shown to me, and we insist that all our people discuss the side effects as well as the effectiveness of the drug.'

Here the real Roy Vagelos is starting to emerge: the honest man who finds himself troubled by the moral nature of many of the people who surround him. I put it to him that he doesn't let his people flog the hell out of drugs, because the ethics of that would worry him.

'Exactly. We have an ethical code which is absolutely rigid. And that is absolutely right for Merck. There is no one at Merck who feels we are hurt by that. Our credibility is so good that even though we are at a disadvantage with some of our competition who will stretch things about their products or talk about our products in a negative sense, we don't feel we are hurt by that. But it's hard for Merck people. I had one marketing person who told me you cannot ask the same salesman who has promoted breakthrough drugs to also promote drugs which aren't breakthroughs. He said psychologically they just can't do it. Well, I got rid of that man, because I think you have to do it, you have to be straight. You can't talk about a slight improvement as if it's a breakthrough – and I can tell you there are people on the market today with drugs I consider to be slight, slight improvements, making great strides in their marketing. That couldn't happen at Merck. So we are at a slight disadvantage, but we enjoy that. We don't mind. That's our ethic, that's our character, that is the strength of the organisation. I do not have to worry that our people are out there describing our products in a way that I would not be proud of, in a way that I would not be proud to see on the front page of the *New York Times*.'

Vagelos acknowledges that ethics had always been a strong part of the Merck culture, even before his time. 'The spartan nature of the company and the dedication to health, the work ethic, the fact that it is willing to work in its community, I think all those were part of the company for years and years before I came. And they helped me because you respond to your environment and I felt very comfortable with that, it was a positive influence when I came. In every large organisation there are some bad apples: we've found people doing things that were done for the so-called good of the business but were being done in a way that was outside our code, and they were immediately fired. There was never any hesitation. When people see that a couple of times, they realise it's not just talk. We have shed some very high-level people who were found to be doing things that were just not the Merck style.

'There was one person who was making sales in an Arab country by guaranteeing that our products had no input from Israel, and that person was instantly got rid of. It was true, but we just didn't like him saying it. There was another person who was making derogatory comments about certain types of patients in a fun way in talks to sales people. It was just in very poor taste, and the person was done away with immediately.'

The sense of ethics seems to go deeper at Merck than merely in the way drugs are sold; it seems to run right through the company, like a thread weaving through a cloth. If so, the president must have strong views, must have feelings, about corporations having responsibilities beyond their desire to make a profit?

'Sure. After all, I'm a doctor. Don't forget I spent ten years at the National Institutes, I was a physician at a university for nine years, training people, and at no instance was I maximising my earnings potential, personally. So you can see that although maximising the earnings potential for the stockholders is important, I have other objectives as well. Delivering new drugs and getting them to people is terribly important to our company. That has been demonstrated, I think, with our action with river blindness, which is going superbly well and is today preventing blindness in thousands of people. It makes everybody at Merck feel great. We got so much out of that in terms of the psychological good feelings among the Merck people. They loved that. They love the forward looking moves we make. The fact that we have no smoking anywhere within the grounds – people really like being in a company that is responsible to its own people and to the outside world, where they know that what we do is going to have an input. It's not like selling toothbrushes and combs.

'Our main work is directed at important diseases. We don't work in trivial areas. We invest for years and years because we think these are critical areas. Things like Alzheimer's disease and cancer, these are the really important areas, things that we want to do. Making a new widget that would make a lot money, I guess we wouldn't back away from that, but we wouldn't go out of our way to do it. At least I wouldn't, it wouldn't interest me, and I don't think it would interest most people at Merck, because they really like what we do. There is something about the way we do things that makes people willing to sacrifice for and really go for. So they work very hard and it brings out the best in people – they are not just putting in an eight-to-five day. We do step out and take on extra responsibilities, it's nothing new for us. We pick things up early and move with them. We tend to be ahead of the wave. We're that way in research and we are that way in other parts of the company.'

Vagelos is passionate about his commitment to corporate responsibility: his passion is matched only by his enthusiasm for scientific discovery. There are strange things being said here, however: strange, at least, for the president of a major multinational. For instance, that he wouldn't be interested in profitable products if he felt they were trivial; and the fact that the company gives things away, although they cost money to make. There will be critics of this line, who will argue it is the job of the corporation to make money, and make money only.

Vagelos shakes his head sorrowfully, as if contemplating the foolishness in the world, and then unleashes a broad grin: 'Well, they can only accuse us of that when our profits start to decline. And, frankly, I wouldn't be interested in a company that didn't do those things, so they would lose me as part of the company. I'm a free agent, after all. I'm not indentured to anybody. Any stockholders who want to get rid of me can do so. But I don't believe we received any negative comments on the Mectizan donation programme, just the opposite. It was extremely well received. They expect it of our company, historically. Now, who are the stockholders? They're pension funds and so on, who couldn't care less about any good things that we do: they're interested in the bottom line. But so are we. I see this as something we do as an extra, we throw it in. It's a freebie as far as the stockholders are concerned. Obviously the money for Mectizan comes out of something, but no one can accuse us of having lost our profitability, or our growth potential, or our returns to stockholders. The stockholders may benefit from it in an indirect way because people just like to work at Merck, and they work harder. I don't think we are cheating the stockholders.'

Vagelos sighs, and pauses: he has made his stand against narrow self-interest, and delivered his tirade. He is immune from his shareholders, anyway: the results from the laboratories keep them at bay, at least until the results start to fall.

But all the passion for research, and the passion for involvement, prompts the question of how big the company has to be to achieve all it wants to. For example, in research. 'A lot bigger. I don't know precisely, but fifty to a hundred per cent larger would cover most of the critical areas that could take large-scale involvement of the Merck type of approach. I know we are not big enough today to do all the things that are important and where science has the leads – where, if you were working in the areas and were expert enough you could jump on the lead. We did that in 1975 with Proscar. I mean to me, that was clearly an open book, and there's Merck out there all alone now, because we recognised it, we committed to it, and we were not going to accept anything but going into the clinic and seeing that it didn't work. And so we were going to go all the way and we have.'

Vagelos is not alone in wanting his company to get bigger. Everyone is bothered by the size question. But what size is the right size for a drugs company?

'I recently put down my ideas on the number of important new drugs since I came into the industry. And it turns out it is at least one per year, on average. We currently have four per cent to five per cent of the industry research. Which means if you are going to be an average laboratory, you'll get one out of twenty important new drugs. If you're twice as good, you'll get one in ten. I don't know any industry which in the long run has been so fragmented and remained successful, but I think we need to do better than that. We've done very well recently. I would like to see us continue with that and so I think we have to have a larger percentage of the R&D in enough fields so that we can cover our future. And therefore if companies started passing us significantly in numbers, say two times our size, we would be at a terrible disadvantage. That would be a big worry.' So it is important to be number one in the industry? 'Yeah. I don't mind someone being a little bit bigger, but fifty per cent bigger, I would begin to worry. Everybody worries about us. Have you ever read anything about another company where they didn't compare to Merck? We are an obsession, an absolute obsession with the other CEOs. They see me coming down the street and they start talking, they start having bizarre thoughts on how they are going to get rid of me. They can't wait for my retirement.'

He laughs as he says this, a long throaty chuckle. Vagelos has a so-so sense of humour; he makes jokes, sometimes even funny jokes, but they are self-congratulatory rather than self-deprecatory. For a man so full of himself, so confident of his abilities and his importance, the notion of retirement must be painful. He says he will retire when he is sixty-five, in October 1994; is it enough time?

'I'm not finished yet. Is it enough time? It had better be. The way I'm changing things, it ought to be enough. There are demographic changes and customer changes coming that we are gearing up for very heavily. I see our customer base changing radically. It is moving towards large organisations, and we are evolving, and hiring different kinds of people to deal with it.'

Different kinds of salesmen, right? Vagelos pulls a face at the very mention of the word. 'Salesmen? Different kinds of people. People from medical schools, medical people with MBAs. The whole spectrum of people at Merck ten years from now will be different. We'll have different kinds of customers, and we'll be ahead of everybody, with a different kind of approach. Our strength is that we see things before they are seen generally either in research or in the trends, and we gear up to deal with them. It will be just as dramatic as the changes that took place in research. We said that only biochemistry and molecular targets are going to be hit and we did it just like that. These are the things that are going to be exciting in the year 2000. It will be a different world. And Merck will be one of the survivors.'

Vagelos is clearly a man of strong feelings – about science, about business. His management of Merck, its emphasis on technology, its social commitment, is in itself an indictment of the bulk of American capitalism. Yet he rarely comments publicly on anything except drugs. He is not a well known man, even in the United States. He is not nearly as well known as many less successful businessmen. Why is that?

Vagelos chews on the question for a second or two, puzzled a little by it himself. 'I do not see myself as a politician. I see myself as someone who can influence universities, who can influence training and development of people. I have a tremendous concern that American industry has lost its way, that we have turned to people that don't understand the technology of our businesses. Our automobile businesses are run by people who haven't been concerned about making competitive automobiles. They've been more concerned about the politics and about how the government feel about the market, and that's just not my bag. I don't stand up and talk about what is wrong with American business. It's very clear, only they won't talk about it. It would be inappropriate for me as a non-businessman to say so. I don't consider myself a businessman. I don't consider myself anything really. When I'm in a medical school I talk with scientists because I understand what they're saying. I can talk with business people but I feel more comfortable in a technical *milieu*. I've read things like *Barbarians at the Gate* and I couldn't even conceive of doing what they do. So we live in our spartan way. We don't have a jet. I have to keep turning down requests from our people. They'd like a jet. We're very straight-laced. I feel that way because it means I can look a workman in the eye and talk about what we are doing here; sure I make more money, but they know I work very hard too. So we don't have our executives flying off to nice vacations in company planes, we are very, very spartan and I think everyone appreciates that.'

Somehow every line of conversation with Vagelos comes back to an ethical issue. The drugs business has been heavily criticised and I wondered whether he agreed with any of the criticisms. Vagelos sighs wearily; he is depressed by the thought of the question: 'Oh yeah. I think at some point Merck, and I assume the other companies as well, recovered their loss to inflation. So in the US we have started a policy that we will only increase our prices by the level of the consumer price index. But all our colleagues are going along at double that rate, and ultimately that is going to be very destructive for the industry. Obviously we don't collude in price fixing but I would feel a lot more comfortable if we were not having pricing discussions in Washington all the time. And some of the commercial practices in the industry are absolutely deplorable. We wouldn't do them at Merck and I wish some of our competitors wouldn't do them to us. In the long run it's destructive of the industry.

'But otherwise the industry does so much good. If you just think of the last fifteen years and all the new drugs. I mean the good that the industry does is so remarkable and the potential for the future is so great. I can't imagine why anybody doesn't want to work in our industry. Why should anyone want to do anything else? And if we could just get rid of some nagging little things, I would be a lot happier. You don't need the other stuff. Unfortunately some people feel that they do.'

Vagelos is subject to these violent mood swings: at one moment he is castigating the industry, at the next praising it wildly, then off into a fresh low. It is the way he feels about it, and in a way he is right. It is a curious business: one with the potential for great goodness, but one, also, with the capacity for mind-numbing badness. Little surprise then, that an honest man shipped up on its highest peaks should be a confused individual.

I get up and shake his hand. Vagelos rises. He is tall, able to tower above any man in the room. Together we walk out. Heading through the door, Vagelos stops. 'Come here,' he says. I follow as Vagelos takes me to a corner of the reception area of his own office. 'See this?' he says. 'My colleagues gave it to me.'

On the wall there is a framed picture. It shows a black line marking out Merck's stock price since the Second World War. Like most stock price graphs it squiggles along, moving up and down. On it various events are marked; the invention of this; the resignation of whoever; and so on. There is a point marking the appointment of Roy Vagelos. From there the line just goes up and up and up. That is the point of the gift.

We stand there for a few seconds looking at it, and then I ask a question. Do you think this would be a very different company if you had never joined it?

'Oh, sure – absolutely. That's not to say it would not be as good. It could be better. But in a different way. My background is so different, and my way of doing things is so entirely different from everybody else's. I wouldn't say there aren't other ways to be successful, it's just that I wouldn't be able to do it any other way. You have to buy an entire individual, and you cannot take a person and tell them how to do something. I would be a total loss, I would be a total loser if they put me in this job and said, well, "Do that job the way Paul Girolami does it." You know, be Paul Girolami. I would be a total failure.'

What does he think of Paul Girolami?

'I've only met him a couple of times. I find him a very interesting man, but we're different. Sure, he's been successful, enormously successful, but with an entirely different approach.'

We shake hands again, and then I set off, heading down the seven floors, and out through the company's strangely modest and old-fashioned lobby. I head out through the doors, past the security guards, past the No Smoking signs, and make my way back into the other world of New York. From there I head for England. That last comment has captured my attention. What, I wonder, is so enormously successful about Paul Girolami? What is so different about him? And what has he done that Roy Vagelos could not do?

PART THREE

The Incursor: Glaxo

12 Badlands

Sir Paul Girolami walks into the room at precisely three minutes past noon. He leads the way: the flunkies tread carefully in the footsteps of their leader. Nobody, but nobody, walks in front of Sir Paul. That is just the way it is.

Sir Paul is a short man, no more than five feet six inches, and he walks with a slight stoop, an arching of the back which has the effect of emphasising and exaggerating his smallness. Today he is wearing a plain, grey suit, single-breasted and neatly tailored, and a pale blue shirt with a blue and white polka dot tie tightly knotted around his neck. He is wearing black leather half-brogue shoes, and carrying, as if it were some ancient but lucky totem, a battered old brown leather briefcase, slim, and frayed around the edges.

He hesitates at the doorway, pausing for a few seconds to cast his eyes around the assembled journalists, gathered to hear Glaxo's first full set of financial results for the new decade. His eyes are the first thing I notice about Sir Paul. They are huge, oval-shaped and composed largely of white. The brown pupils shrink in the centre, narrowing away from the white around them, as if in fear. The eyes dominate his face. They swivel, fixing a momentary flash of panic on objects of their displeasure, then swivelling on, round and round, revolving in constant and disquieting motion.

Sir Paul turns from the doorway, heads to his right, and collides with a television monitor. Six monitors are distributed around the room, each black, and with a blue display flashed up. On the blue, etched in white, the words: 'Glaxo, 1990'. Sir Paul's nose hits one on the zero. Nobody laughs. Some of the reporters manage a wan smile, but the flunkies stand rigid and stony-faced, unsmiling. They are not amused, and neither is Sir Paul. He pulls himself away, gives a little shake of the tattered briefcase, and walks along the centre of the room, shaking his head to himself as he goes.

It strikes me as a strange little scene. Sir Paul, so calm and composed, surrounded by his minders, confronting – via its inanimate electronic presentation – his formidable financial and economic reputation. There is a method in it, however, just as there is a message in his stoop and his tatty little bag. Don't mind me, he seems to be saying, I'm just a little old man who happens to have wandered in here, perhaps by accident, on his way somewhere else, and in a minute or two I'll find out where I am and be on my way. Nothing to worry about, nothing to be frightened of. Nobody of significance.

It's an act: a carefully contrived and carefully presented image, intended to confuse. The truth is different. Sir Paul is a man in complete control of himself and of his company; a man who is closer than he has ever been to control of his industry. It is an industry he had set out to conquer many years ago, and which, even if it has not fallen yet, has trembled at his name and learnt to fear his skilful generalship of his forces and resources.

The results announcement is being held in Whitechapel, an area to the east of London, about two miles from the fringes of the City, but further away in spirit than it is in distance. This is part of a different London and a different England from the one Glaxo now inhabits: an England of twisted dreams and forgotten promises.

There is a symbolism in the location which explains what Glaxo are doing here. Whitechapel is an old area, sandwiched between the new England and the old Britain. It is largely unmodernised, littered with relics of its own and the country's past. There are wooden signs hanging above timber and garment businesses, inscribed with their owners' names and with dates that stretch back into the early nineteenth – even into the eighteenth –

century. These businesses were around at the very start of the industrialisation of the world, they have seen it all happen, but have not prospered from their longevity. If they had, they wouldn't be here, they would have moved on. Whitechapel is not a place for the successful or the prosperous.

To one side of the area is the City, a teeming financial centre, full of Europeans, Japanese and Americans hustling their way through the money markets. To the east, another couple of miles on, is Docklands, a massive area of redevelopment, where skyscraping post-modernist office blocks and trim, mock-Georgian executive homes are rising out of the rubble and dereliction of Britain's trading past. In between are areas which have missed out on everything.

There are traces of modernisation here, but it is modernity of the now reviled sixties. The tower blocks look nastier and feel nastier than the slums they were built over. There are some new businesses, but they are mostly importers, bringing in cheap clothing from the sweatshops of South East Asia, and they have a temporary look to them, as if they might only be here for a few weeks – until they make enough money to go someplace else. There are long and winding concrete subways, stretching dismally beneath the roadways. The subways are covered with graffiti, some of it political but most of it just partisan obscenity; each of the underground passages reeks of beer, urine and blood. There is litter everywhere and, stuck away in corners and under arches, are huddles of newspapers and cardboard boxes where the dispossessed curl up for the night.

This is the England that promised so much and delivered so little. Tucked away down a side street, however, there is one brand new building, a snazzy business conference centre, all chrome, glass and plastic, plonked down like a small respite of neatness in a sprawling wasteland. This is where Glaxo has chosen to release its results. We too, it seems to be saying, have come from this sort of background. We too have come out of England's past. But we have broken away from it. We have made the leap and this location is just to remind you how far we have travelled, and how difficult it has been, and how bad it all was back then.

Sir Paul is sitting down now. He introduces himself, his long, thin eyebrows raised, his eyes blinking in the bright light. 'I feel I have to say we have had another excellent set of results,' he starts out. 'It has really been a very impressive year.'

The evidence is there on everyone's laps. A press release records the bald facts. Glaxo's turnover for the year ending in June 1990 is £2.8 billion, up from £2.5 billion the previous year. Its pre-tax profits are £1.14 billion, up from £1.006 billion the previous year. Nineteen eighty-nine had been a significant milestone for the company. For the first time in its history, and after a decade of achievement, Glaxo had passed the magic one billion figure, an achievement that pushed it into the very top ranks of UK corporations – indeed into the top ranks of global corporations.

Sir Paul runs through the results. He looks at each figure in the notes in front of him and hesitates for a moment. Then, as he recites each one, he speaks with an elderly air of astonishment, as if he had never seen such a big number before, and as if it had taken him completely by surprise. 'This particular year has been a bit of a watershed,' he explains to the press. 'I have for many years been making the forecast that we would continue our rate of growth while introducing new products. Two of those products have been launched this year, and three more are close behind.'

Sitting beside Sir Paul is the American chief executive of the company, Ernest Mario, a thin, shallow-faced man, with close-cropped grey hair. He is taller than the chairman, but he sits back in his chair, slouching almost, so that his eyes can flicker upwards and not downwards to the boss while he speaks.

'Our new products are the most exciting challenge any pharmaceutical company has ever faced,' continues Sir Paul. 'We accept that challenge. Indeed, we created the challenge for ourselves.' He continues for a while in the same vein. Corporate speak at Glaxo, a manner of speaking stylised and perfected by Sir Paul Girolami, is the language of the self-made man. There are no references to other individuals, no bows to luck or good fortune, no hint of admission that factors other than tremendous ability and dedication may have had a role to play. Instead, it is the constantly upbeat language of success: striving, working, struggling, forcing, shaping. And through it all is the constant theme of the self-imposed challenge.

It is his language that betrays Sir Paul's laid-back and languid manner. Language, as always, is more accurate: the observer, paradoxically, must watch what he says and not how he acts.

The challenge he is talking about is certainly self-imposed. Glaxo, at this junction in its history, is a company with nothing to fear. It is the master of all it owns, the master of all it surveys. It has the world's top selling drug, Zantac, which is now the biggest selling medicine of all time. It has a rate of growth which nobody in this industry, or in any other, can match. And it has over a billion pounds sterling sitting around in the bank waiting to be deployed in its next campaign. Any challenges would have to be self-imposed: there isn't anyone out there to challenge it.

Sir Paul has finished now. He turns to Ernest Mario at his right and asks him to speak, referring to him condescendingly as Ernie – everyone else in the company and the industry calls him Ernest, pronounced 'Ernst'. Mario is wearing a blue-grey suit this morning and a blue shirt with a burgundy tie striped with thin black lines. He speaks forcefully and positively, but with none of the serene calm that emanates from his master.

'We are making a huge investment, under the guidance of Sir Paul, in the US this year,' he starts out, skilfully slipping in a small note of deference. 'And this year we will spend £500 million in research, which translates to $950 million at current exchange rates – rather more than the number two company is spending.'

Competitiveness is not so much a tactic at Glaxo: it is more a state of mind, a state of hyped up combativeness that has infiltrated the minds of the men who run the business. There is no secret about what turns Glaxo on. It wants to be the number one drugs company in the world. So far, fifteen years or so into the gameplan, it is a goal that just eludes Sir Paul. Not by much, but by a little. This year has seen a step along the way and it is too important to leave out of the presentation: Glaxo has taken over from Merck as the number one spender on pharmaceutical research and development. Even though the figures are largely the result of a high pound and a low dollar, it is the first opportunity to refer to Merck as the number two company. Little swipes and kicks like that are not missed at Glaxo.

Mario moves on, detailing the ins and outs of the financial results, the movements in working capital, the currency fluctuations, the relative market shares in different countries and different products. Reporters scribble away with their pencils, noting and marking the material of which first and second paragraphs on the financial pages are made. More interesting, however, are Sir Paul's movements. While Mario speaks he sits back in his chair, his eyes gazing wistfully out of the window, into the cold and drab day outside. From time to time his eyes roll up towards the ceiling, stare at it for a second or two, and then roll back to the window. He has the expression and manner – the contentment and composure – of a man listening to a much loved symphony.

Mario moves on to the new products. This is the challenge the chairman spoke of. There are four of them: Zofran is an anti-emetic to prevent the nausea and vomiting associated with cancer and chemotherapy and radiation treatment, already launched in the UK, France, New Zealand, and with other launches due soon; Flixonase is a steroid for the treatment of inflammatory conditions, with regulatory approval for first use in the UK; Serevent is a drug for treating asthma, with product licence application already filed around the world; and then there is the big one, Imigran, a truly novel and original drug for treating migraine, with licence applications submitted in Europe and the US, and with launches scheduled around the world in 1991.

'This is a really significant product for us,' says Mario with an air of enthusiasm. It certainly is. If Glaxo is to maintain its momentum, if it is ever to achieve its goal of becoming the dominant drugs company in the world, then Imigran is the product it will ride. Migraines are the perfect ailment for the modern profit-minded pharmaceutical combine, and it is no accident that Glaxo has been seeking a cure: the complaint is both very common and is suffered by people in the rich, industrialised countries where medicines can be paid for; and it is repetitive, meaning that the drug user will have to take it repeatedly. Both factors spell out a drug with a potential for sales well in excess of one billion pounds a year.

'So let's move to question time,' announces Sir Paul at the end of Mario's *spiel*. As he speaks, his mouth opens up into a smile of infinite wisdom, as though he were addressing a gaggle of respectful and well behaved grandchildren. It goes down well. The pack gathered here today follow a narrow scent: money and profits. On that score at least, Glaxo leaves a heavy trail.

There is a question about what Glaxo plans to do with its cash mountain. Sir Paul turns to John Hignett, his finance director, sitting at his right, and, with a playful, impish look asks: 'What are we going to do with it, John?'

Hignett glances back at his employer: 'I'll leave that to you, chairman,' he answers. 'In the meantime, we'll look after it for you.'

'The answer is that we're keeping it,' says Sir Paul.

There are smiles at that, showing a respectful admiration for an old man's joke. Another question. Someone asks when the patent on Zantac will expire. There have been stories – stories which whirl around the stock market and send it into a spin – that the patent may be useless after 1995. These stories are bad for confidence and bad for business. Sir Paul is keen to deny them. 'The patents on Zantac will last until the year 2000,' he reassures his audience.

A question is asked about a drug called Losec, manufactured by a Swedish company called Astra. The drug is a new type of ulcer treatment, radically different scientifically, and starting to make inroads into the market. It has rattled Glaxo through the year, partly because it is a head-on challenge to the company's only really successful product, and partly because, in the United States, it is licensed and marketed by Merck.

A frown appears on Sir Paul's already wrinkled brow. He leans forward slightly, taking up the question himself, brushing aside his flunkies. 'We've always said that the Astra product was one we didn't see competing with Zantac,' he says. 'It isn't really a genuine competitor.' This is the end of the answer, although, as the Glaxo functionaries sitting around the room know, not quite the end of the story. Losec has played a role in the product's one-per-cent drop in market share across Europe – from fifty-four to fifty-three per cent. Zantac has suffered over the last year. The company has spent much of the year dreaming up schemes to belittle and discredit its rival. But for now the official answer is repeated once more: Losec is no threat.

There is a question about the recession, asked in the context of a world economy which, in September 1990, appeared to be both heading downwards and gathering pace along the way. It is a standard question: reporters like to ask company chairmen about the state of the economy, and about how it affects them. It is one of the questions they have ready when they can't think of anything else to ask.

Sir Paul's eyes turn towards the ceiling. For a second or two he is flummoxed for a reply; he is unsure of the correct response. 'I wouldn't like to say it made no difference to us,' he starts. He explains how the demand for medicine, however, is little changed by the overall state of demand in the economy. Then he offers this caveat: 'But to the extent that our employees are affected by economic conditions, in terms of their morale, we are not able to ignore it.'

It is a conventional response, received limply. What Sir Paul means to say, but is reluctant to spell out, is that the economy makes no difference, since nobody chooses to die or to suffer mind-numbing pain to save a few pennies. Nor are its prices heading anywhere but up, regardless of the amount of money people might have to spend. In reality the corporation is immune from recession. Whatever else happens Glaxo will keep on growing.

The results announcement ends after about fifty minutes. The reporters drift away from this strange limbo of an area, back to their offices and deadlines. The corporate functionaries drift away also: back to their high-class and luxurious Mayfair headquarters. For another year the game is over. The results are posted, and their team has won again. Another season is about to begin and, for a team that plays as hard as this, there is no time for relaxation or celebration.

Sir Paul leads the way out, walking with a distracted expression on his face and clutching his battered briefcase. The flunkies follow in his wake. For them, the story goes forward from here: to new blockbuster drugs, new fortunes, new heights of corporate power; or just, in a vague sort of way, forward. Most of the important men among them are new to the company and have known it only as an incredible success. That experience is shown in the smug and satisfied smiles they wear on their faces.

But for Sir Paul the story goes backwards as well: back to a strange little pharmaceutical firm he joined when he was still young, twenty-five years ago. To a vision which inspired him, the struggles to make the vision real; the stretched finances and desperate gambles, the moments of inspiration and genius, the bruised reputations and egos that fell along the way.

From here it all looks smooth and easy. But way back there, in the mid sixties, it was all very different. For Girolami and for Glaxo, it has been a wild and scary trip, a trip which is etched deeply into the lines on the man's face.

13 A bonny baby

On a corner of Lombard Street, twisting down from the Bank of England, past the site of the original Lloyds Coffee House, there is a blue plaque marking the turning into Plough Court. It reads: 'In a house in this Court Alexander Pope was born in 1688.' Head into the Court, an alley no more than forty yards from one end to the other, and you find nothing else to mark the birthplace of the famous English poet. Nor is there anything to mark the birthplace of Glaxo. The building the company and the poet shared has been demolished, replaced by a hi-tech black office block, looming over the Court and all but obscuring it. The new building is occupied by the Hokkaido Takashoka Bank, and the Bank für Gemeinwirtschaft, and by a few other faceless financial institutions as well, which is, in its way, a small lesson in English history.

Had Pope and the druggist's that was to become Glaxo been in the building at the same time, the poet would most likely have showered the company men with satire and scorn. But Pope was long gone when, in December 1715, a twenty-four-year-old Quaker named Silvanus Bevan took a lease on the building and opened an apothecary. It was a good location. Lombard Street was at the very centre of the City at a time when English capitalism and finance were about to embark on their most brilliant and expansive period.

Quakers played their own small role in the expansion. Like the Jews they were a small sect with a disproportionate influence: their religion excluded them from the mainstream of English life, shunting them aside into trade and commerce; there, with a religous commitment to thrift, education and hard work, together with a healthy interest in commercial success, they generally succeeded. Bevan was typical of his times. Although he styled himself an apothecary, he was as much a general practitioner as a druggist, diagnosing and dispensing medicines for the vast majority of the people who could not afford the fat fees charged by the small group of practising physicians. Bevan also dabbled in amateur science, and was introduced to the Royal Society by no less a person than Sir Isaac Newton.

Bevan died unmarried, handing over the business to his brother Timothy who, in 1775, in turn handed it on to his son Joseph Gurney Bevan. Joseph was another devout Quaker, and also a expansionist businessman. The shop he inherited had built up a reputation for wholesaling and dispensing drugs; Joseph began exporting the drugs, as well as textiles, to the ports of the Mediterranean and the colonies of North America. As the years wore on, however, he became a keener Quaker than businessman. The rough and tumble of the eighteenth-century drugs trade troubled him: the high prices of medicines and the nasty business of debt collection. Eventually he retired, and became a happier man as the editor of a small journal called *Piety Promoted*.

The company stayed in Quaker and humanitarian hands. In 1794 Joseph Bevan had sold it to a Samuel Mildred, who sold it on, in 1797, to William Allen for the sum of £525. Allen attached his own name to the pharmacy, later adding the surname of the two nephews who joined him in the business, Hanbury, to create Allen & Hanbury, a name which survives as a subsidiary of Glaxo to this day. Allen was a more ruthless operator: he had no compunction about chasing debtors or establishing solid lines of credit. He was also a deeply religious man – one diary entry reads 'Experienced some degree of comfort in striving against evil thoughts' – and a minor figure in English social history. He was a close friend of Thomas Clarkson and William Wilberforce, and played a leading role in their eventually successful campaign to abolish slavery within the British Empire.

But Allen, though he was a wealthy and successful man, was still running a pre-industrial operation. There was just the one shop at Plough Court, where customers from the City would come in with their prescriptions and ailments. Each order would result in a tonic or tablets being prepared by hand by the staff at the back of the shop. There was nothing very sophisticated about it. As late as 1868 the total staff amounted to just a clerk, three laboratory men, two warehouse men, a shop porter plus two errand boys, and seven dispensers.

It also included Cornelius Hanbury, now managing the firm. Cornelius understood the need to move towards industrialisation, at a time when the drugs business itself was just beginning to industrialise. In 1874 he took over an old match factory in Bethnal Green, then a semi-rural area to the north-east of London. The first product line to be manufactured at the new factory was cod-liver oil, a foul remedy extracted from fish livers which had been a folk medicine for centuries in the coastal villages of northern Europe. Two other products were to be just as significant in the development of the company. One was malted extract, made from malted barley, and used in a range of medicines and in baby foods. The other was throat pastilles, manufactured to recipes Cornelius Hanbury had learnt while travelling in France, and had introduced into Britain. The tremendous popularity of the pastilles, in an England then growing rapidly more wealthy, ensured the success of the company.

By the turn of the century, Allen & Hanbury, still controlled and run by the Hanbury family, had discovered another major product: dried milk. Dairy milk in those days could be a dangerous drink, particularly for babies, since it was often infected with tuberculosis. Dried milk, by contrast, was fully sterilised, and much recommended by doctors and medical authorities for babies. Allen & Hanbury established a factory for manufacturing the milk in Ware in Hertfordshire in 1896, and was soon to lead the British market. The milk was marketed at mothers, under a separate trade name, Allenbury's, and with different milks for the first and second six months of a baby's life;

it was followed by malted baby food, and malted rusks for older children, and accessories such as baby feeders and baby soap. On the back of its increased product range, the company began expanding overseas, following the flag of the British Empire into Canada, Australia and South Africa.

Cornelius Hanbury died in 1916 at the age of eighty-seven. He had built the company up to a substantial size – its turnover in 1914 reached one million pounds – and the business was in many ways typical both of the drugs business and of British industry at the time. It had grown from a small retail outlet by recognising the growing demand for branded consumer goods in what was the world's first wealthy consumer market. And it had expanded into the colonies, where military and political domination had prepared the way for commercial expansion. Yet it remained in the hands of its founding family, some of whom were skilled businessmen, and some of whom were not. It had the faults and flaws typical of British companies at the time: conservatism and a soggy lack of professionalism in its management. They were flaws that were to be ruthlessly exposed when a more dynamic competitor appeared on the scene: an ambitious New Zealand trading company with a product called Glaxo.

Glaxo was the brand of baby milk dreamt up by Joseph Nathan, an individual from a rougher school than the old gentlemen of Allen & Hanbury. Nathan was a Londoner by origin but he had settled in Wellington in New Zealand in 1857, setting up as a general merchant. He imported ironmongery and groceries from England, distributing the stuff in the distant colony. Towards the end of the century, with the development of refrigerated ship containers, he switched the business around, exporting frozen meat and butter from New Zealand to the UK. He later dabbled in dried milk as a way of using up the surplus skimmed milk from his creameries and butter factories; the first effort collapsed when the patented process he had bought for drying the milk turned out to be a dud. But by 1908 the process had been successfully mastered, and the company, Joseph Nathan & Sons, launched its dried milk in the UK.

In the same year, Joseph's son Alec came over to Britain to head up the UK branch, and to launch the product. Although the company may have had trouble with the technical processes, under Alec Nathan's direction it was quickly to master the arts of product marketing. His milk product was launched with full-page advertisements in the *Daily Mail* announcing the 'Food that Builds Bonny Babies'. Later advertisements were to stick with the Bonny Baby theme – it was to become a company slogan – with the additional, cheery tag line 'The Sunshine Baby Food'. Clearly these were people who had no qualms with the hard sell.

The new baby food made steady inroads into the market, catching up with Allen & Hanbury's, and eventually overtaking it; by 1921 Nathan & Sons had a turnover of £1.5 million from the food alone, outstripping its rival's total business. In the 1920s, Allen & Hanbury stepped into the production of modern drugs when it started manufacturing insulin, a product which was to secure the profitability of the company for the next twenty years.

At the same time, however, Glaxo was experimenting with modern drugs. In 1919 Alec Nathan had recruited a twenty-eight-year-old chemist named Harry Jephcott, to monitor the quality of the milk coming from New Zealand and to set standards of production. His resources were slender: a twenty-foot-square laboratory in a warehouse. Jephcott, however, was a man to make much of slender opportunities. He realised that adding vitamins to the baby foods would give them an important competitive edge and secured for Nathan a licence to manufacture vitamins in the UK. The first result of his work was marketed in fine style, and with due scientific seriousness, as 'Sunshine Glaxo – the baby food reinforced with sunshine vitamin D to build strong bones and teeth'. In 1924 Jephcott followed it with Ostelin, the first vitamin concentrate to be made in Britain, and the first pharmaceutical product to be launched by the Glaxo department of Nathan & Sons.

By 1935 Jephcott had completed his transformation, renaming his part of the company Glaxo Laboratories, with a separate base in Greenford west of London, and with himself as managing director. There he deepened the company's involvement in drugs, manufacturing vitamins and purified anti-anaemic liver extract. He was not a contented soul, however; so frustrated was he by the company's commitment to food products that he rather obtusely considered resigning to become a fruit farmer in New Zealand. But in 1939 he took over from Alec Nathan as managing director of the parent company, eventually renaming it Glaxo, and set about chasing his own dreams and visions.

The Second World War gave him his opportunity. In 1945 he visited the United States on behalf of the Ministry of Supply to report on the production of penicillin. With government backing, he set up a specialised antibiotics factory at Barnard Castle in Durham, and negotiated licences with Merck and Squibb to use their technology for penicillin production. By the end of the war, his plants were producing ninety per cent of the British supply of the new drug. Building on this success he kept on moving forwards. In 1945 he took over from Alec Nathan as chairman of the company; in 1947, the newly-knighted Sir Harry Jephcott arranged for the business to be listed on the stock exchange, and got rid of the remaining Nathan & Sons businesses. The bonny baby had eaten the parent, which was not a very sunshiny thing to do.

Jephcott was a man of his time: no more and no less. The prevailing mood in British industry at the time was for consolidation. There was a trend for bringing together companies in similar lines of business to create ever larger combinations. The belief was that this would somehow make them stronger and better, and Jephcott was an enthusiastic and dedicated disciple. Over the next fifteen years, he was to attempt to pull as many of the British drug companies as he could under the Glaxo umbrella.

Allen & Hanbury, meantime, had fallen prey to its own lack of vision. The business had maintained its profitability, but only just; in 1955 it made profits of £105,000, slightly less than it had made in 1925. The company, under the direction of its last family director, John Hanbury, had lost its way. It had misunderstood the arrival of the wonder drugs: it was still manufacturing traditional pre-modern concoctions using traditional techniques as late as 1957. Some efforts were made to license in new drugs from the United States, but it generally chose badly; efforts were also made to develop its own drugs, but here it failed to grasp the need to treat common illnesses to make a financial success of development.

And so it went on, withering away. The company became desperately short of capital – in the late fifties it only had £100,000 to play with – but the family refused to surrender control by listing it on the stock market. By 1958 the rot had gone too far for it to have any realistic future as an independent company. On Tuesday, 8 April 1958, an agreed takeover by Glaxo was announced. The price was £633,000.

For his money, Jephcott has bought one of the most respected and established drugs companies in the UK; he himself, and his company, was regarded as a *parvenu* by the rest of the industry. This put him in a new league. Allen & Hanbury was allowed to continue within Glaxo very much as a separate entity; there was no wholesale reorganisation or reshaping of the company. Jephcott was more interested in continuing his marauding through the industry; he bought Evans Medical in 1961; and Edinburgh Pharmaceutical Industries in 1962. Later the company bought British Drug Houses in 1967; and Farley Infant Foods in 1968.

All these companies were slung together within the ever-larger Glaxo Group. It was one thing to merge the companies into one, however; making them work was another. By the end of the sixties Jephcott's strategy was tired and hackneyed. He had succeeded in transforming Glaxo from a scrappy baby food company into a respected British drugs house. It was an achievement of sorts, but an achievement rapidly running out of time; the company had become bigger, but it was yet to become significantly better in any of its product areas. It was still badly out of tune with the world drugs industry as it had grown up in the United States, Switzerland and Germany.

At the end of the sixties Glaxo bore very few similarities to the then giants of the industry, Hoffmann-La Roche or Merck. Dragging the company into the modern world was to take brilliance of another sort. And that brilliance, when it came, was to be found not in the expansive traditions of Glaxo, but in the older, more scientific, traditions of Jephcott's one really significant acquisition, Allen & Hanbury.

14 The great inventor

David Jack is a small man, no more than five foot five high, and he walks with a bustle, rushing around, glancing at his watch, his eyes darting around the place, all with an air of great hurry and purpose. It suits him. He is like a small bundle of pure energy dropped into a calm setting; he fizzes and splutters, sometimes poking with his finger, sometimes reeling back in a long chortle, provoking and questioning everything around him. The energy, the hurry, the curiosity, each is a clue to the man. Jack is one of the greatest unsung heroes of European capitalism. He is not, though, a great businessman, neither is he a great financier; he is, instead, a great inventor.

Like many great inventors, he was born in Scotland: in Fife, in 1930. His accent and his humour and his caustic, rough and tumble outlook on life are still distinctly Scottish. He started his career in his native Fife as a pharmaceutical apprentice, and went from there to both the University and the Royal Technical College in Glasgow, graduating in 1948 with a first-class degree in pharmacy and pharmacology. He taught briefly, in Glasgow, and spent two years in the armed forces doing his national service. Then, in 1951, he joined Sir Harry Jephcott's Glaxo Laboratories as a research chemist: he imagined a spell in industrial research might be a useful stepping stone in the academic career he then planned for himself. He found industrial work interesting, however, although not at Glaxo. He figured there was no real future for him there, and left in 1953 to take a job with a company called Menley & James as a senior development chemist. It turned out to be a lucky move. Menley & James was acquired by the American giant SmithKline, and Jack quickly found himself heading up a department of a hundred scientists developing drugs for the American company.

His fascination with drugs had grown by now, and in 1960 he won a doctorate in medicinal chemistry from the University of London. His work up to then, however, was pure development; inside, Jack was an inventor, and he wanted to invent things. Tiring of his work he applied for a job as head of the School of Pharmacy in Glasgow, but was turned down by the interviewing panel. But one member of the panel took to his mixture of sharp opinion and sharp curiosity. He was Cyril Maplethorpe, then the managing director of Allen & Hanbury. Maplethorpe suggested Jack apply for the vacant post of director of research and development at the company and, when he applied, immediately hired him.

Jack had found his place. Allen & Hanbury's research was located in Ware, and had a hundred and twenty staff. It was a very modest research centre, with very modest achievements to its name. The situation had one decisive advantage for a man of ideas and ambition, however. It was flexible.

Sir Harry Jephcott may have built up the company from its origins as a baby food manufacturer into a modern drugs house, but by the sixties he was losing his way. He had one striking flaw: he had completely and spectacularly missed the whole point of the business. He still believed that the point of the drugs business, the road to success, was to merge companies, and to license in drugs from the United States. Jack, by contrast had grasped the point; and the point was him.

'The man who created Glaxo was Sir Harry Jephcott,' Jack was to recollect later. 'He turned it from a low-technology group into a high-technology pharmaceutical business. And he did it really by getting in on the early development of penicillin, and by licensing in. After the war it was easy to license in because there were very few truly international drug companies.' So far, so good. But, Jack goes on, 'In all honesty Jephcott was very suspicious of research unless it was brought to him by the government. For example, Glaxo worked on interferon because of the Medical Research Council. Similarly, it got into cortisone because of government encouragement. Same with vaccines. But speculative research? Jephcott reckoned that was just like gambling, which of course it is.'

Jack, however, was a man with a taste for canny, calculated gambles. Joining Allen & Hanbury was a risk for him: he didn't know how good he would be at experimental research, neither did he know how supportive the company would be. He had, though, secured a retreat for himself: he had a permanent job waiting for him back at SmithKline if this new venture did not work out.

Jack handed Jephcott and Maplethorpe a list of demands before accepting his new job: he wanted an increased level of resources for research; he wanted the time to develop a full research programme; and he wanted to have final control of everything the research department did. Both men agreed. Soon afterwards, however, Jephcott went back on the deal, proposing a plan to merge the Allen & Hanbury laboratories with the Glaxo research centre. The idea angered Jack. 'It wasn't that I didn't want to work with Jephcott, I had no choice but to work with Jephcott, he was the chairman,' Jack recalls. 'But I didn't want to go along to Glaxo in Greenford every month to be chastised for doing what I thought was right.'

Jack realised Jephcott's way of doing business was doomed: licensing in would become harder and harder as the American drug companies grew larger and expanded their international operations. The only way to go was for the company to start developing its own original medicines. He refused to go along with the merger scheme, insisting the separate Allen & Hanbury research centre continue as an independent entity. Fortunately, for the future of the company, he won the battle.

In the beginning the prospects were not encouraging. 'At Ware there were only difficulties as far as I could see,' Jack recalls. 'There were a lot of nice people working there, but there was not a single viable project. I used to walk through the laboratories, and sit down next to the researchers and say "Right, what you doing?"

and "Why are you doing it that way?" And my purpose was to find out whether I had people with anything between their ears. It was a very disruptive process for the laboratory, but it worked. A lot of them were all right. All they needed was a bit of focusing.'

He found one man in particular who was to prove invaluable. Roy Brittan had joined Allen & Hanbury after graduating from London University's School of Pharmacy in 1955. Over the next twenty-seven years Brittan was to be Jack's right-hand man, his foil and sidekick. He was well suited to the role. Although a sharp man, his academic career had not marked him out as a first rate scientist. His appearance had not helped him, either. A bad motorcycle accident as a young man had left some scarring down one side of his face, and he had one deaf ear, which, according to one friend, he used much as Nelson used his one blind eye: there were things he conveniently didn't hear. But as a manager and motivator of a team of scientists, he had found his role in life. Jack and Brittan worked together instinctively as a team. During more than two decades of running the research department they never communicated once on paper, talking endlessly, discussing and chewing over the possibilities of their projects.

Jack's scheming was helped along by the retirement of Sir Harry Jephcott in 1963. He was replaced by Sir Alan Wilson, a businessman by profession but also a distinguished scientist: he was a Fellow of the Royal Society, the sign of acceptance by the English scientific establishment. Wilson took a more sympathetic view of Jack's projects than Jephcott had done. 'To say that Wilson encouraged research would be to go too far,' recalls Jack. 'He was a remote man by nature. But he didn't interfere and he made the money available. So he liberated research, and if that is encouraging it, then he encouraged it.'

Wilson, with his lofty, academic, reserved and disinterested manner, helped create a rarefied image for Glaxo in the sixties. Also contributing was Arthur Hems, the head of research and development at Glaxo Laboratories, the company's other research department, and another Fellow of the Royal Society. Hems was an able and distinguished scientist, yet very little of commercial value came out of his laboratories. Even so, he was an influential figure within the company, and his prominence was an indication of the way it was going. Wilson and Hems had turned colonial Glaxo into the very embodiment of the English establishment's enterprise of its period. It was unambitious; it was restricted to the United Kingdom and the Commonwealth; it was addicted to cosy, monopolistic deals with the government; and it was, at its core, deeply uncommercial in its habits and attitudes. It had lost contact with its entrepreneurial roots and had caught some of the English disdain for trade. During the decade it picked up the nickname 'the only quoted university on the stock exchange', a badge which stuck for twenty years, and one which, for a time, the company was to wear with pride rather than with embarrassment. Universities, after all, were a classier line of business than commerce.

Ironically, more than a decade later, Merck was to start aping the university, with results as spectacularly successful as Glaxo's were dismally poor. There was, however, a crucial difference between Merck today and Glaxo in the sixties. Merck imitated the methods of the university, while shifting the objective to practical discovery. Glaxo imitated only the objectives of the university – the accumulation of knowledge – and combined it with the peculiar disdain for trade which is a distinctive feature of British academic life. The result was a hopeless squandering of its research efforts.

Jack and Brittan, meantime, back in Ware, were setting their own agenda. Their research efforts started modestly enough; the team restricted itself to investigating versions of other drugs to see if they could improve on them; and to the traditional screening of hundreds upon hundreds of chemical compounds to see if they could strike anything with interesting effects on the body. During those routine investigations they were to start looking at the range of treatments for asthma.

Asthma is a common ailment, affecting about one in twenty adults, and a greater proportion of children. The symptom of an asthma attack, the wheezing and difficulty with breathing, is caused by a narrowing of the airways within the body. The narrowing itself has two causes: a contraction of the muscles surrounding the bronchi (the tubes leading up to the lungs), and an inflammation of the lungs caused by allergies to foreign proteins, most often pollen.

By the fifties, the most common treatment of asthma was Riker & Co.'s Medihaler, a pressurised inhaler which gave almost instantaneous, although short-term, relief from an attack. It was a flawed and dangerous product, however. Patients with worsening attacks regularly took more of the drug than was safe, accidentally killing themselves through over-stimulation of a heart already weakened by a lack of oxygen. There was plenty of room for improvement, a task which Jack's team set for itself in the early sixties.

They worked the conventional routes, testing continually until a compound was struck. A breakthrough was made in 1966 when the team came across a substance called salbutamol. It turned out to be both more active on the bronchi than any of its predecessor drugs, and also more potent in relieving the asthma attack. Once discovered, it was quickly developed. It was launched in 1969 as the Allen & Hanbury Ventolin inhaler, and a year later as Ventolin tablets. Six years after joining, David Jack had led the company towards its first significant and novel new product.

It was still a flawed product. Although it acted on the bronchi it had little or no action on the inflammation of the lungs that also contributed to asthma attacks. A steroid was also needed to reduce the inflammation. The researchers found one through a rather different sort of scientific investigation. It is common at drug laboratories to keep a library of thousands of compounds that have been developed for one investigation, to be pulled out later for possible use against another disease. Glaxo Laboratories had long specialised in steroids, and had a huge back catalogue. Among the samples the Ware team found a compound called BDP, orginally prepared for use on the skin. They found it had the desired effect on the lungs, and developed the drug. It was launched as the BDP Inhaler in 1972, to be used in conjunction with Ventolin. Together the two compounds were the most potent asthma treatment yet discovered, and were, in time, to become the most widely used medicine for the condition.

The discovery of the asthma treatment was not a heroic piece of science; it contained no new insights into the nature of the disease; neither did it contain any fresh developments in medicinal chemistry. But it was a great piece of invention: a scavenging around among elements already known and a new way of locking together those elements to produce something both different from, and superior to any of the existing products. It was typical of the type of innovative thinking the Ware group was to specialise in, thinking that was later to transform the company.

'David Jack, to my mind, was one of the very best pharmaceutical research directors there has ever been,' one former board director at Glaxo was later to recall. 'He is not a great scientist, he would never get an FRS, but he has this incredible ability to spot the application for something. David Jack will not only take his own research projects he will take over other people's as well, and he will spot opportunities for them. I will never forget his development of Ventolin. It is a magnificent product, but all he did was to put two and two together and make about ten out of it. Other people couldn't even put the two and two together. This is the skill of the developer. Usually he had to call on his scientific skills, but that product was a good example of his abilities, because it was right under Glaxo's noses and they hadn't spotted it.'

Ventolin was a radical departure for the company Sir Harry Jephcott had created. It was a new and effective drug for an ailment common throughout the industrialised world. It had all the ingredients for a major, worldwide success; Glaxo had the patent on it and could do what they liked with the drug.

What they made of it in the next few years was to be the first real test of the skills, abilities and ambition of the company. Glaxo's reaction would reveal the strengths and weaknesses of the business. And, with hindsight, its reaction to the opportunity presented by Ventolin was to set the stage for everything that was to happen to the company over the next twenty years.

15 The numbers man

Modesty is not among Sir Paul Girolami's attributes. On 18 June 1985, he gave a talk at the London School of Economics. It was something of a homecoming for him: he had been a student at the LSE some thirty years earlier, and in these familiar surroundings he may have been tempted to dwell and reflect a little longer than usual on things past. His subject that evening was the development of Glaxo: where it had come from, where it had been, and where it was going. He rambled along in easy enough style, stopping along the way for little anecdotes about dried milk and bonny babies, but moving on eventually to the substantial issues involved in the transformation of the company. He analysed the various factors at play, weighing each one judiciously in the scales of hindsight. Each had a role, he conceded, and many men and molecules had played their part. Yet as he spoke, it became clearer that he had one particular theme to place before his audience. Ladies and Gentlemen, he seemed to be saying, only one overpowering force wrought the transformation of Glaxo from a deadbeat British drugs house into Europe's most successful commercial organisation. And yes: it was me.

The early part of his talk that evening was a powerfully reasoned intellectual rebuttal of the techniques Sir Harry Jephcott had devised for stitching together Glaxo. He mentioned the string of acquisitions from all around the British drugs business. 'There was no clear industrial strategy behind these acquisitions,' Girolami sneered. 'With the exception of Allen & Hanbury, there is little evidence of any long-term benefit, either financial or industrial, to the Group. Moreover, many of the activities acquired were only rationalised after a good many years of ownership, while others were only able to survive under the cover of a growing and prosperous Group.'

For Girolami these were not light words, neither were they lightly spoken. He was talking not just about the company's past but about his own. The Group in the sixties had suffered from muddled thinking, from confusion, from a failure of concentrated brain power. He himself had felt the frustration of being surrounded by men whose minds were dated and tired, who lacked the clarity to see what needed to be done. And through those years he had argued and fought and struggled to put right all the mistakes that had been made. Like most old warriors, however, the battles that may seem distant and forgotten to others are still fresh and vivid in his mind. So, looking back that evening, it was impossible for Girolami to resist another skirmish over the old ground. No benefit, he reiterated. No rationalisation. No logic. These were the same words he had used many years earlier in another, more fraught and more dangerous context.

Over twenty-five years the story of Paul Girolami and the story of Glaxo have been intertwined, threading into one another until they became seamless components of the same quilt. The way he sees it, the company's destiny is his destiny, and vice versa.

Like Glaxo, Girolami was an immigrant to England from another country. Again, like the company, Girolami is an immigrant to the drugs business from another trade. He was born in 1926 in Venice. The Girolamis were an old artisan family, with a traditional mosaics business in the city; they were craftsmen in the finest sense of the word, skilled with their hands, but also men of great artistry. And their city, itself a place of supreme artistry, is a fitting place for Girolami to have his roots. Venice is one of the great European cradles of capitalism, a place which exploited its position as a pivot between east and west to build great trading wealth, and a place where merchants were able to combine vision, energy and ruthlessness to create their commercial empires.

Girolami, in his own way, was to become one of the few modern-day inheritors of their tradition of commercial grandeur.

If he has inherited any of its spirit, however, it is only as a distant memory. He left the city at the tender age of two when his father moved to England to manage a branch of the family mosaics business. Paul was raised as an Englishman; apart from a certain stylishness in the cut of his suit, there are few traces of the Italian left in him. As a young man, he showed no aptitude with his hands – a feature he readily admits to – and so any thought of continuing in the family trade was unthinkable. He went instead to the LSE, where he studied economics, and afterwards studied to become a chartered accountant, qualifying in 1953.

Accountancy was only a stepping stone for Girolami. In 1954 he joined the firm of Cooper Brothers (later, as Coopers & Lybrand, to become one of the largest accountancy practices in Britain), to serve out his apprenticeship. He stayed with the firm for twelve years, becoming a founder and director of its consultancy practice, widening his experience by advising a range of companies on their financial affairs. By the age of thirty-six, however, Girolami had tired of peripheral involvement in other people's business. His time of learning was over, and he knew what he wanted to know. It was time for him to stake out some real influence in an important company.

Casting around for a new job, he was made three offers; Glaxo was one of them, and also the lowest paid of the three. He accepted it – the job was as financial controller of the company – because, he said later, he 'liked the feel of the place'. This is typical Girolami talk: a calculated imprecision carefully created to hide rather than reveal. In reality, he is not a man to make any move for such a whimsical or sentimental reason. He took the job at Glaxo because he recognised it as a place where he could wield the most influence most quickly, and where his distinctive ideas on industrial strategy could best be tried out.

Financial controller is not a very important job within any company. It is a technician's role. The controller is really the man who counts the beans and little else. It is, however, a way into corporate life for accountants who, in Britain more than any-where, tend to conceal some of the sharpest business brains behind their calculators and ledgers. With formal business training a rarity in Britain, accountants are among the few schooled in commercial disciplines, and the profession serves as a stepping stone for many whose real ambitions lie in strategic management.

Anyway, Girolami did not stay long in the job which gave him his entry point. Within two years, by 1968, Sir Alan Wilson had promoted him to financial director. This was a posting much more to Girolami's tastes. At the age of thirty-eight it took him right to the strategic heart of the business, in a position from which, with skill and the occasional flash of steel, he could exert real influence over its future direction.

The financial director's job is a key posting for a young executive with ambition. It sounds boring, and in some ways it is, but unlike any other corporate slot it has flexibility. The finance director, if crafty, and cunning, can spread tentacles out into the rest of the organisation; there are few parts of the company that he cannot claim at least some legitimate interest in. It is one of those undefined jobs, where a skilled practitioner of the arts of corporate politics can stealthily extend his influence.

Almost immediately, Girolami began operating beyond his own area. Wilson was working on taking Glaxo deeper into the European continent, where, with its colonial roots, the company had failed to build a presence. Girolami was one of his key aides: he worked on the reorganisation of Glaxo subsidiaries in Italy; he created new companies in Spain; and he created joint ventures in Germany and Italy. In 1972 he began building joint ventures and a sales network in Japan, a country that was to remain an obsession with him throughout the rest of his career.

In his manoeuvrings, 1972 was a good year for Girolami. That year the rival British drugs company, Beecham, then close on twice the size of Glaxo, launched a takeover for the company. It was a bid to increase Beecham's dominance of the British market. Beecham offered the Glaxo shareholders a mixture of shares and convertible loan stock (bonds which can be turned into shares):

the effect of the two inducements was to give Glaxo's shareholders an immediate twenty-per-cent profit on their holdings.
Glaxo's response was quick and audacious. It proposed forming a
new company, Glaxo Holdings. It would be owned by the same
shareholders as Glaxo, and would itself take over Glaxo, using a
mixture of ordinary shares and its own convertible loan stock. The
effect of all the asset swapping would be to yield an immediate
eighteen-per-cent gain for Glaxo's shareholders, closely matching
the Beecham offer but leaving the company unchanged and run
by the same management.

The bid was an early example of the kind of financial conjuring
tricks that were to dominate the corporation a decade later. At its
time, however, it was novel. And it was, on Glaxo's part, a
brilliant piece of financial engineering; the asset swaps were
imaginative and deadly, killing the Beecham bid stone dead soon
after it had been announced. In the end it turned out to be
unnecessary: the Monopolies Commission ruled against the bid.
But the skill of Glaxo's defence had made an impression. From
then onwards, as Girolami trod the company corridors, he could
trade on the knowledge that he was the man who could protect the
business and its people from any raiders. For him it was a
significant victory and, close on twenty years later, he is still
unable to resist the occasional swipe, often pointing out how
Glaxo has consistently out-performed Beecham since the bid was
made.

Yet the corporation Girolami was starting to exert his influence
over was not a successful organisation. The mistakes and the
myopia of the Jephcott era were starting to take their toll on the
business. It had expanded through the late fifties and sixties
through acquisitions in the British market, but its failure to bring
anything to the companies it bought was beginning to drag the
business down. At the same time, its softness, and its lack of
commercial edge, meant the few products it had were being
squandered.

One former executive, who joined the company as a marketing
man in the early sixties, recalls the atmosphere and culture of the

company like this: 'Marketing people were viewed very, very suspiciously, and I think had virtually no say in the management of the business. All the really important decisions were essentially technical or financial. Not many decisions in those days were strongly influenced by the market place. It didn't necessarily ruin the company but it did mean we didn't get anywhere near the proper exploitation of our products.'

Ventolin was to go down in the company's history as the great warning. The product David Jack and his team had laboured to produce was not to become the financial success he and his colleagues had hoped for. It was launched in 1969 in the UK and achieved good results there: the UK was the strongest of Glaxo's territories. In time, but in a casual way, it was launched in the Commonwealth and Latin American countries where Glaxo had subsidiaries. Over the seventies it was launched in Europe as a network of subsidiaries and joint ventures was built across the continent. But it was never launched in the United States, the world's biggest, richest, and most profitable drugs market (it finally made it onto the market there in 1981).

This laid-back, lazy approach to marketing the new drug was a severe disappointment to David Jack. He had tried to persuade Sir Alan Wilson to set up a base in the United States but was unsuccessful: Wilson reckoned the company did not have the resources to mount a foray into the American market, and was not about to risk the company on such a dangerous adventure.

Elsewhere in the company the early failure of Ventolin was equally painful. A former board director at Glaxo recalls his reaction: 'I was always a great proponent of the potential of Ventolin. It should, by the conventional rules of the drugs industry, have been the world's number one pharmaceutical product before the arrival of the first of the ulcer drugs, Tagamet. But it was miles behind in the US: the resources were not put behind it, and even if they had been there wasn't a company to sell it.'

According to this source, the senior men in the company were scarcely even aware of what they were doing: 'I don't think they really understood what Ventolin could do,' he says. 'There was a complete failure to comprehend the nature of the product.' The product had been a test for Glaxo, and it was a test it failed. It lacked the nerve and ambition to make a succes of the work done in the laboratory, and it squandered its chances to become a major international company. Its financial figures began to tell their own depressing story. Between 1973 and 1974 its profits stagnated while its turnover scarcely rose. The company seemed trapped in a cycle of low and declining expectations.

Inside the company, however, the mood was starting to change. Much earlier, David Jack had started reworking its attitudes to research and development, working against the grain of the company to turn it into an experimental drugs business. But at the corporate heart of the company, nothing had changed. Nothing except Girolami. The numbers man, now in his forties, had carefully watched the trends within the business and had worked out his own response.

Business in the sixties and the seventies was dominated by a desire to sidestep risk. Risk was viewed as a bad thing: there was no way you could control it, and what you couldn't control you shouldn't deal with. That, at least, was the prevailing view. Glaxo, just as in Jephcott's time, was simply a creature of its time. It was in the hope of taking the risk element out of their trading that companies would spend their money wildly diversifying out of their own industries, buying into businesses they knew little about. Glaxo had believed it could contain the risk by buying more and more of the British drugs industry. Beecham thought the same way. Yet risk had become central to the drugs business, and the company that failed to embrace risk by its own nature, would fail to embrace the industry.

Girolami realised this crucial truth. To take a risk, he figured, naturally carried with it the risk of failure. But not to take risk, paradoxically, was not to ensure any kind of success. With risk you might fail; without risk you certainly would. The whole panoply of decisions taken to sidestep risk, ironically, only increased it. As the company diversified, as it looked one minute

at food, the next at medical equipment, the next at wholesaling –
all businesses Glaxo was then involved in – it was unable to
concentrate on any single item. And as its concentration was lost,
so was its performance: the risks then increased.

Many years later, he was to instruct colleagues in that simple
truth. 'Having all your eggs in one basket', he would tell his junior
staff with one of his waspish half-smiles, 'concentrates the mind.'
And then he would add slyly: 'Because you'd better make sure it is
a good basket.'

It was a brilliant piece of logical thinking. The argument was
partly about motivation: the concentration on the single objective
would focus the minds of the individuals within the company,
since they knew its future and their jobs were at stake should they
fail. It was partly, also, about channelling the resources of the
organisation towards a single, crucial point: the business equiva-
lent of a *blitzkrieg*.

His philosophy was to become fasionable in the mid eighties:
indeed, by the end of the decade it was the stuff of business-school
textbooks. But when Girolami formulated it he was fifteen to
twenty years ahead of his time. In terms of deep strategic
thinking, it was a masterpiece. And Glaxo was to soon act upon it:
over the next few years it was to start to pile its eggs increasingly
into one basket. For the first time it was becoming a company not
of its times, but ahead of its times.

16 The roll

One dark evening in 1973 David Jack and Roy Brittan made the journey from Ware to Hatfield, a small, dismal dormitory town to the north of London. Together they headed for the town's polytechnic. They made their way to the lecture hall and settled into their seats. Around them was a jumbled, oddball audience; students, pharmacologists, scientists. The event was a lecture by James Black. He was a man who, by then, already had a formidable reputation within the drugs industry. While working for the British chemical and drugs company ICI in the sixties, he had discovered the first of the anti-hypertensive heart drugs, Inderal. The drug had been a huge success for ICI, establishing Black's genius as a researcher. Black himself, who has since won both a knighthood and a Nobel Prize for his work, had by then moved on from ICI. In 1973 he was working in the UK research laboratories of the American giant SmithKline French. For them he was studying ulcers, and ulcers were the subject of his talk that day.

It was also the reason Jack and Brittan were in the audience, listening so attentively. A year earlier, in 1972, the pair felt they had finished their work on asthma, and were thinking of new projects to work on. One that came to mind was acid secretion, the process that creates ulcers. They had started investigating the way acid secretion works within the body and were thinking about what type of compound might inhibit it; but they had not, as yet, progressed very far with their project. To them Black's lecture was to be a revelation.

He certainly had something to reveal. Numerous companies at that time were rooting around for a cure for ulcers. They provided a perfect market for the modern drugs company. It was a common ailment, it needed to be treated, and it was suffered mainly by people in the rich industrialised countries where governments and health systems could afford to pay for a drug. And a drug, if it worked, would have no trouble winning acceptance: the only cure for an ulcer then was expensive, painful and risky surgery. No doctor would recommend a surgical cure in preference to a drug cure if one was available.

Among the companies rooting around for a cure were Pfizer and Lilly in the United States, as well as Glaxo and SmithKline. Before it was possible to find a cure, however, the scientists on the trail needed to find out what was causing the acid secretion. One theory knocking around was that the process was controlled by a naturally-occurring substance called histamine. Earlier research had shown that histamine was a powerful stimulant of acid secretion both in animals and humans. Yet the current state of scientific knowledge still made it very doubtful whether blocking histamine would be any use in blocking acid secretion; it was known it had a role in the process, but what role, precisely, was still a mystery.

This was the subject Black was to talk about. His research at SmithKline had shown that histamine was indeed a physiological controller, and that the way was now open to creating drugs to inhibit the substance, and so control acid secretion and cure peptic culcers. It was, in its way, a historic lecture: it marked a genuine breakthrough in biochemical knowledge. But for Jack and Brittan there were other reasons for listening with such rapt attention. They now knew which path to follow in developing their own drug.

Back in Ware, the two men set about stepping up their search. James Black had told them what to look for, but he had not told them where to find it, the other half of the riddle of discovering any drug. Two other men, John Clitheroe and Barry Price, joined them in the hunt. It was not an easy task, however. Three years after the search had begun they had found nothing. And both men were ready to dismiss the ulcer project as a waste of time. It was the same year that Black's work at SmithKline culminated in the launch of its ulcer drug Tagamet, a drug received with wide praise in the medical world, and described as the 'state-of-art in medicinal chemistry'. Jack and Brittan were well behind in this race, and it seemed as if their attempt to crash the ulcer market was dead.

'We were ready for one last throw,' David Jack later recalled. That last throw was a realignment of the molecule structure of the compounds they were looking at. One compound worked on by the chemistry team led by Barry Price was a thing called raditidine. With the molecular alterations, it looked promising. And, sure enough, as the team hauled it through tests during 1976 it proved to be the compound they had been looking for. Raditidine worked as a histamine antagonist, blocking the process of acid secretion. Just at the point where they were ready to abandon the search, Jack's team had disvovered their ulcer drug.

With hindsight, the inventor is almost embarrassed about the discovery. 'Raditidine's not an interesting story,' he complains. 'To tell you the truth, I'm not interested in it.' Pressed, he shrugs aside any credit. 'It was a straight piece of medicinal chemistry, because all the original thinking had been done by Jim Black. He showed histamine was a physiological mediator, and he also found the first clinically tolerated H2 blocker.'

And so he had. But Jack, the inventor in him twisting and turning and finding fresh angles and novel approaches, has this to add: 'It does however show you something very important,' he says, a smile starting to play upon his face. 'The second prize in this business can be bigger than the first.'

Glaxo had lost the scientific race to find a compound to cure ulcers; they had started late and it had, in truth, never been a race they were likely to triumph in. But the company was about to set itself a steelier objective. If it was not to be number one with the science, it would be number one in the market. It might not be as lofty or noble a prize, but it would certainly be far, far richer.

There was a mountain to climb, however. Soon after Tagamet was launched it started climbing towards the top of the world's drugs market; five years after its introduction it was, with sales worldwide worth $620 million, the biggest-selling drug in the world, and the biggest-selling drug ever. Yet in those five years, while Tagamet was riding towards the peak of its success, the men at Glaxo were stealthily plotting its downfall. To overtake Tagamet, they would need to rework and reinvent all the accepted ways of making and marketing drugs. Their new ulcer drug was given the trade name Zantac. Sitting there in the laboratory, however, it was a problem for the company. The new drug was blatantly a 'me too' product, with nothing more to say in its favour. Copies had long been part of the drug industry; most successful compounds would, within a few years, attract a small platoon of followers. But in the past none of them had made very significant inroads into the market: around ten per cent of their competitor's sales would be the maximum aspiration of a 'me to'. After all, after Librium and Valium, the drugs industry had been all about innovation: the prizes were meant to go to the innovators.

Nineteen seventy-six was a bad year for Glaxo, just as it was a bad year for England. The long, steamy summer saw unemployment rise above one million for the first time since the Second World War; the country had just been humiliatingly bailed out of its financial problems by the International Monetary Fund; and the talk was of irreversible decline, the country becoming an impoverished and strife-torn backwater. Glaxo was just entering the bleakest period in its history. Group profitability started to stagnate through 1976 and continued over the next few years: from a peak profits figure of £87 million recorded for the financial year ending in 1977, profits declined slightly to £86 million the following year, and headed sharply down to £72 million and then £66 million in 1979 and 1980. To the outside observer, it looked as though the company was washed up.

Inside, however, a change was starting to take hold of the business. The cultural shift, so evident in men like David Jack and

Paul Girolami, had begun to spread throughout the company: they were becoming an aggressive group of fighters who were determined to take on the market and win.

'What was right about Zantac was first and foremost that it was market-driven,' recalls one former board member. 'If it had been science-driven, as it used to be in the past, then I don't think the product would ever have been developed, on the grounds that it wasn't new. At the time that it was being developed it really was a "me too". Scientifically it was thoroughly uninteresting. The management in the past might have been driven by a scientific goal, but they would not have been driven with this frankly commercial end in view. And previously even sales and marketing would have said: How can we sell it, it doesn't have an edge? But this time there was a different attitude. Which was, we want to beat the opposition in the market place with a product which, to all intents and purposes, is the same as the product that is already there, but then when we get it there we are going to make absolutely certain, and a lot of preparation was done for this, that it is launched internationally, in all the major markets in the world, and that we are going to take our share of that business.'

It was a new and very different goal for Glaxo to set itself; the aggressive determination behind it was new as well. Yet setting the goal was one thing; accomplishing it was to take many years of intense and fevered marketing, taking the company in new directions, and developing for it bold and risky strategies.

The campaign started back in the laboratories in Ware. There, David Jack had one more major contribution to make to the development of Zantac. 'He was the man who determined that if this product was to make any headway in the market it had to be developed very quickly indeed,' says one employee from the time. 'He knew that other people were following in the market place and therefore things had to go quickly.' Traditionally in the drugs business discovering a compound is just a first, tentative step toward the market. The processes of development and testing are so complicated, and the results take so long to come through, that it can take ten years before the drug is ready to be launched.

Glaxo didn't have ten years, Jack figured. Ten years was too long: by then the market would be lost forever, and Zantac would be just one among several 'me toos' jostling for space on the chemists' shelves. Some way had to be found of telescoping the development process and stealing a valuable lead on the competition.

He wrestled with the riddle and, eventually, came up with an idea he called 'parallel development'. Typically of Jack, his solution was a neat mixture of clever science and savvy business. The long-accepted procedure in the drugs business was to take the development of a drug one step at a time: start with the rats and see what happens; if it works in the rats, try it on the monkeys and see what happens; and so on. There was a way to short-circuit the cycle, however. It was to do all the testing work simultaneously.

The parallel development project was taken up: long-term testing for toxicity took place before the results of the short-term tests were known, for example. There was one catch, however. Parallel development multiplied the volume of work and it multiplied the dangers. 'Some very courageous decisions were made in the group at that stage,' recalls one witness to the events. 'The development strategy we adopted was very expensive and it was taking a tremendous risk.'

The risks were reflected in the fast-rising cost of research and development at Glaxo: the total spent on the laboratories rose from £17 million in 1976, the year the compound was discovered, to £40 million in 1981. And it happened at a time when the company's profits were falling: in fact the rise in research expenditure was one of the main contributors to the profits fall. The risks were all too clear. Pushing profits down to finance research spending risked laying the company open to another raid such as the one launched by Beecham only years before; and bunching the development process risked spending vast sums only to discover that the money had been squandered on a dud product.

Paul Girolami, however, was by now bestriding the organisation. It was his ideas, his insights into the essential riskiness of the drugs industry, which, together with David Jack's inventive genius, were now holding the company in thrall. There are moments in a corporation's history when it stakes its all and sits back to see whether fortune will swing with it or against it. This was one of those moments.

It could have gone either way. Some nine out of ten drugs that come out of the laboratory fail to make it through development: some bug or side effect kills the project. Although enough was known about Zantac to lower the odds from a one in ten gamble, the likelihood of success was never more than fifty/fifty. Yet fortune on this occasion favoured the brave. As test followed test, and as the details of the licensing application gathered into file upon file, Zantac pulled through its development without a serious hitch. Parallel development worked triumphantly: despite the cost, the drug was ready to be launched only five years after it had been discovered. And a five-year head start on other competitors had been stolen.

But Girolami's appetitite for chance was not yet satiated. He had realised Zantac was an opportunity to take a major slice of the ulcer market, and had been ready to stake the company to achieve that ambition. But he realised something else as well: that Zantac was also an opportunity to turn Glaxo into a major world company. He was ready to stake the company on that roll of fate as well.

There were three more risks to be taken. One was to take the drug back to the laboratory before it had even been launched. Zantac, the way it had originally been developed, came in a twice-a-day dosage, to be taken for six weeks to cure an ulcer. But for the drug marketeers at Glaxo that was not good enough. They wanted it to come in a dosage that could be taken by swallowing one rather than several pills a day; people don't like taking medicines, and skilful marketeers are acutely aware of the need to tailor the product to consumer whims. And they wanted a continuous dosage as well. Tagamet had been developed as a drug which people took to cure an ulcer once it started hurting, and Zantac had imitated it. The next step was to refine the drug so that patients could take it every day for the rest of their lives to prevent an ulcer from developing again: naturally, a drug taken every day would be vastly more lucrative than one taken for only six weeks. 'That was a marketing decision,' recalls one former director. In other words, the scientists had made their discovery and had lost interest; but the marketing men were still pushing for more. And more meant sinking more money into research before the product had yet been put on sale in any form.

The second risk was this. Glaxo had traditionally licensed its few original products in the United States, allowing them to be sold by other companies. It did not have its own company there, so it had little choice. Girolami resolved to change that. In 1978, he masterminded the purchase of a small American drug marketing company. Even so, this was far too small to handle a major nationwide marketing campaign in a country as big as America. Girolami resolved to use the drug as a way of establishing the company in the United States. He still had a dilemma to solve, however: it would take too long to establish the drug and the company at the same time. By the time that was accomplished, the patents would probably have expired and the opportunity lost forever.

Negotiations were held with Merck for them to take the licence on the drug; Merck were close to agreement, and the deal was almost signed when the negotiations were abruptly terminated. Girolami had changed his mind. The chance to have the biggest of the American drugs houses sell Zantac was thrown away, and Girolami tied up a deal instead with a business he felt more at home with: Hoffmann - La Roche. 'Roche had this excess capacity problem,' recalls a former colleague of Girolami. 'They were desperate. Glaxo was poised to make an agreement with Merck, but then at the last minute we pulled out. Again the marketing view prevailed. Girolami clearly saw that if Glaxo did a deal with Merck we would never be in a position to turn the product into a Glaxo product. It would always be a Merck product. Merck would launch it and would do a very good job with it. They might even put more money on the bottom line, but it would have diminished our motivation to establish our own company over there. The Roche arrangement was a temporary arrangement – you couldn't get a temporary arrangement with Merck, they didn't have a shortage of products for their salesmen. So that was a great commercial decision. I think what the company was doing at that time was wrestling with how it should achieve the real marketing impact of this product. And it was having to try out entirely novel ideas, and break away from the traditional ideas, to achieve anything.'

The same colleague goes on to recall how the atmosphere and culture of the company had changed decisively. 'Within the Group, for Glaxo anyway, there was a lot of quite unconventional thinking. And the point about it was that it was market-driven thinking. Unconventional thinking in a company that had a reputation for conservatism, and market-driven thinking in a company that had reputation for being dominated by science. Those were two quite dramatic changes.'

Glaxo had been captured by Paul Girolami's ambition for the Group, and in more than spirit. In 1981 he was made chief executive, giving him power over the organisational as well as the mental levers of control. There was, naturally, one last dramatic and daring risk he wanted to take. He wanted to put the price of Zantac way over the top: he argued it should be priced higher than Tagamet, a startling contradiction of the conventional wisdom, which held that a copy of a successful drug had to be priced lower than its rival to stand any chance of winning a place in the market.

Girolami wanted to burst that piece of wisdom wide open as well. 'Of course, everyone else in the industry was expecting us to undercut Tagamet,' recalls a one-time board member at the company 'But that's poor marketing. What is the advantage in that? Particularly if you are going to start saying that your product is better than the other guy's product. The industry was stunned but, of course, it was another classic piece of marketing.'

The board was stunned, too, by the new chief executive's audacity. Many voices were heard in the company saying the decision was a terrible mistake, that the product would be doomed by making it too expensive. But Girolami stuck to his logic, and pushed the decision through the board. Employees from the time recall that he finally agreed to a price about thirty per cent above Tagamet's as a compromise, although he himself would have preferred a still higher price.

All the pieces of Girolami's puzzle were now in place: all the company's eggs were firmly planted in one ulcerous basket. His vision of how to run a drug company was being realised: research money had been staked on one product; more research money was being staked on refinements; the company was being established in America with a novel and untried marketing agreement; and its pricing was way above what anyone ever thought possible. Every single conventional rule of the drugs industry had been broken and a new one put in its place. And now, in 1981, the drug was ready to make its debut. A new decade was starting. And Paul Girolami's one great roll of the pill was about to be cast.

17 The ulcer wars

In 1986 Glaxo's senior management flew from its Clarges Street headquarters to San Francisco. They were joined there by other senior marketing people, top salesmen and managing directors from each of the operating subsidiaries around the world, who had been told the event was an announcement, a presentation, of a major new product. Shaking off their jet-lag, the hundreds of salesmen gathered there for the first morning in an atmosphere of mystery and excitement. The company grapevine had not prepared them for this meeting: normally a new product would have been trailed within the company several years before it was actually launched, and yet they had heard nothing about this.

The first speaker was a man called Bernard Taylor, and he strode up to the podium clutching a sheaf of papers, and backdropped by a large graph. Taylor was a tall, lanky man, with a long square face and a very proper, English manner; around the corridors of corporate headquarters he was nicknamed 'the headmaster' for his schoolmasterly mixture of gentle authority and old-fashioned formality. He had been in the company since 1963, working his way up through the marketing hierarchy, managing the Australian subsidiary with great success in the seventies and coming back to headquarters to work on Zantac in the early eighties. He was now chief executive. To have the chief executive making the first presentation that morning only heightened the air of excitement.

Taylor unveiled part of the graph on the backdrop behind him. Along the horizontal axis, it showed the years from 1986 to 1991;

along the vertical axis it showed the numbers which seemed to range from zero to one billion dollars; between these axes was a stark, black line which headed straight upwards. 'Well,' asked Taylor, peering out over his spectacles, 'what do you make of that?'

There was bafflement in the hall at the question. A few people in the hall protested: there was nothing in the upcoming product line, they argued, which could achieve a billion in sales in five years. Taylor cast his eyes around the room and asked if anyone had any ideas on what the product might be. Nobody did: they all repeated that nothing had that level of potential. Eventually, Taylor decided to stop teasing his audience. He turned to the graph behind him and uncovered it fully. There was a lower half, up to now concealed. It showed the product starting at zero back in 1981, reaching one billion dollars in sales by 1986, and then moving ever onwards and upwards to two billion in sales by 1991. Now it was clear. The product could only be one thing: Zantac. 'This is an incredibly important product,' explained Taylor. 'And you have to treat it as such. You have the ability to make sales of another one billion dollars. Nothing else in our portfolio can do that. I know, because you've told me. Now go ahead and do it.'

That day marked the start of the second stage of the great push on Zantac. Behind it lay five years of extraordinary success. The ulcer drug launched in 1981 as a copy had surpassed the drug it had been designed to imitate, had become the biggest-selling drug in the world, and was now, with one billion dollars in sales, the biggest-selling drug of all time. Girolami's roll of the pill had worked. And it had worked beyond anyone's wildest expectations: even his own.

Making it work, however, had taken five years of skilled and fast footwork: the selling of Zantac had been one of the most intensive and fiercely fought marketing battles the drugs industry had ever seen. Zantac had been registered in all the major markets around the world in one go; this was a worldwide campaign and there were to be no pauses along the path to establishing it. It passed through its regulatory hoops with ease.

There were no serious side effects to the drug, and no significant barriers to its registration.

It worked and it was safe. At the same time, however, there were no significant advantages. Scientifically it was much the same molecule as Tagamet. For the marketing people, that posed a tricky problem: Tagamet was already well established in the market, the doctors were used to prescribing it, and habit, they knew, was the most powerful marketing weapon of all. There was only one way to solve that problem: they would have to create some differences.

When any drug is launched, it invariably has a good side effects profile; it will have been tested on up to six thousand individuals, enough to prove it is safe, but too few to be certain it has no side effects at all. As it goes into the mass market, its 'side effects profile' will slip. It will pick up what is known in the industry as 'background noise': during intensive registration by doctors of their experience with the drug, it will start to pick up some side effects. Tagamet, after five years on the market as the most widely prescribed medicine in the world, had started to develop a profile. The studies had shown it had minor side effects: it interacted badly with some other medicines, particularly with heart drugs.

It was not a serious problem for Tagamet, but it was enough to give the Glaxo salesforce a foot in the surgery door. One Glaxo marketing executive recalls that: 'You couldn't say Tagamet was an unsafe drug because by any reasonable standards it was very, very good. But by concentrating on the areas where it could be improved, the salesforce could say that Zantac was a better drug.'

The first line of attack developed by Glaxo was to identify the side effects profile of Tagamet, and use it to lever their drug into the market: it was a classic example of what advertising people call 'knocking copy'. Questioning Tagamet's safety was a neat line of attack. It could not be proved that Zantac was better: it had not been used widely enough yet for its side effect profile to emerge. But, by the same logic, it could not be disproved. This is the kind of information which, in the hands of skilled marketing professionals, can be twisted into a decisive advantage. Doctors are generally cautious people, particularly in the United States where the threat of being sued for negligence makes them fearful. Any doubts over the safety of a drug will be an immediate deterrent to their prescribing it.

One difference in side effect was established immediately. To push the advantage further, however, the marketing department needed more, and they came up with dosage. When Tagamet had been launched in 1976, SmithKline had released it in a form that required the patient to take it five times a day – four times a day in one dose, and then the fifth time at twice the dose. 'Pretty complicated stuff,' recalls a Glaxo marketing man with a wry smile. Glaxo, by contrast, released Zantac in a much simpler form: one pill, twice a day. Doctors, they figured, would presume it was easier for their patients to remember that simpler instruction.

There was more to dosage than how often the pill was taken. Glaxo had put more of the active chemical into each pill than SmithKline had put into Tagamet. It was a small difference of substance, but it allowed the marketing people to compare one individual Zantac pill with one individual Tagamet pill. In the long term, there was no qualitative difference between the two, but on a one to one basis, it could be argued Zantac was stronger.

'Glaxo, with luck, got the dosage spot on,' recalls an executive. 'That meant the salesforce could go around saying that Zantac was "better than Tagamet". Doctors interpreted that as meaning that Zantac was better at healing ulcers than Tagamet. In fact, we didn't have any data until as late as 1988 to show that there was really some small advantage in preventing relapse. We didn't know that then. But we could produce graphs showing a green line for a Tagamet pill and a blue line for a Zantac, and the doctor could look at them and say, oh yes, better product. Now, it wasn't that what we were saying wasn't right, it's just that the impression given by those pictures was that Zantac was a better product overall.'

It was clever, though rough, marketing; accurate but selective information, pushed into the market to undermine Tagamet slowly and gradually to create the impression that Zantac was a more potent medicine. And it worked: in the years after 1981 the copycat drug slowly edged the originator to the sidelines.

A significant enough victory in itself, it was not enough to satisfy Glaxo; nobody there would relax until Zantac was the biggest-selling drug of all time. But to take it to that position would mean stacking up yet another deck of risky cards.

Zantac had originally been launched as a twice-a-day medicine: that had been one of the factors behind its success against Tagamet. By 1983 and 1984, however, there were rumours circulating in the drugs industry that Merck was about to step into the market with its own ulcer drug. The rumours were well founded: the company had licensed in from Japan another drug called Pepcid and was working on refining it into once-a-day form. 'We were frightened that Merck would do to us what we had done to SmithKline,' recalls one marketing executive.

It was a powerful fear. Merck not only had the technical expertise to get the drug right, it had the marketing strength to cripple the still young American subsidiary, Glaxo Inc. The marketing people were determined to crunch it. The laboratories, despite some resistance, were ordered to come up with a once-a-day drug as well. When they succeeded, Glaxo beat Merck onto the market by some twelve months, restricting the appeal of the rival drug.

There was more to come. Soon after becoming chief executive in 1985 Bernard Taylor looked at the sales forecasts made for Zantac. They showed a prediction for 1988 of £500 million in worldwide sales. He decided that was too low. In his opinion, the drug had the potential to cruise on and on, to reach a figure much closer to one billion pounds. To achieve it, though, required a massive investment: in manufacturing plant, in marketing spending, and above all in teams and teams of salesmen. He put forward his plans, but met with resistance from the board of the company. This, some members of the board figured, was taking Glaxo to the wilder shores of optimism: no drug had ever reached sales of one billion pounds; for that matter very few drugs companies at that time had ever reached sales of one billion pounds across their whole range. To suggest just one drug could take on that target by itself looked like pumping money into a pipe dream. 'The arguments were rife,' recalls one board member from the time.

Yet the marketing men at Glaxo had discovered something very interesting. Traditionally, in the drugs industry, a medicine is launched with a big promotional splash, and then the marketing spend trails off to the relatively low level needed to support its position. With Zantac, something different had been tried: no matter how high its sales went, the marketing men just kept spending and spending. And it worked. The more was spent on promotion, the more money – doubled, tripled and then quadrupled – came back in sales and profits. As one marketing whizz later recalled: 'The best way of making more money at Glaxo was to spend more money on Zantac. It was absolutely fantastic.'

Just as fantastic were the profits. Girolami's decision to push the price up high was a smart one: it helped establish the reputation of the product, but it also helped increase the already lush profit margins on the drug. Even by the standards of the industry, Zantac was a particularly lucrative property. For every pill sold, Glaxo made a marginal profit of more than ninety per cent. For every extra dollar in sales it could achieve more than ninety cents turned into pure, instant profit.

Armed with that ammunition, Taylor's ambitious plan to push the levels of investment up again, and to crank Zantac up to the one billion dollar level were eventually endorsed. The money was spent, and the pill rolled out again. As soon as the decision was made, however, the arguments started all over again. Taylor decided, in 1986, that his earlier forecast of one billion dollars had still been too low. He was now betting on two billion. And he wanted more investment in order to hit that target as well. Once more he won the debate, and yet more money was to be pumped into Zantac. The marketing men from what had once been such a sleepy company were now riding high, and they were ready to test the outer limits of how big and how profitable a drug could be.

The answer came back: very profitable. Late in 1988 Sir Paul Girolami hosted a press conference in London to announce

Glaxo's results for the year. For him it was a triumph, the culmination of everything he had believed in and fought for over more than two decades. That year's financial results were an elegant testimony to the way his series of gambles had paid off. Turnover passed the two-billion-pound mark and profits were up to £832 million. Zantac was just a shade under one billion pounds in sales, at £989 million, and still growing strongly. The American subsidiary had proved itself by turning in sales of £751 million, and it had taken its share of the US ulcer market past fifty per cent for the first time. It was, for everyone present, a dazzling display of financial power and success.

Yet the real message of the conference was different: it was the first time Girolami felt confident enough to reveal his true ambitions for the company. Much was made of the fact that the year's results marked a new turning point for the business: with these sales and profits figures it was now the second largest drugs company in the world. From there only one more hurdle needed to be cleared. 'We want,' Girolami let slip, 'to be the largest drugs company in the world.' It was a significant statement: Girolami may have harboured the ambition, nursing it within himself, since 1965, but this was the first time he had revealed his desire in public. Now the gameplan was clear: to overtake Merck, to overrun its lordly citadel, and to occupy its position of dominance over the world pharmaceutical industry.

Given Glaxo's extraordinary growth rate, it did not strike anyone as an impossible goal: that year the company had been the fastest growing major drugs business for the sixth year running, and the momentum had only to be maintained for Girolami's ambition to be fulfilled. It was not much of a surprise to anyone, either: the rest of the industry had been staggered by Glaxo's audacious arrival on the world stage but, by now, they respected it, feared it and had even begun to treat it as a model to learn from. In terms of style at least, it was already close to being the world's dominant company. Yet, as one board member was later to remark privately, 'It is strange how as soon as you announce a goal it starts slipping away from you.'

18 Life at the top

John Ansell is a medium man: medium height, medium looks, medium weight, medium ability. Not the greatest individual in the world, but a very long way from the worst; he is an average sort of guy. He joined Glaxo in 1985, hired to work on ulcers in the company's international marketing department, the section charged with coordinating sales strategies for Zantac around the world. It was a small department then, only four people, working from the Clarges Street head office, a low-slung, grey and very ordinary office building just off Piccadilly. Together with his colleagues, Ansell contributed much of the statistical and brain work that turned Zantac into the world's number one drug: it was they who figured out the potential size of the ulcer market, who worked out the unending relationship between higher promotional spending and higher sales, and who laid the intellectual groundwork for Bernard Taylor's second push that turned the company's minor triumph in establishing the drug into the unstoppable juggernaut it had become by the end of the decade.

He thought he had done a good job. He had no reason to think otherwise, and his pay packets seemed to reflect a reasonable level of corporate satisfaction with his achievements: he was paid thirty thousand pounds a year and got regular bonuses of up to twenty per cent of his annual salary. It was a good, well paid job with the most commercially successful company in Europe: a business executive in his thirties could be well satisfied. Yet three years after joining, he left a sorry and disappointed man.

He describes his feelings on leaving the company like this: 'It was a bit of a relief, really,' he explains with a wan smile, 'because there was nobody there who was particularly interested in your future, and even working on Zantac you tended to start going around in circles after a while. The department was in a constant state of reorganisation: I think it has had five different heads in five years. That makes it difficult for everyone, because each time it changes everyone in the department has to prove themselves all over again. Sometimes people succeed and sometimes they don't. It just depends how they feel. But it is a very unstable situation to be working in. As a result, the level of job satisfaction is not high. The main source of satisfaction is the pay packet. Glaxo's philosophy is to pay people well. It's the main thing they do for their people. If people want other things, then they shouldn't work for Glaxo.

'The company's attitude to career progression is that it is something for each individual to do for himself. They have no particular policy of developing people's careers. It's a company that people want to join, because they are so successful, so why should they bother? If they want someone with a particular expertise, then they buy them. And if they no longer need that person five years later then they dispense with them. They certainly won't find anyone within the organisation – because nobody will have bothered to train anybody up. So that's another reason why satisfaction is so low. They release these employee surveys showing satisfaction is very high, but when they did their own survey for internal use it showed that satisfaction was rock bottom.'

Ansell's own break with the company came shortly after he had organised a major conference in Tokyo, aimed at improving the position of Zantac in the Japanese market, the one major arena where it has failed to make a big impact. The conference went well, and he was praised within the company for his work on it. Yet his work on Zantac was starting to run out of steam: there was less and less marketing work to be done on the drug. One of his bosses pushed for him to be transferred to another project, but that request was turned down: the view higher up was that he knew about ulcers and that was all he was needed for. 'I found for the first time that year that I didn't get a very good salary rise,' he recalls. 'Higher up they were turning around and saying: why is this guy costing us so much? They were not saying: well, he's done a good job here, what can we get him to work on now?'

Soon afterwards, the view that he was costing too much prevailed, and he was offered voluntary redundancy. Sensing that his time was running out, he decided to take it and left to join a pharmaceutical consultancy. Within Glaxo there was no sorrow at his leaving: 'They just said fine, okay. There is not much sentiment there,' he recalls. Nor was there much opportunity to discuss his decision with his bosses or his colleagues: like others before him, after he began to sink, the waters closed in above him, and he was gone. 'It is not a very open place,' he remembers. 'If anybody left it was almost as if they had never existed. Unlike most other companies, within Glaxo, once you were on the way out, you suddenly became a non-person. It is not because most of the people themselves are mean, it is just that they think they will have nothing to gain from associating themselves with that person.'

Life at the bottom may be hard and dispiriting but it has its good points: there is camaraderie, loyalty, and ambition. It had once been like that at Glaxo. It may have been a stuffy and, in many ways, a hopeless old company, but it had its qualities. Things had changed at the new-look Glaxo Girolami had created: it had become a tough and mean-spirited place, riddled with rivalries and jealousies.

Life at the top has its good and bad points too. Success hits different people and companies in different ways: it depends how you handle it. Some take it well, with a certain grace and generosity. Other take it badly: they maul and they scrap and they sneer. And as the eighties drew to a close it was becoming clearer that Glaxo was taking its success very badly. With the ultimate prize so close at hand, there was no hint of generosity here; no grace; just more fighting.

The first outward sign of the internal tensions within Glaxo came on 10 May 1989. On that day a boardroom reshuffle was announced at Glaxo: Sir Paul Girolami had appointed a new chief executive, Dr Ernest Mario, and the previous chief executive, Bernard Taylor, had resigned without notice. He simply got up and walked out of the door. The announcement was a surprise to outsiders: there had been no hints, no indications, no rumours of a clash between the chairman and the chief executive. But to insiders the axing of Taylor was no surprise at all; for the last eighteen months the corridor gossips had had little else on their tongues.

Taylor had been made chief executive early in 1986, soon after Girolami himself had given up that role to become chairman of the company. By any standards, he had been a remarkable success in the role. During his time in the job, the company's sales had risen from £1.1 billion to £2.5 billion, and its profits from £403 million to one billion pounds. It was hardly a failure. Certainly Girolami did not see it that way: Taylor was his man, handpicked for the job, and he shared with the chairman a passion for selling drugs and a commitment to high prices and ruthless marketing that had been Girolami's special contribution to the industry.

The two men had worked well together at first. Their views locked together neatly, and the firm was running smoothly uphill in its challenge to Merck. But as successes piled up and the battle became ever more intense, the tensions between the two men began to grow. The space between them, once no more than a whisker, grew ever larger.

Not long after Taylor was appointed to the chief executive's post, gossip began to filter through the ranks that Sir Paul Girolami, forever a man driven by his own logic and desire, had developed a fear: he was nervous about Glaxo being taken over by a hostile rival. 'Girolami was unhappy that the share price was still rather low,' recalls one insider. 'He felt the company was vulnerable. In fact, he was shit scared about it all through 1987.'

Sir Paul himself denies this: he says the only time he was frightened of a takeover was around 1981, when, he claims, both

Merck and Hoechst were preparing bids for Glaxo. The truth of what thoughts were inhabiting his mind is impossible to prove one way or another. But it is clear that to others in the company the chairman's fears seemed very real; they also seemed strange and bizarre. As far as they could figure out, the company was not vulnerable at all: there were no rumours in the City; no hostility among the shareholders; the sales and profits figures were tremendous; there was, in short, nothing to worry about at all. But Girolami did not see it that way. Within his mind, there was a threat, and it was a threat to everything he had built up over so many years. And at Glaxo, when the chairman had something in his skull, no matter how strange or unjustified, action had to follow.

Taylor, according to these accounts, was the man charged with finding some action to take. Glaxo, despite its growing success, kept a low profile for itself. Girolami was not a man to court City or public esteem. Nor would he seek the rewards or adulation of fame, and although he was the most successful English business-man of the decade he never became a well-known public figure. Partly because of diffidence and partly through an inner sense of tactics, he preferred to wage his war privately and secretly. The press office had needed people of little linguistic creativity: two words would suffice, in any language – 'no comment'.

Should a hostile bidder emerge, however, this reticence would be a liability: the companies that survive a raid are the ones who are not ashamed to blow their own trumpet. So in 1987, re-portedly at Girolami's prompting, Bernard Taylor decided to launch a PR campaign. It was directed mainly at the financial markets, and in particular at the stock analysts who largely determine a company's share price. The one thing that really turns the drug analysts on is new product information: they understand how dramatically a new drug can lift a company's profits, and most drugs analysts are engaged in a constant search for the next wonder drug. For that reason, raising the prices of pharmaceutical shares is fairly easy: you just have to feed the market some laboratory results.

Traditionally, the company had kept the drugs it was working on a close-wrapped secret: revealing what was being planned risked giving away too much to the competition. In 1987, however, it began holding elaborate briefings for analysts, detailing for them – and, in turn, for the press – everything the laboratory was investigating. It worked in the short term: the briefing created much attention in the City and for a time the share price raced upwards. But that excitement soon wore off and the company was left with nothing more to say: it had unloaded everything with one burst of enthusiasm. The share price drifted down again, never to a low level, but below what Girolami would have liked. He was said by staffers to be angry, and he turned his anger onto Taylor.

Shortly afterwards, still fretting about the imagined takeover of his domain, so his colleagues say, Girolami floated another brainwave. This time it was even wackier: privately and discreetly, he started sugggesting to senior colleagues that the company should move its headquarters to the United States, reincorporate there, and sever its ties with Britain. 'Paul is very keen to see the company become more American,' recalls one former board-level executive. 'It is very difficult to see why. He is a man of incredible intelligence, he is not going to be easily fooled, and he would always give you a very vigorous debate on the subject, but he had this view that if he were free to do it, it would be a good thing to move the headquarters to the States. That, more than anything, reflects his view that it should become an American organisation. From a financial persepective, of course, it would be a good thing. Glaxo's share price would go up overnight.'

Financial perspectives, of course. Yet those were the only real perspectives Girolami ever had: the numbers man in him was coming to the fore. A move to America was always a wild idea: Glaxo had by this time risen to become the UK's fourth largest company, measured by market capitalisation, and to flit the country would have been a nasty swipe at its often fragile economy. The news would certainly have been harshly received by the Conservative government, of which Girolami was a strong supporter, and to which the company contributed through generous donations to party funds. The idea was a potential bomb, as likely to explode the company as solve its imagined problem, and Girolami was eventually persuaded from pushing it beyond a suggestion. Or so the story goes. Again, the desire to shift to the US is something Girolami denies. The truth is impossible now to establish. All the same, that the people around him believed this to be his thinking is unquestionable, and they go on to say that opposition to a move, particularly from Taylor, was to further sour the relations between the two men.

Other disagreements contributed to the malevolent atmosphere. Taylor was unhappy with the progress of the company in Japan and Germany, as were many people in the company. These were the two most important markets after the United States and Zantac had done poorly in both compared with its successes elsewhere. Taylor figured its stumbling performance was the result of joint ventures and alliances that had been struck in both territories to market the drug. It was clear that they were not working well and his solution was to tear the contracts up and start again. There was a problem, however: both deals had been struck by Girolami, and Sir Paul was not a man who liked to be told he had done a dud deal.

The poison between the two men had now gone deep. Girolami had decided that Taylor was a man to be disposed of. 'It was very clever,' recalls one former board colleague of both men. 'He didn't do it all of a sudden, but he took his power away piece by piece. He chopped him up like a salami.' Over the course of a year, more junior colleagues began to notice how Taylor was not a good man to be associated with: decisions he was pushing for began invariably to be defeated; he was sitting on fewer and fewer committees; and the chairman's scorn for his former favourite became ever clearer. 'Poor Bernard,' recalls one insider. 'I think he was the last to know.'

Eventually, however, even he would find out what was happening to him. The crunch came during the last weekend in May. At a hotel in Venice, the city of Girolami's birth, and a perfect spot for a kill, the chairman met with the head of the American subsidiary, Dr Ernest Mario. Mario had joined the company from Squibb three years earlier; he had made a tremendous success of the US company, and was, in Girolami's view, a man who carried with him no baggage from Glaxo's past. He was to slot into the role of the chairman's favourite. Girolami offered him the job of overall chief executive and Mario, inevitably, accepted. Taylor was to be left with his title, but he would now report to Mario. Although the PR department bravely tried to make out it was only a reshuffle, Taylor had plainly been demoted to an insignificant position. He promptly resigned: the outcome, it seemed to everyone in the company, that Girolami had been planning all along.

Mario at once became the man who would inherit the crown. It was not clear when: Girolami was sixty-three in 1989, suggesting he might step down some time in 1991. But he had, as yet, given no indication of when he might leave, and had changed the company rules to allow the chairman to stay in office until the age of seventy. He might go; he might not. In the meantime, as Mario well knew, the post of heir apparent to Sir Paul Girolami was a dangerous one to occupy.

Taylor had been the chosen successor, and he had been cut away. Soon after Girolami had first lost faith in Taylor, he had found another heir apparent. His name was John Burke, a young and talented pharmaceutical executive who had been head of Merck in the UK, and vice-president for Europe. He had been approached by Glaxo in 1985, and joined the company because he felt he had gone as far as he could at Merck: the main board of Merck was a sanctuary for Americans, and he was an Englishman. Within a year of joining the company, and still in his early forties, he was promoted to the main board of Glaxo. He was the youngest of the executive directors, he was close to Girolami and, to everyone in the company, was clearly destined for the very top.

Then, in 1988, he suddenly left. He had arrived in a flash, risen quickly, and left just as suddenly. Among the corridor gossips it was assumed he had overreached himself, had made his bid too early, and had been cut down by Girolami. He himself has a slightly different angle on the story: 'I left because I became unhappy with the way Glaxo was run,' he comments tersely. Whatever the truth of the matter, the relationship between the two men had clearly degenerated. Burke had come a little too close to the top; and then he was gone.

The way Glaxo was run was the way Girolami chose to run it. After ten years of control, the company had become Sir Paul's plaything; it was a reflection of his character. In conversation, Girolami likes to talk about how he manages by intuition. There is truth in this: he has the gambler's instinct, and gamblers listen to and obey their inner voices. But he goes on to describe intuition as no more than logic working at the speed of light. There is truth in this also. Glaxo is very much the creation of its chairman's ruthless and unbending logic: a logic unhinged from any trace of sentiment, and one which has bequeathed a company driven by rivalry and neurosis.

Not least at the top. 'I would say people respect the chairman,' recalls one insider, 'but they don't like him. He just isn't a likeable man.' Aspects of his behaviour became the stuff of jokes at the company. People noted the way he almost never acknowledged the existence of even those people in the company he knew, when he passed them in the corridor or joined them in the lift. They giggled at the corporate videos circulated to staff, in which the chairman would make a point of putting down an expensively-hired interviewer presenting the programme. Even in small ways, the chairman was unable to stop himself swiping and cutting at everyone he met.

These were minor points; others were more serious. It took a year for Girolami to find a heavyweight finance director: nobody with the right qualifications, went the rumour, wanted to be the chairman's numbers man. His managerial style became ever more disconcerting for the staff. 'You might be managing some far-flung territory,' said Bernard Taylor in a magazine interview before he left the business, 'and you'll run into him by chance in the local hotel. He may not actually come and see you, but you know he is there for some reason connected with your business, though you may never know what. It's non-plussing.'

This was Girolami unbound, freeing himself from the restraints of civility or compromise. The tyrannical side of his nature, in the late eighties, was bubbling to the surface. In 1987, David Jack, the inventor, and one of the last significant links with the Glaxo of the early days, had left the company, retiring to a quieter life. Soon afterwards Taylor, another key executive with roots back into the early sixties, had been cast aside. Others, too, in more minor positions, but also with roots back to the Glaxo of the sixties, had resigned or retired early.

There was a pattern here. The men with the memories had all gone. Like all leaders in whom the tyrannical spirit is strong, Girolami did not like to have around him men who knew; men who remembered him when he had been a small fish, who remembered the battles fought, who had struggled with him and who could treat him as an equal. Some had gone willingly, some had been carved away, some had just wearied of the whole business. As far as Girolami was concerned, the point was not how they had gone, it was simply that they were no longer there. Only he was left.

As he had effectively said in his London School of Economics lecture, it was me. This was now the Girolami version of history, and the Glaxo version too. And as the nineties began, the chairman was to grind the point home ever more firmly. During the first year of his second decade in charge of the corporation, he commissioned two sculptures. They were, inevitably, of himself, and they were to be placed in the London and United States headquarters of the company. There they would stand, monuments in cold stone to everything the chairman had achieved.

19 The chairman

The chairman's eyes were rooted on the floor as he spoke. 'I've had a very boring, banal sort of life, and there's nothing really exciting to talk about,' he was saying. 'That's maybe what has shaped me.' This was his response to a question about his past, about the people, events or experiences that had influenced him, that had created his character.

It wasn't a good start. But, then again, it was unlikely to be. People had warned me about talking to Sir Paul Girolami. He would be difficult, troublesome, they advised. One of his former board colleagues even told me to forget the whole thing. 'No point talking to Paul,' he said. 'He'll only confuse things.'

I had persisted, however. Arranging the interview had taken a year of filing requests and firing off faxes. For month after month nothing happened, and it seemed as if nothing would. There is a culture of secrecy at Glaxo, a firm refusal to disclose any significant information: it is a company dedicated to controlling its universe, and information is an instrument of control. Even the men who had left the organisation, and who were most helpful in providing information, were reluctant to allow any of their comments to be attributed directly; the Glaxo culture had moulded them, and they still hadn't shaken it off.

Ten months or so into this stonewalling, there seemed to be a breakthrough. It came after I explained how much information Merck had provided: as I explained, I could feel their competitive instincts rising. Soon afterwards, I was offered an interview with Dr Franz Humer, a board director appointed in 1989. I asked again about a meeting with Sir Paul. Well, I was told, let's see how this goes first. So it seemed a kind of test: if I was nice, I could get to see the chairman.

I was nice. Dr Humer is a stout Swiss who joined Glaxo in 1980, has worked as a manager in territories around Europe, and who has risen to be the director responsible for product development. He has learnt the company lines well, and speaks them fluently.

Asked how Glaxo became such a success, he answers: 'The leadership by the then chief executive and now chairman, Paul Girolami, who projected the company, projected the people into a spirit, into a winning situation. He woke the whole company up. I'm very much talking about a motivational sense. He made it truly international – wherever we meet, that is where the centre of the company is. He gave it depth, width, vision, which did not exist before.

'A clear focus came to the company. You could see and feel Paul's presence very quickly throughout the company at that time. Paul still travels eighty to ninety per cent of the time, so he is always around, he always understands. And it doesn't matter to him if a market is big or small. He visits Greece, he visits Portugal, less frequently but with the same spirit and approach as he travels to the States or Japan. So you always have the feeling the chairman is right there with you. He gave people a tremendous sense of power and autonomy, which makes people come up with ideas, and creativity, and makes them work twenty-four hours a day. Paul was very much present, you could feel it. He made the changes.'

It is an extraordinary testimony to the transformational powers of one individual, and it is expressed through the kind of concepts – omnipresent, beneficent, inspiring – usually used by churches to describe their God.

So I was aware of the sort of presence which, at least in the minds of the people around him, I was being ushered into. We met on the third floor of Lansdowne House, a swank new post-modernist office building in Berkeley Square, London. The Glaxo board and senior officials decamped here from the Clarges Street building around the corner two years previously, presumably because its late eighties' opulence was better suited to their elevated status than the functional sixties' minimalism of the older base. It is a pricey and swish piece of real estate: the sign above the door says Saatchi & Saatchi, and this is also the head office of that great eighties' bubble, the company which, for a short time, was the world's largest advertising agency.

The offices are slick, with the decor and operation of some fabulously expensive hotel: the receptionist, you notice, knows your name as soon as you walk through the door. Over to one side of the marbled lobby there are a couple of comfy, old-fashioned cloth sofas, and next to them a fireplace and a bookshelf, with various leather-bound and dusty tomes in it: the collected works of Dickens, and some very old, bound editions of *Country Life*. In this small corner, at least, the offices have been mocked up to look like a Georgian sitting room.

I had been waiting there about fifteen minutes when Sir Paul came out, flanked by his PR man, a tall, lanky, stressed-looking individual called Geoff Potter. We shook hands and headed off to the boardroom. A long, oval-shaped wooden table dominates the room; the place looks rich and calm. There is little in the way of ornamentation, although there is a portrait of Sir Paul on the wall, plus pictures of the other past chairmen.

'By nature I'm not that analytical or that abstract, I'm very much moved by impressions,' says Sir Paul, recollecting the time when he joined Glaxo in the mid sixties. 'In those days it was a name, and a big name. But it was considered to be a company which had failed in its potential, because it was talked about quite openly as a takeover target. So much so that I sometimes wondered if I'd have a job to go to. Quite frankly, then, it was a company which somehow or other had failed to live up to the potential of the people it had in it.'

As an answer it is quite plausible, but underneath it there is a catch: Why should a man of Sir Paul's undoubted ability want to join a business which he thought was a dud? Sir Paul appears taken aback by the angle of the question, and the pitch of his voice rises a notch or two as he searches around for a reply. 'No, that's quite an interesting point, I have to say,' he starts. 'When you take something on, you look at the big things and not the little things, and when I looked at Glaxo I saw the big thing, which was the quality. The fact that there are faults doesn't put you off. In fact the absence of faults would put you off. Because what the hell would be the argument for going? If I'm going to make a contribution, I have to improve the thing. I'm rationalising a bit, but all I'm saying is the fact that it wasn't perfect doesn't matter. The quality was there: there has been a continous line – sometimes quite thin – of quality, at Glaxo. That doesn't mean I didn't see a lot of other things that disheartened me. Quite frankly, there was no sense of purpose. There was no strategy. I was learning, the development of my contribution to the strategy wasn't really manifest until many years later, but those early years of acting as custodians of the business rather than – we the directors – leading it, forging it and framing it, defining where we should go, led me to the second stage. It was shaped almost by accident, rather than saying I'm going to try to change it in the way I think it ought to change.'

Sir Paul is a bashful man in conversation: he hesitates over his words and stumbles through his sentences. But only the delivery is modest. The words themselves are loud with self-confidence. Asked how much he contributed to the creation of Zantac, he answers: 'I think it's well known that I was the finance director but I was effectively the chief executive in the last few years, certainly from 1975 onwards. And this was not just because I was trespassing on other people's territory, it was because I was encouraged to by the chairman. So, obviously not the discovery of it, but everything else I think I can say was my doing.'

With hindsight, always a great bestower of wisdom, Sir Paul figures he not only made all the right moves with Zantac, but took few chances along the way. 'I wouldn't say we were stacking up on its being a success: we made great efforts to make it a success. There's no succesful product *per se*. Management make it a success or they make it fail. There is nothing in the ingredients of

Zantac that make it the best-selling drug in the world. It had to be made such. I could tell you a story of how we could have failed dismally with Zantac . . .'

How?

'Oh, I'm not going to tell you. But it could have been one minor product. There is no drug which can be automatically a success. Anyone who has that view should sell their shares. People say, oh, anyone can do it if they have the product. Baloney. Look at the tremendous job SmithKline did with a second-rate product like Tagamet. Tremendous. It's still selling; it has no right to be selling.' A broad, thin grin crosses his face. 'So we didn't do such a good job.'

'I think the fundamental thing was the company saw a very clear objective ahead of it, was very realistic about its limitations and about its strengths, and decided to make the most of it. There was no magic formula. There was a commitment to success, a commitment to a highly focused business, and at the same time we recognised that we didn't want to diversify, that we wanted to go against the stream and sharpen our focus on one business, and do that one business extremely well. I'm not suggesting it would be the right form for anyone else. I wouldn't be so arrogant. But from the Glaxo point of view that was a turning point. Because from that point on all our talent, all our energies said, gee, we know what we're going to do, we better do it well. In other words we are putting all our eggs in one basket. It's a bloody nice basket, but all the same we are putting all our eggs in it.'

There was something surprising about the fact that the money from Zantac was put back into research. A company of fearsome strategic imagination seemed to have fallen for the Roche syndrome of squandering the fortune from its one blockbuster on the search for another.

'I think the mistake made by the industry generally is to look at research as an optional extra. You can't disassociate research from our business. It *is* our business. So as you expand the business you have to expand research. Now, you ask, are there any guarantees of success? No. There are no guarantees.'

But it can't just be hoping . . .

'No, that's not managing the business. You get these learned books on managing research, but from a corporate standpoint you manage research as you manage a business. You manage it because marketing starts with research. We're not concerned with academic research, we're concerned with curing the common illnesses. Will we succeed? The answer is we're bound to succeed. The question is when, and, second, whether you succeed better than your competitor. It's not one of these roulette things. That's a misconception, a complete misconception. Every product we look for, we shall get one. Whether it's successful or not depends on whether it comes out before our competitors'. Our real risk comes from our competitors, whom we do not underrate.'

Competition is an issue that excites Sir Paul: one that gets under his skin. Yet competition in the drugs industry is intensifying all the time?

'I'm quite clear that the industry is consolidating,' he says. 'I said it many years ago. Most of the major companies are badly structured – look at Beecham before it went in with SmithKline, and so on. They had problems with position because they clearly had no long-term strategy. Or if they did have one, it was probably the wrong strategy. They ended up in a situation they couldn't get out of except by merger. Then many medium-sized companies are coming together to create some form of critical mass.'

And is that something you need to react to?

'No. We never react. On the whole, I would rather compete with strong competitors than with weak ones, because we'll be better if we compete with strong competitors. It's more fun. I don't think you really improve your own quality unless you have to fight for it. In the nicest way. So we are aware of it and we welcome it. We have to compete, but we are part of a great strategic industry with a very important role to play in world society, and I want to belong to strong industry. Having said that, am I going to participate in it? No. We don't need to. Why do we need to be larger just for the sake of it?'

For Sir Paul to say the drugs industry has an important role to play in the world is a curious turn of phrase. Could he mean the company is responsible in some way for whether people can afford its products?

'I don't think we have a responsibility for people as such, no. Even governments don't have a responsibility for that. People are responsible for themselves.'

It was time, I sensed, for a change of subject. When, I asked, will he retire?

'Not for some time yet.' He pauses for a few seconds of deep hesitation. 'My contract goes to seventy and I might go on until I am seventy. I think I'll retire when I ought to retire. A couple of years, maybe. I hope in a way that I won't be necessary much beyond that.'

Do you have a problem with the notion of a successor, with the idea of someone taking over your empire?

'It's very difficult, this type of self-diagnosis, but I'm not actually conscious of that. I could walk away tomorrow. I think actually we have got the successor, although it's one of the most difficult things in the world, isn't it, to find a successor. But I still think I can help him a bit. It does worry me a bit. Because it's a common and quite natural fault that having been associated with a company for so long, you can't give it up. But, you know, I am wholly committed to the success of the company, and that would be wrong. I have often examined myself for that flaw, and I think I am not very guilty.'

Sir Paul turns to his PR man and asks: 'Don't you think, Geoff, I'm not very guilty?'

Geoff shakes his head: 'No, no.'

'This troubled me because I was finance director for many years and we had the problem of finding a replacement when I moved up. We had a lot of trouble finding anyone to replace me. But then I found something quite interesting: because I was afraid of falling into that trap I was falling into the opposite trap of maintaining inefficient people. So there is a double edge to that sword. This is not an authoritarian group. It is a group which respects leadership, but there is no one around this table who wouldn't say, if I did have faults, come on Paul, you're being a bit bloody . . .'

How would he reply?

'Oh, really! We put a great premium on leadership and not on command; we have very few control mechanisms, we put our trust in our managers, and they thrive.'

You said once you wanted to be the largest in the world.

'Of course we want to be the largest. But there is nothing in our strategy which says our aim is to be the largest, because that would endanger our whole future. There is a great deal of satisfaction in doing the best you can, and in fulfilling your potential. Whether that takes you to first, or third, doesn't matter. I don't think we'd be turned on by buying something and saying, hey, now we're the largest, great. Because what the hell have you done?'

But to be the first through internal growth, that would be quite something, wouldn't it?

Sir Paul's face lights up at the thought, as if a switch had been turned on inside him. 'That would be something, yes. But we're going to get there. It'll only take a bit of patience and we're going to get there. I'm sure Roy Vagelos doesn't agree, but that's a healthy thing. I'm sure he'd say: like hell, Paul. But that's fine. There are no hard feelings; one of us is going to be wrong and it doesn't matter which, frankly.' He laughs. 'Nobody's going to get hurt.'

What does he think of Merck?

'I think they are a great company. We do admire them in a way that we don't admire any others. We compare ourselves with them, we measure ourselves against them. It's a great company.'

But they are very different from you?

'Sure, sure. But that's fine. I think they are both valid approaches, and they both work, so the world would be worse off if one supressed the other. The world can do with a lot of approaches, you know, and the race is a long one.'

And that was it. My audience with the chairman had run out of time. We stood up, and Sir Paul shook my hand briefly before leaving. I wandered over to have a look at his portrait. It shows him in a grey suit sitting in an armchair, peering out of the canvas with one of his waspy, enigmatic smiles. It is an unremarkable representation: recognisable, but it misses the eyes, and their sly, combative sparkle. It also makes him look younger than he is now: the hair is fuller, and the lines less deep on his face. I commented on that to Geoff Potter, and was told there was a fresh portrait now being prepared. Well, yes. I should have guessed a new portrait would be needed. The chairman, clearly, will be around for some time yet. And the race is indeed a long one.

Epilogue: Two companies, two drugs

I found the great inventor sitting in the foyer of the Royal Medical Society. He was resting beneath the arched columns and forbidding portraits of the grand, classical building, itself a monument to European medicine's rich heritage. I introduced myself and shook his hand. Together we walked off to find some mid-morning tea and biscuits.

David Jack is an old man now and his age is carved into his skin. His face is lined with the memories of past struggles, and his jowls droop with the cares and worries of so many years.

'Roche is a kind of warning, you know,' he says, as we sit down. 'How do you follow a huge success? That's one of the biggest problems a drugs company can have. The only thing is to have another huge success. Or two. Because a huge success creates a way of living, it creates an organisation, and it puts the company into a kind of orbit. And these orbits are not stable orbits. Unless some energy is fed into the thing it will fall back to earth. For many years, Roche failed to be adventurous enough. They failed to find any fresh energy.'

Energy and orbits? They are, appropriately enough, scientific metaphors, and they neatly capture the trajectories of the combatants in this battle. The two companies spin around the globe at great velocity, and with strangely predictable destinations; and they need new energy, new momentum to keep spinning, or else they fall.

Everyone in the drugs business knows about Hoffmann-La Roche, and worries about it as well. It lurks in the back of their minds like a kind of industrial myth: the story of the business which was bad and which paid the price. They all want to avoid its fate. Yet there is a paradox here: it was also the business on which the industry was most closely modelled. How can you copy the story without copying its ending as well? The implications of that paradox are best revealed through the story of two molecules: one of them Zantac, with which we are already familiar, the other the drug Losec, the novel ulcer cure invented by a Swedish drugs company called Astra.

Zantac, seemingly secure in its poll position as the world's top-selling drug, has created its own earthquakes and reactions around the industry. It has created opposition. Here is one former board member at Glaxo talking candidly about the arrival of its enemies: 'The industry has never seen a two-billion-dollar product before. It is now so big that it is going to attract the most dreadful and intensive attacks. You see, the industry has never seen an attack on a two billion dollar product before, either. The fur is going to fly. Our friends at SmithKline never thought about the penalties of success as well as the rewards of success, and there are very severe penalties. You can see them all the time. One example; people are now going to prison in Greece for producing fakes of Zantac. Glaxo never had that kind of problem before, but it is becoming serious. You can make a lot of money from Zantac, the real thing, and you can make a lot of money from forging it. Just as morphine and cannabis attract unsavoury characters, so Zantac is beginning to attract unsavoury characters too. People can make it without any threat to themselves until they try to sell it, so they will. It is better than forging bank notes.

'The other end is the generic threat. Zantac has two forms. The form Glaxo sells is form two, which is the more stable form, and the patent will last until the end of the century. But the patent on form one expires in 1995. Now there is going to be an enormous challenge to Glaxo's attempts to keep the form two patents as the significant patents. There are going to be very clever chemists trying to work on the development of form one, and there is so much money at stake that the development is going to be done.

Now, we all know that you can't have a two-billion-dollar product without competition as soon as somebody else gets the opportunity to make it. It's the action–reaction thing. Every great success story such as this brings with it an exactly opposite opportunity for somebody else.'

The second drug in this story, Losec, was developed by Astra after it was first discovered in 1979. It has an original mechanism for curing acid secretion: unlike Zantac, it is a genuinely new invention and not a copy of an existing cure. It took a complex route from the laboratory to the pharmacy, however. It was withdrawn from development in 1984 when laboratory rats developed tumours after being subjected to high dosages of the drug. For a time that killed the project. But within two years Astra had solved the problem and the project was up and running again. Two years later, in 1988, the drug won its first regulatory approval, in Sweden. Other approvals followed.

But, and this is the most significant part of the tale, Astra had also made a marketing deal with Merck for the American launch of the drug: it had the stamp of approval from Merck's laboratories, the most respected in the world; and it had their marketing muscle to push it into the world's most important market. Now, for the first time, the two most forceful companies in the industry were about to go head-to-head with a similar product in the same country. This conflict, more than anything, would test the differences between their two models of the corporation.

Almost immediately, Glaxo was worried by the drug. 'It used to be the case that you didn't do trials on a rival's drug until they had actually launched it,' recalls one insider at the company. 'Glaxo changed that.' With its control of the ulcer market to protect, Glaxo set about systematically rubbishing the new product. One move, played in 1989, was to drop the development of a compound called sufotidine, a highly potent version of Zantac; the move was widely publicised to draw attention to the dangers of potent ulcer drugs and to make an implied criticism of Losec. Then, in 1989, it published a report in the *Lancet*, the main professional paper for the medical community in the UK. In it

Glaxo reported results of clinical trials on Losec which showed it had the potential to create cancer in rats. It was aimed as a knockout blow, pitched to raise a scare over Losec, to blow the rival right out of the market before it had a chance to establish itself.

But the punch rebounded badly on Glaxo. Astra responded with its own series of allegations: it complained that Glaxo would not make its information available before it published it, and it questioned the accuracy and impartiality of Glaxo's science, complaining that 'the study lacks appropriate controls' and that Glaxo 'misinterpreted the results'.

In propaganda at least, Losec was starting to have the upper hand. The impression was being created that Glaxo was twisting the results to smear its rival. A suggestion to that effect in a report in London's *Financial Times*, however, generated an angry response from the company's scientists: Dr Richard Sykes, David Jack's successor as head of research and development, wrote to the paper protesting angrily at the suggestion, and rejecting any charge that his scientists would warp the scientific evidence to suit a commercial end.

Nonetheless, the impression seemed to stick. Merck, which by implication Glaxo was accusing of trying to push an unsafe drug through the regulatory system, sat on the sidelines. Yet their concern over Glaxo's tactics was evident. I remembered Ed Scolnick's comment on the affair: 'We didn't do that, another company did that. You'd have to ask them why they did it. We certainly wouldn't do anything like that.'

Within Glaxo itself there were many qualms about what the company was doing. John Burke confirmed that one of the reasons for his resignation was his unease over the hyped-up aggressiveness towards Astra. 'As far as I was concerned, the drug had been approved by Roy Vagelos. Merck wouldn't be doing it if there were any questions about the drug,' he said later. Others tell stories of fierce internal battles over Glaxo's stance. 'There was a lot of disagreement over how to undermine Losec,' recalls one insider. 'Some of us felt the cancer link should only be used as a last resort, but that was not accepted. It was felt that there was a lot we could do, and so this very aggressive stance towards Astra was taken up. It's an example of what happens to a company when it gets to the size where panic takes over. The panic goes in waves throughout the company. The people lower down, at the nerve endings, see the competition coming and they put up proposals. Then the wave of panic reaches the top level, and suddenly panic is everywhere. They say we must do something, get the new drug off the market. But it's unrealistic. It's just not a good appreciation of what a pharmaceutical company can hope to do. You can't just get something off the market, but they think they can.'

They were wrong. Losec won its marketing approvals despite Glaxo's claims that it could cause cancer, a good indication that Glaxo's tests were not generally accepted as valid; and by 1990 the new drug was confidently expected to win at least a quarter of the world ulcer market. All Glaxo had achieved was to win a blast of publicity for its chief rival, and to reveal its own anxiety over the damage the drug could do to Zantac. At the same time, it had dismayed many of its best people to the point where they were considering resignation. It was an 'own goal'. The episode revealed questions about the willingness of Glaxo to subordinate science to marketing; and it had revealed how its top executives – in reality the top executive – thought he had a right to determine which drugs should and should not be sold. It seemed as if the power and ambition of the corporation, by now bloated, had finally reached too far.

Sir Paul Girolami was deeply shaken by the episode. He clasps his hand to his forehead when asked about it, leaning forward on the table, wrinkling his face up into deep frowns. 'It wasn't a tactical error, because there were no tactics behind it,' he explains. 'I know it's difficult for an outsider to believe this, but when that study was made it was done in absolute good faith. The fact that it didn't a hundred per cent clinch the argument with the profession, I don't think matters. It was done in good faith. It wasn't a marketing technique – which is difficult to see because it could have been – but if it had, it would have been wrong and it would have backfired. It's not nice, though. I don't like that situation.'

Yet whatever Girolami's protestations, he has failed to convince either the industry or even the most important of his former collaborators. The great inventor reflects on the episode with a sorrowful expression on his face. Its implications are clearer to him than to anyone else. 'Astra are a successful, innovative company, in my view,' he says. 'Will Losec turn out to be carcinogenic in ten years? I don't know. And knowing that, I am very unsure if it was wise of Glaxo to have a public argument about it. Of course, I don't know the circumstances in which the decision was made. But it was not the sort of thing I would want to be involved in.' He pauses for a few seconds, lost in his own introspection, and then he adds: 'Controversy of this sort doesn't do our industry any good.'

There was a moral to this story. When Losec appeared on the scene Glaxo faced a test of its integrity and a test of its intentions. The company proclaims boldly in the mission statement printed at the front of its literature that its purpose is to make medicines to promote human health. Here it had a chance to prove the truth of that statement, to demonstrate that it put the advancement of health before the quick buck. It had a clear choice. And it chose the quick buck.

Of course, to the people who know Glaxo, this was entirely unsurprising. The truth of this was brought home with shattering clarity towards the end of my conversation with David Jack. Here, after all, was a man who was responsible for creating some of the most profitable and successful scientific products in the world. And yet is he a satisfied man? Is he proud of his achievements? Hardly. I recalled another Glaxo executive who had told me Jack had been unhappy at the company after Girolami moved him from the research laboratories to the head office. The executive went on to explain how Jack had been unhappy because he was no longer working with friends: there was nobody in the head office he could call a kindred soul.

'The first seventeen years at Ware were lovely,' he recollected. 'That's when we were building a real research organisation. But moving to the Group job was a foolish move for me. It was much less of a job. It was remote. People used to come to talk to me once a month, that was all.' There is sadness in his face as he remembers. We finish our tea and get up to leave. As we are walking away, another question occurs to me. I asked him whether Glaxo's success was all just an accident?

'It was all chance,' replies Jack instantly. 'Everyone knows it. Even Girolami knows that good science and good scientists are a prerequisite for success. Although, I can tell you quite frankly, I don't think he had any great regard for scientists, or for science as a way of living.' The inventor chuckles to himself as he plays with the irony of that thought. 'Science as philosophy would not be his first choice of subject. It would be economics. His whole purpose is to make money. I don't think there is much folly in his mind about doing good.'

And you?

'My own attitude was a little different. As far as I was concerned my main job was to find better medicines for common illnesses, and to get them used. Anything that stopped the better use of my drugs I was against. If the price was too high I was against that.'

Then you must have thought the price of Zantac was too high?

'Certainly I did. My fear was that if the price was too high the drug might not be used. It was our own little thing, you know. I believe that the greatest threat to the drugs industry is not a lack of innovation, because there will always be plenty of problems to solve. The biggest problem is the trouble the government and society will have in providing good healthcare for an ageing population with greater and greater need. The economics of the provision of healthcare is the big problem, and if the industry doesn't see that, then, in my view, it is looking down the wrong end of the telescope.'

So you used to tell Sir Paul Girolami that he was wrong?

'Of course. But he has changed the way of thinking there, and made it, although obviously a more profitable place, also a more uncomfortable place to work.'

Did he mind being told he was wrong?

The inventor laughs at the thought. 'Very much. Paul will tell you he did everything himself, and that he didn't make any mistakes while he was doing it.' And then he laughs again, adding: 'Like all of us.'

And with that parting swipe at memory, the great inventor turns away, his mind still on new inventions and new ironies. Yet the story is not over. Merck is still there, leading the field, still number one. Glaxo is still there, with Girolami still at its head, and its ten-year challenge turning into a fifteen- or twenty-year incursion. The battle continues. And, as Sir Paul Girolami puts it, the race is a long one. Nevertheless, for many of the people in this story, there is a sense that the Astra episode marks a turning point which crystallises the nature of the conflict and makes its outcome clear.

That thought arrives from two directions. Among the scientists there is a deep feeling of unease at the way Glaxo fights. It is natural enough. The company clearly holds science subordinate to marketing: making money is more important to it than making medicines. For the scientists that is a depressing and degrading configuration. The commercial people suffer another angle of unease. It seems to them that Glaxo made a tactical error, that it blundered. That is worrying, because Glaxo had been, for ten years, a company of supreme tactical mastery, which never blundered. Now it seems to be making all the wrong moves.

Though these may seem like different concerns, in reality they spring from the same fault. The paradox was: how can you copy the story without copying the ending? It related to the Hoffmann - La Roche story; and the solution lies with what went wrong with Valium.

There are many reasons for Roche's failure: it was unlucky, it was out of touch, it grew too quickly, it lost control, and so on. All these, however, relate back to one theme: the company didn't really care about the product; it didn't put the drug – the central purpose of the corporation – at the centre of its universe. Nobody set out with any great desire to ease mankind's anxiety: they set out to find a profitable product in a market that was already booming. The company did not sell the drug with such evangelical fervour out of any great desire to alleviate stress: they sold it to improve their financial ratios – margins, market shares and profits.

Consider the similarities with Zantac, and with Glaxo. Its trail was not triggered by a particular desire to cure ulcers; it simply wanted its own competitor in a very profitable market. Its wildfire marketing was not motivated especially by a desire to improve health; it too set itself above anything else financial targets.

In both cases, the companies succeeded brilliantly. The mobilisation of skills and resources behind their campaigns are impressive displays of intellectual and practical achievement. Yet for all the razzle and flash, they are also very empty displays: a lot of sound and fury signifying nothing.

What, after all, are the achievements of Glaxo? For all the effort, the trials, the anger and the rage, its main impact upon the world has been only negative. It devoted a lot of time and energy to replacing one perfectly adequate ulcer drug with another, very similar, drug which happens to cost considerably more. The net effect had simply been to raise the cost of treatment.

Does it matter that Glaxo is only interested in the numbers? Not in the sense that numbers are bad, that profits are wicked. There is nothing wrong with the numbers in themselves: they are an essential element in any commercial enterprise. But profits and margins are an elusive goal: strangely, those prizes are most likely to be won when you aren't playing for them.

Talking to Roy Vagelos, I asked him at one point whether he had any systems for controlling Merck. 'Systems?' he replied, with a look of disdain. 'That is a kind of business-consultant type of baloney. It is people, in every sense and in every job. I depend tremendously on the people and I lean upon them. For example, I find that the people who came from Washington University with me still like to talk about what's going on, because we've come to trust one another, and it's trust that we're building. You can only do that when you get people whose quality is the same as yours, whose excitement is the same as yours. It's very exciting to talk to them – the trouble is, there's too much excitement around.'

It sounds simple – even too simple to be true – but it has the crystal-clear accuracy of truth: for Roy Vagelos and his colleagues their journey into the drugs trade is a kind of adventure and a kind of experiment. And although it may seem glib, behind it there is a web of complexity. A drugs company, by the very nature of its business, has advanced far into the post-industrial world: manufacturing is an insignificant part of its business; what counts is the intellectual content in its product – the knowledge stored in both its research and marketing projects. As in any post-industrial business, information is its key resource, and the manipulation of that information is its key activity, just as materials and their manipulation were the resource and work of the industrial corporation.

But materials and information require very different handling: things can be dealt with mechanistically; information and creativity can be managed only with leadership, vision, and moral certainty. Why? Because information, in part, and creativity, in total, are human activities, and people do not respond to numbers. Goals such as profits, margins, and especially the more esoteric financial targets of earnings per share or returns on shareholders' funds – the targets that gripped the business world during the eighties – are dry. The head may be able to comprehend their importance, but the heart doesn't connect.

The heart connects instead with nobler purposes: with the advancement of knowledge, the alleviation of disease, the relief of poverty. A corporation which upholds values such as these, which allows some idealistic blood to run through its veins, will succeed because it will create a community fired by a common purpose and sharing a common consiousness. Wherever industry is dominated by information and knowledge, the consciousness of the enterprise is all that counts.

That is why, ultimately, Merck succeeds, because it puts the product first, and builds around it a streak of idealism; and that is why, ultimately, Glaxo is fated to replay the tragedy of Hoffmann - La Roche. It is a brilliant attempt to impose the logic of an industrial corporation on a post-industrial industry: tactics, strategy, and logic have been mastered and marshalled with great expertise. But it is a hollow enterprise, lacking purpose, and lacking soul. So, the conflict rumbles on; the race still runs. The battle between the light and airy genius of Roy Vagelos and the dark and brooding genius of Sir Paul Girolami is really no contest at all, however. It is more of a lesson.

Index